The Adventures of Space and Hobo

By Kenneth L. Birks

Published by Straight Arrow Publishing
Ten Year Anniversary Edition, Revised 2024

Cover Design by Matthew Wright

www.spaceandhobo.booksbyken.com
Copyright © 2014

Unless otherwise indicated, all Scripture quotations are taken from
The Holy Bible, New King James Version
© 1982 by Thomas Nelson, Inc.

Ken writes from the redeemed perspective, as this journey is rich with God's fingerprints at every step of the way. And at a deeper level, while the particulars are Ken's unique story, the journey he describes is one that we either have or must travel.

Caught in the Pursuit of a Lost Soul
By Kenneth L. Birks

In panic, crying out in desperation, I yearned to be free.
In captivation, You flashed my life flashed before me.
Like a fish with a hook in its mouth, I was caught.
Not ready to submit, I fought the hook, trying to spit it out.
Jerking the line periodically, I knew You were still there.

Why do I run, fighting Your hook, resisting being captured?
Freight train hopping from place to place, I often wondered.
With the hook set reeling me in periodically, I resisted.
Letting go again and again, I returned to sin and stubbornness.
How long will Your patience last, I wondered, in my distress.

Breaking me down, Your patience exhausted me, little by little.
Raging on, the battle for my soul continued in non-committal.
What was it resisted? Your unfailing love or fear of surrender?
Lost in a spiritual maze of philosophies, I stood in wonder.
What was it discovered so long ago, drawing me so near?

Not giving in, stubbornly refusing, I stood in denial.
Lost in confusion, I desired but didn't quite know how.
Blindsided, caught in a hypnotic trance, I finally decided.
In a moment of intense struggle, worn out, I caved.
With the battle over, I was wrapped in the arms of Your love.

With Your patience taking opportunity, You waited to intercept.
Outwitting stubbornness and deception without force, You drew.
Leading to a moment of awe-inspiring revelation, my spirit leapt.
It was You I looked for all along. Why did I wait so distraught?
Forever grateful for Your pursuit of a lost soul, I was caught.

The Adventures of Space and Hobo
by Kenneth L. Birks

Table of Contents

Foreword by John R. Houghton	1
Introduction	3
1. A Lost and Wandering Soul	5
2. Coming Home from Vietnam	11
3. Readjusting to Civilian Life	23
4. East Coast Hitchhiking Adventure	27
5. Jack and the Minnesota Group	33
6. Meeting Hobo	37
7. Texas: Surprise, Surprise	45
8. New Orleans and Destinations Unknown	55
9. Gulf Coast Hitchhiking Adventures	63
10. Florida Gulf Coast Adventures	67
11. Christmas in Jail	77
12. Florida East Coast Adventures	83
13. Jesus Freaks	91
14. Leaving Florida	95
15. Houston and onto Los Angeles	101
16. Discovering More of Arizona	111
17. Mardi Gras, Here We Come	119
18. Heading North	127
19. Madison, Wisconsin	139
20. Homeward Bound	147
21. Back in My Hometown – Wenatchee	157
22. Discovering Canada	161
23. Going Home—So Long, Hobo	175
24. Home—But Still Lost	179
25. Conversion at Last	187
26. Alaska: Established in the Journey	197
27. Sent Out and Launched into Ministry	209
Epilogue	217
Space and Hobo Reviews	219
About the Author	221
Other Books from Kenneth L. Birks	222
Reviews and References	225
Connect with Ken Birks	227
More Pics	228

Foreword

by John R. Houghton
Consultant and Life Coach

I've had the pleasure of serving with Ken Birks for years as part of an eldership team in Roseville, California. When I first met Ken twelve years ago, I was impressed by his theological astuteness and sober-minded approach to church life. He had been a pastor, but it was more than that. He seemed to understand the boundaries and guidelines of scripture as they pertained to the local church and God's expectations for those He loved and saved.

Over the years, I discovered that underneath this exterior of Biblical knowledge, there was a powerful story of redemption. Not that each of us who has experienced God's grace doesn't have an exciting story of redemption, but Ken seemed to have some pieces that didn't all come together for me. As I learned more and more of what we had in common—our music, our former lostness, our belief that God was always working in our lives, even when we were unaware of Him or His workings—a mystery began to emerge. How had Ken come to know Jesus and the love of God in his life? I knew it wasn't. 'boy grows up, goes to church, enjoys Sunday school, dedicates his life at Summer Camp, goes to a young adult group, becomes a solid Christian citizen, gets married, and fulfills his lifelong dream of becoming a pastor.' I knew it was a different story embedded and fashioned out of the times we grew up.

The Adventures of Space and Hobo tells the story of Ken's vagabond life after Vietnam. It explores the on-the-ground confusion and chaos of the Vietnam War and its effects on a generation and those who served. Named "Space" by a new friend, Hobo, Ken and his traveling companion hit the road to partake of all the possibilities of that generation in search of adventure and uncharted experiences. They were looking for what was genuine and authentic and the hidden mysteries behind it all. The story takes us step by step along the path of awakening a lost soul on his way to understanding himself, his path, and the meaning of his life.

Along the way, we discover the futility of expecting different surroundings and new happenings to fill what's missing in our lives. And we discover the grace of God. We watch as His patience, protection, and kindness take every opportunity to express His love and intercept the consciousness of a young man looking for more but not knowing exactly what. We see the diligent pursuit of a God who won't let go and can outwit our stubbornness, deception, and complacency. We see Him as God who knows who belongs to Him and won't stop until we look with awe at how he has called and led us, without force, to a moment of awe-inspiring revelation and an actual change of identity, heart and mind.

The Adventures of Space and Hobo narrates the empty and exhausting search for "something more" that characterizes Ken's generation. Ken tells the story of the God who was there all along, waiting at the end of their road with open arms, as the searchers realized they were looking for a Person and their authentic selves, not just an exciting experience.

Introduction

This is the story of two Vietnam Vets who allowed fate to guide them while navigating through the spiritual maze of the 1970s. As they traveled by freight trains and hitchhiked through our nation's cities, they used their wits and street knowledge, traveling as vagabonds. Looking for the next free ride to nowhere, they mooched off whatever resources or people coming their way.

The purpose of writing this book isn't to glorify the drug-crazed lifestyle I once led or the crazy things I found myself involved in but to show how our gracious Heavenly Father is long-suffering and full of loving kindness towards us, even in our most sinful states. He never gives up on us but continually draws us unto Himself.

God demonstrates His own love toward us in that while we were still sinners, Christ died for us. (Romans 5:8 NKJV)

I am unbelievably fortunate to be alive and in a sane mind today. During those lost years, I abused my mind terribly with all the drugs I took. I am very thankful to the Lord Jesus Christ for saving me and giving me a sober mind that allows me to enjoy everything around me without the aid of mind-altering drugs.

For God has not given us a spirit of fear, but of power and love and of a sound mind - 2 Timothy 1:7.

In writing the book, some 30 years after the events, my memory isn't as sharp as I would like it to be. All the stories are accurate to the best of my knowledge and memory, but some details might be more generalized. By remembering the basic timeline and sequence of places we visited, I remembered quite a bit as I pieced the story together. In writing the book, I am sure there were many stories and places I failed to mention simply because I couldn't remember the details. The stories I have chosen to share are those that have stood out to me with the most details placed.

The latter part of the book shows how God can take any life—no matter the person's condition—and use that life as an instrument of His righteousness. Then, through the Holy Spirit's leading, this person can become the person God has destined them to be.

A Lost and Wandering Soul
Chapter One

The warm sun of the Tempe–Phoenix area was a nice respite from what began as a harrowing hitchhiking experience. Traveling through Colorado from Minnesota, I got stuck in a snowstorm while sitting on the side of the road waiting for a ride, wearing clothing that was not suitable for winter-like weather. I was shaking from head to foot from the cold. Fortunately, someone finally stopped and gave me a nice long ride from Colorado to Arizona. I was able to sleep through the night, waking up to the warmth of the Arizona sun.

The Adventure Begins—Tempe, Arizona

I had been hanging out in a park just outside Tempe, Arizona, for a few days with some other hippies who seemed to have nowhere to call home. We would hitchhike to Phoenix each day around noon to get a meal at the local St. Vincent de Paul food kitchen. During the day, we would hang out at supermarkets and panhandle. There always seemed to be a lot of pot floating around, so we spent a lot of time getting high. In the evenings, we would hit the local bars and spend what little money we had made that day panhandling. We eventually found a cave not too far from the park where we all slept at night and stashed our packs during the day.

It was the autumn of 1972. I had ridden a freight train from Washington State to Minnesota with friends. After spending a week or so there, they all wanted to return to Washington, but I was up for more adventure, so I struck out alone with no destination in mind. In my mind, I was lost and knew there was nothing back in Washington that seemed to strike a chord within me. So, with my pack on my back, I struck out for Arizona, hoping to meet up with whatever came my way. In the back of my mind, I thought about going to Phoenix, Arizona, but I didn't quite know why, except a few days earlier, we were all browsing through a record store, and the latest album by Grand Funk caught my attention. It was titled "Phoenix." So, for some reason, Phoenix got lodged in my mind and seemed as good of a place to go as anywhere. So, following my intuition, I struck out for Phoenix.

The trip from Minnesota to Arizona wasn't my first time taking off alone somewhere. Earlier in the year, I quit my job with the railroad and decided to hitchhike across the country from Washington State to Pennsylvania and go back to visit an army buddy. After returning home from Vietnam, I was at a loss about what I wanted to do with my life. I wasn't ready to settle down and had a tough time figuring out where I fit in, so I finally got fed up and hit the road.

G.I. and Childhood Memories

While in the army, I began to encounter many new things, but it was a very confining environment that didn't allow me to experience the things I had a yearning to do. I wasn't even exactly sure what it was I wanted. I just knew I needed to get out and away from all that was familiar and see what the world had to offer.

I grew up in East Wenatchee, Washington, a small town in North Central Washington. We lived in the outlying area with apple orchards all around us. My parents were genuinely religious and went to church every Sunday, which meant my three brothers, two sisters, and I went along. During the summer, we attended Vacation Bible School—not only ours—but sometimes those held by other churches to keep us out of Mom's hair.

Looking back on our family, I have concluded it was somewhat dysfunctional. We were a typical family in many ways, such as always having food, shelter, clothing, family dinners, chores, and regular vacations. However, communication and learning how to bond with one another were very lacking. My parents were not good at communication and didn't teach us how to get along and connect. As a result, there was always bickering, yelling, and commotion. As a result, I have had bonding issues throughout my adult life.

Our church didn't believe in going to movies, dancing, playing cards, or going to carnivals. So, we grew up without much of a social life, living on the outskirts of town in more of a country setting. All of this caused me to be somewhat socially awkward with an introverted personality, from which I developed a rejection complex.

Even though our family had its problems, and despite being raised in a strict religious environment, my brothers and I had relatively good childhoods. We had a vacant lot near our home where we often played baseball, football, and other activities with all the neighbors. The field also had a hill we used for sledding in the winter, where all the neighbors would congregate and play in the snow. We would build go-karts in the spring and summer and race them down the hill. We also had neighbors with horses and ponies, which we rode often. Unlike today, where you have to be careful where your kids play, we were able to roam all over our neighborhood and the country around us, including a big canyon about half a mile from our home where we would often roam. Badger Mountain was also within hiking distance, where we frequently hiked and explored.

Joining the Army

Following high school graduation in 1968, I decided to join the army rather than get drafted. There were several reasons for this: I didn't want to be a grunt and get shot or have to shoot someone. My driver's license was revoked because of too many speeding tickets, and I knew I would be drafted at any time because I had already taken my physical and was classified 1A. Not wanting to be a grunt (infantryman), I enlisted, hoping I wouldn't be in the middle of the fighting. I asked my recruiter what I needed to do to accomplish that, and he told me to sign up for aviation, which I did. As it turned out, it was good advice because I ended up in a General Support Helicopter Company assigned to work on Chinook Helicopters in Phu Loi, Vietnam. Phu Loi was located about 25 miles north of Saigon and was the scene of fierce fighting during the 1968 Tet offensive.

In Vietnam, I became heavily involved in drugs—everything from pot and LSD to heroin. Even though the army was a confining environment, I enjoyed the camaraderie I experienced with the other potheads in my company, something I had never quite experienced during my growing-up years. In addition, it helped to make my tour of Nam more enjoyable. As I look back over that time, I have many fond memories.

While in Vietnam, I had a genuine spiritual awakening. But after returning to civilian life, I wasn't ready to settle down. Instead, I greatly desired to experience freedom and the so-called hippie lifestyle. So, there I was in Tempe, Arizona, with no direction home. It had been just over a year since returning home from Vietnam, and I now found myself in Tempe, living the life of a hippie with a sense of being lost. I was very unsure of myself, but at the same time, I was looking for adventure while trying to navigate this new lifestyle I was now enjoying.

Assigned to Phu Loi Vietnam

This phase of my life began with my Vietnam tour, where I started expanding my horizons after being raised in such a restrictive environment. Growing up with so many restrictions caused me to be open to drugs and the acceptance of those around me. Enjoying this newfound acceptance is what drew me to those who were involved with drugs and considered outcasts. However, we were all in this thing together, which produced a bond I had never experienced. I remember when I first got assigned to my unit in Phu Loi and met my new bunkmates for the first time. Frank's first question, my new bunkmate asked me, was, "Do you smoke pot?"

My response was, "Yes, of course!"

He said, "Great! Now I have someone to smoke with."

I thought, "Wow! My time here isn't going to be so bad!"

I soon realized Frank was the type of guy who didn't want to identify with the known pot users. He was a great Huey helicopter mechanic and wanted to keep his job. So, Frank and I would go off alone in the evening to smoke pot rather than hang out with the others. However, it wasn't long before I began to drift away from Frank's company. Hanging out with just him didn't meet my need for acceptance and belonging. I craved more of a sense of belonging than what I was getting from hanging with Frank.

Because of Frank's desire to hide the fact that he was a pothead, he was the type of person who was very susceptible to the use of heroin. Heroin was just beginning to come into play amongst us, and Frank was one of the first among those I was hanging out with to get addicted to it. Heroin was so much cheaper and easier to use without being detected that many people you wouldn't suspect used it. It was reported about 15% of all G.I.'s in Vietnam from 1970-1971 were using heroin, which was the period I was there. Frank tried to get me to use heroin repeatedly, but I resisted. I remember reading David Wilkerson's book *"The Cross and the Switchblade"* several years earlier about how he worked with junkies in New York City. After reading about the junkies in his book, I thought, "I would never do that." I enjoyed smoking pot and even dropping acid occasionally, but heroin, or "skag," as we were calling it, didn't interest me.

Reckless Behavior

I did many crazy, stupid, and reckless things while in Nam. For example, there was a time when I was getting ready to go home on leave for the Christmas holidays, and I was at the Tan Son Nhut Air Base located near the city of Saigon in Southern Vietnam. The United States used it as a significant base during the Vietnam War (1959–1975), stationing Army, Air Force, Navy, and Marine units there. Before boarding my plane home, I had time to kill, so I decided to venture over to the PX (general store). A Papa San *(a term used to describe adult Vietnamese)* approached me and wanted me to buy a bunch of items from the PX for him. He gave me quite a bit of money to do so. I didn't want to do it, but he kept bugging me until I finally gave in. As he continued bugging me, it reminded me of a negative experience I had when I first arrived in Vietnam on my first trip to Saigon with some of my buddies. One of my friends and I had somehow become separated from our buddies and were alone on the streets in our brand-new fatigues when a Vietnamese man hit me up. He wanted to exchange his pesos for my Military Payment Currency (MPC). Of course, I wasn't interested in doing so, but he kept bugging me and upping the ante to the point that I finally gave in. He then showed me a roll of cash that was more than triple what I had in MPC. We made the exchange and then headed back to the USO located a couple of blocks from where our friends and the two of us had all agreed to meet later in the afternoon.

When we met up with our buddies, I began bragging to them about the incredible deal I had just made and took out the roll of pesos to show them. As I unrolled the cash, I realized he had suckered me. There were only a few pesos on the top of the roll, and all the others were just paper. The pesos he had shown me were good, but he switched on me once he realized he had a sucker. I was outraged. I felt stupid for having been suckered by such a simple ploy. He had spotted my brand-new fatigues and knew I was an easy target. I was thinking about this when the Papa San at the PX began pestering me about purchasing the items for him. It was payback time. I decided it was my turn to get back at them for what they had done to me months earlier. I took his money, went into the PX, walked out a back door, jumped into a taxi, and headed to the airport. Unfortunately, I had told him I was leaving on a plane, and he followed me there, but he wasn't quick enough. I was entering the gate area and boarding my plane when he caught up with me. We made eye contact, but it was too late. I felt terrible for him but, at the same time, figured he had swindled other G.I.'s out of their money, so it was payback time.

Beginning to Have a Sense of Being Lost

During the final months of my Vietnam tour, I began to sense I was lost. I was losing my points of reference and sense of belonging. I was shuffled from one company to another because of the rehabilitation process I was put through. It began to mess with my head. All my old buddies from the 539th were gone or shuffled around. The South Vietnamese Army was taking over our post because the U.S. Army was in a troop withdrawal, and the war was winding down. One of the last LSD trips I did before returning home from Nam did a number on me. A sense of being lost came over me big time. I was in a hooch[1] with a bunch of guys I didn't know. We were all tripping on acid and smoking pot when I realized how lost I was. I didn't understand why I was there or what I was doing. I was very disoriented. This sense of being lost and disoriented stayed with me during the next couple of years after returning home from Vietnam. I was lost in my mind and didn't know what to do. This disorientation is part of what prompted me to take off hitchhiking around the country.

I was waiting in line at the St. Vincent De Paul Food Kitchen with some of my buddies from Tempe one day when the man in front of me turned to me and said, "You're lost! Aren't you?" He saw it in my eyes. I was a lost and wandering soul looking to connect with something that would put me on the path to discovering who I was and the destiny and purpose I had begun to seek while in Vietnam.

---

[1] The term we used for our sleeping quarters in Vietnam.

Coming Home from Vietnam
Chapter Two

My trip home from Vietnam was quite an experience in itself. I was under guard, along with another person, from the time I began processing out until our plane landed at Travis AFB in California, just north of San Francisco. The reason for the guard was the army was booting me out with a general discharge under honorable conditions. The discharge papers read, *"Unable to Adapt to Military Life."* My downfall with the military began the first day I arrived in Vietnam as I began to get stoned on pot and other drugs daily. The drug use had caused me to take on an *"I don't care"* attitude, which led to a couple of Article XIII Court-Martials. As a result, I got busted in rank from an E-4 to an E-1—buck private and fined to the extent that I had little money on my return trip from Vietnam.

The Rebel—Unable to Adapt to Military Life

Because of the drugs and the people I was hanging with, I became somewhat of a rebel in Vietnam.

I remember one day, while passing the day away in the boneyard (the salvage yard for wrecked helicopters), one of my buddies, Mark, said to me, "I know what you are. You're a revolutionist."

I had never really thought of myself that way, but it was what I was becoming. I was the one who had thrown the first smoke grenade into the Officer and NCO barracks in the middle of the night while they were sleeping.

I was also one of the main instigators when we tear-gassed them during the night on another occasion, though I wasn't directly involved. We all knew they would blame me for it because of the smoke grenade incident, so I sat that one out. We were all bent on doing our own thing without being harassed by the authorities or the "pigs," as we called

them. After one of our buddies had gotten busted for pot and sent off to LBJ (Long Binh Jail), we were determined to harass them back. The middle-of-the-night attacks were our way of getting back at them and letting them know if they continued to mess with us, there would be consequences. On another occasion, I was responsible for organizing what we called a "Far East Woodstock" with two other buddies. We mass-produced flyers several days before the event and put them all over our post at Phu Loi. As a result, we had several hundred people who came and went throughout the afternoon while we listened to the Woodstock Album and got high on pot and LSD. We had set up a big awning made from a parachute on our company baseball field with a stereo system blasting the music extremely loud. We had no permission to do this; we just did it, not caring about the consequences we might receive. Our commanding officer called the military police on us and

tried to break it up. He got up on the hood of the MP jeep and began to make a big speech that what we were doing was unlawful and that there would be consequences for our actions. He told everyone how he and the other company officers had been tear-gassed just a few days before the event. I then got up and began to yell back at them about how we were not leaving and that there was no way that they could make us go. We were adamant about staying and not giving in to their rhetoric. While the MPs were there and tried to break it up, we were playing Jimi Hendrix's version of the *"Star Spangled Banner"* from the Woodstock album. It was quite a scene. They eventually left us alone.

Our festival happened on the weekend. I was supposed to be on duty, in military clothes at my place of duty, in the boneyard. The following Monday, my buddy, John, and I were called to the Company Commander's office and were issued Article 15s for not being at our place of duty and being out of uniform when we were supposed to be on duty. I received a temporary reduction in rank and a $50.00 fine. On the next page are statements about my conduct during this time:

Statement from Platoon Sergeant, Jimmie R. Morgan

Specialist Four, Kenneth L. Birks, was assigned to the single rotor section of the maintenance platoon. His section sergeant wouldn't utilize him as an aircraft mechanic as he is a suspected drug user. His primary job was as the truck driver for the single-rotor section's two-and-a-half-ton truck. On this job, his duties were to perform different functions such as the 520th Transportation Battalion courier, picking up POL products, delivering security guards to the 520th Transportation Battalion, and numerous other runs as required by the maintenance platoon. I continually had to counsel SP4 Birks on the necessary maintenance of his vehicle, not being at his place of duty, missing formations, and joyriding in his truck. On 1 February 1971, he was observed joyriding in the village of Phu Loi, which is off-limits. On 1 February 1971, I relieved him of his duties as a vehicle driver and assigned him to work in the aircraft salvage yard. I also counseled him that he would be at his place of duty unless he had permission to leave and would make company formations. SP4 Birks missed company formation on 5 February 1971 and 6 February 1971—article 15 UCMJ. Punishment was imposed on him by the Commanding Officer on 6 February 1971. His punishment was a reduction to the grade of PFC E3, suspended for sixty (60) days, and forfeiture of fifty ($50.00) dollars for one month. SP4 Birks' job performance in the aircraft salvage yard was poor.

Salvaged parts, such as instrument panels, were damaged in their removal, and production of the parts back into supply channels was almost non-existent. On 3 March 1971, I assumed the duty of acting 1SGT. SFC Peacock became acting platoon sergeant of the Maintenance Platoon. SFC Peacock submitted statements that SP4 Birks had continued to be absent from his place of duty. The Commanding Officer counseled SP4 Birks on his absenteeism from his duty station. The Commanding Officer informed him that action under AR 635-212 could be initiated against him. SP4 Birks became very belligerent toward the Commanding Officer, saying that he didn't care if he had an action under AR 635-212 initiated against him. His suspended sentence of reduction to PFC E3 was vacated, and rehabilitation transfer was initiated. In my opinion, PFC Birks is unsuitable for military service. He is antagonistic and belligerent toward any authority and will not accept responsibility for anything. He seems to wander around in a daze most of the time.

– End of Statement –

Statement from SFC Peacock

On approximately 8 February 1971, I was assigned to the 539th Transportation Company as a maintenance supervisor on the CH47 section. On 2 March 1971, I had a meeting of all personnel of the Aircraft Repair Platoon. PFC Birks was present at this time. A few days later, PFC Birks was not present at his place of duty, and I observed him at a party not in proper military uniform, wearing a checkered headband on his head, no shirt, and no military boots. PFC Birks is extremely non-productive and has been since I was assigned to the 539th Transportation Company. PFC Birks cannot be trusted to do a job and do it right unless he has someone standing over him and close supervision. PFC Birks is unreliable as a soldier because of his attitude and unwillingness to follow orders to be in his place of duty.[2] He can be highly belligerent towards those in authority.

– End of Statement –

Our time in Vietnam wasn't just about getting high and thumbing our noses at authority; we honestly felt we had a purpose that went along with the revolution that was happening at the time. If we were going to do something about it, we had to be willing to make sacrifices as well, even if it meant getting discharged from the army with something other than an honorable discharge.

Woodstock Influences

We were constantly reminded of the Vietnam Song, *"I-Feel-Like-I'm-Fixin'-to-Die Rag,"* that Country Joe and the Fish sang at Woodstock. We were there to give Uncle Sam a helping hand by disrupting the war by thumbing our noses at our responsibilities and authority, even if we did get kicked out of the army. In my unit, four of us received discharges other than honorable.

Following my Article 15, I was to be transferred to another company within our Battalion for an opportunity to rehabilitate. My buddy, John, was also moved to a company 30 or 40 miles from Phu Loi, which was

---

[2] This statement was an exaggeration. I actually performed all my ground handling jobs very well. It was only when I was assigned to the boneyard that I became reckless in my duties.

a part of our Battalion. I would eventually join him there after my rehabilitation failed at the 165th. My first opportunity to rehabilitate was when I received an Article 15, which was only a 60-day suspension and a $50.00 fine. If I had made it through the 60 days without any other incidents, I would have gotten back my SP4 rank. When that didn't happen, I had to decide whether to get serious about rehabilitating or get out on a general discharge. Until then, I hadn't given thought to getting out of the army early with a discharge other than honorable. But, since things had turned out for the worst, I began to think about it. I decided staying in for another year and a half was going to be too difficult with the way things were now going. So, I decided to do what I could to get a general discharge under honorable conditions.

Once at the 165th Transportation Company, I made it clear to my new Commanding Officer that I wasn't going to rehabilitate but was bent on getting out. He made it clear to me that he didn't want to be a part of the same army I was in, which meant he would do his part in getting rid of me. Within a few weeks, I—along with some others who were troublemakers—was transferred to the company where my buddy, John, was assigned. The 165th was getting ready for a major IG (Inspector General) inspection, and they didn't want us around.

Connecting with John was a real lift for me. While we were in the 539th together, we all developed a strong bond—something I missed. This company was quite different from what we had experienced at the 539th. The potheads were not together at all. They feared being found out and would go into hiding to smoke their pot. Well, neither John nor I were going to put up with something like this, so we immediately began to change things. It wasn't long before all the heads came out of the woodwork and joined us as we smoked in the open. John even went to the Commanding Officer on one occasion and put him on notice.

He told him, "You can mess with the junkies all you want, but don't mess with us. There'll be trouble."

John had a way of carrying things a little too far and ended up getting an undesirable discharge rather than a general discharge, which meant he lost all his benefits. One of the guys came to me and tried to get me to cool it. He said until we had gotten there, there weren't any real heads. He told me things needed to be done in stages. He chose to play it safe and never joined in with the rest of us but continued to hide when smoking pot and ended up a loner.

After a couple of months, I received orders to return to the 165th while finally awaiting discharge from the army. While back at the 165th,

I discovered that all the new friends I had met before I left had switched to smoking heroin rather than weed. As a result, I began to use it again, knowing my time was short, so I probably wouldn't get too addicted. The heroin we used in Nam was almost 100% pure, which meant we could get high just by smoking it in cigarettes. Those who snorted it became addicted more quickly than those who were smoking it. Only the hardcore junkies were using needles.

Demoted to Buck Private

Back at the 165th, I went AWOL for about a week, hanging out at my old company, the 539th. Nobody seemed to mind until I returned one night to the 165th because the movie *"Woodstock"* was playing there. My Sergeant saw me and informed me I had been AWOL. I was immediately slapped with another Article 15. This time, they busted me down to an E1 buck private with fines. The good thing was that it was the final straw. In their eyes, I was beyond rehabilitation and received my discharge shortly after.

During the months after deciding to get out of the Army with a general discharge, I was in constant conflict with the spiritual values I was beginning to develop, which I mentioned in a later chapter. I knew they directly contradicted my path to getting out of the army. I prayed that God would somehow take my crooked path and make it straight someday. Thankfully, He eventually did!

I had joined the army for three years; just after 21 months, on June 21, 1971, I was out for good. I didn't even have to do the three years of reserve duty. The army discharged me with all the benefits. Upon arriving at Travis AFB, California, with little money, I didn't have enough money to catch a flight, bus, or train to my home in Wenatchee, Washington. My friend and I had just enough between us for a bus ride to Oakland and one night's stay in a motel room. I decided to look up my friend, Jack. He had left Vietnam a month earlier than I had under the same circumstances. My friend and I split company the following morning as he was on his way toward Southern California, and I was on my way north to Washington State. I called Jack and found out he was in the hospital for an injury he had just received. His mother came from Fremont and picked me up. I went to the hospital to visit him and then hung out with his brother, Pat, for a few days before hitchhiking home. I didn't have much choice about my method of travel.

On my way home from visiting my buddy, Jack, in Fremont, I got as far as Berkeley before running into a couple of Jesus freaks who were hitchhiking. I traveled with them for a short while before parting ways as we were going in different directions. Even though we had heard about Jesus freaks in Vietnam, this was my first experience with them in the civilized world. Before going to Vietnam, I was unaware that the term existed. While in Vietnam, we heard about Jesus freaks and even saw a news special about them. I was curious when I ran into them but just observed them without getting into any deep conversations. Even though I had a genuine experience with the Lord in Vietnam and had begun to explore the Bible and Christianity, by the end of my tour, I had started using heroin again and losing interest.

On my trip home from the Bay Area, after getting as far as Medford, Oregon, I was tired of carrying my big, heavy duffle bag. So, I decided to go into a restroom and dump some military clothes, including my Class A Uniform, into a garbage can. I had no sense of pride whatsoever at having been in the military. I had become very anti-military during my time in Vietnam, having fallen in with the potheads.

One of my major regrets in life is having been so anti-military during this season. At this point in my life, I completely support our military and am ashamed that I took such a stance during that season.

Influenced by Kent State Shootings

In Vietnam, we heard about all the anti-Vietnam rallies going on stateside and what had happened at Kent State with the shootings by the National Guard. The Rallies and the Kent State shootings influenced us, causing us to do stuff to disrupt things on our end. It was a different world I was returning to, and I had no idea how to adjust to it other than letting my intuition guide me. I was a lost and wandering soul looking for something, but not sure what.

After dumping half of my duffle bag contents into the trash can, I resumed my trip and got a great ride from a lovely lady from Grants Pass, Oregon, to Salem. I had relatives near Salem in a little town called Independence, where most of my dad's family lived. It was a place where our family spent summer vacations when I was growing up. So, I gave them a call, and they came and picked me up. After spending the night with them, they decided with my family to put me on an airplane. So, the next thing I knew, I was on a plane headed home.

Back in Washington, I settled into living at my parent's home for a couple of weeks but was getting restless, not knowing what to do with my life. Then, my neighbor, who was working in an apple orchard near

Chelan, WA, and was home for the weekend, invited me to come along with him, assuring me I could get a job.

Apple Orchards

My brothers and I grew up with apple orchards all around us and spent our high school summers working for a family friend who had an orchard in Manson, Washington, right on Lake Chelan. We also had apple orchards just down the street from where I grew up. So, I worked in those as well. Most orchards had cabins for the workers to live in, which was the case where my neighbor was working.

Even though the apple harvest is in the Fall, there is work in the orchards throughout the Summer. First, during June and July, the thinning of the apples must be done, and then late July and August is the time for putting the props under the limbs so the weight of the growing apples will not break the limbs.

After a few weeks of working with my neighbor, I had enough money to buy a car and take off for California to meet up with my friend, Jack, who was now out of the hospital. While working in the apple orchard, one of the other guys had a dog with pups. He talked me into taking one who was half German Shepherd and Collie. I called him Freak. He was a beautiful pup.

Off to California

Within a few days, Freak and I set out for the Bay Area in the Ford station wagon I had just purchased. As I was cruising down I-5 through the State of Oregon, I picked up some hitchhikers who just happened to have some LSD. We all partook and continued cruising through the night down I-5 into California. Somehow, I could remain somewhat sane even when tripping on LSD and driving without mishap. Now, it's scary to think about drivers like that on the road. About an hour later, we picked up a couple more hitchhikers who were constantly bickering. When we stopped for gas, one of the last hitchhikers I had just picked up struck  up a conversation with me, saying that the person he was hitchhiking with was a leech and he was having a hard time shaking him. He told me to be careful, or I would have a hard time getting rid of him, too. He then told me he wasn't going to continue with us. He took this opportunity to shake him once and for all.

Even though I wasn't necessarily going to San Francisco, as I was going to Fremont on the other side of the Bay, I drove into the city and dropped all my hitchhikers off at Golden Gate Park. I then headed across the Oakland Bay Bridge to Fremont. The guy I was warned about tried hard to get me to take him with me, but I held firm and insisted he leave with the others. I spent the next several weeks hanging out in Fremont with my friend Jack. Most of my drug and hippie experiences were confined to my army time. But now that I was out and free to do whatever I wanted. I was really into experiencing all that I could. Jack was involved during the heyday of Haight Ashbury. I looked at this trip as my opportunity to experience some of this. I enjoyed my time with Jack, but to my dismay, I found the time in California somewhat disappointing. For the most part, we just hung out at parks and got high with his band of friends. We did make a couple of trips to Yosemite and one trip to Big Sur. Other than that, there wasn't much happening. Subconsciously, I was hoping to connect somehow with the destiny I had begun to sense while in Vietnam. Unfortunately, I was coming up empty and was still feeling very lost.

After a few weeks with Jack and his band of friends, I was almost broke. I decided to head back home. On my way home, I stopped by Sacramento to see another army buddy, Kevin, who had been in Nam with me. I spent a few days with him and his friends, going to Folsom Lake and some mud pits with mudslides next to the American River. After sliding down the mudslides into the mud pits, we would jump into the river to clean off. It was quite an experience. On the final day before continuing home, Kevin and I went to the California State Fair and dropped acid together.

On my way to Oregon, I decided to stop in Eugene and look up John, another buddy from Nam. We had gotten kicked out of the army together. John was my friend who went a little too far in his insubordination. He ended with an undesirable discharge, whereas I finished with a General Discharge with all the benefits. We had formed a strong bond because of the process of transferring from one company to another to rehabilitate. We found ourselves amongst strangers as we went through this process. I repeated this process three times until the army realized I was beyond rehabilitation.

While in California, I heard about a Rock Festival happening in Satsop, Washington, southeast of Seattle and Tacoma. When I arrived in Eugene and connected with John, he, too, had heard about Satsop and wanted to go. John and I were on our way to the Rock Festival within an hour. However, we decided to first stop by my home in Wenatchee, pick up camping equipment, and see if anybody else wanted to go. We arrived at my home and waited until the following day to head to the coast for the festival. I discovered that one of my brothers had already taken off for the festival. We then gathered some camping equipment, sleeping bags, and such. Our family always had plenty of camping equipment since we did that for recreation and vacations. Before heading out of town, we stopped by the pool hall, where I hung out when I didn't have anything better to do. We wanted to see if anyone was hanging around and if they might want to go with us. Neither John nor I had any money, so we were hoping to get someone to go along to help with the gas. I still didn't know many people, having been gone for nearly two years. But I did meet a few of my brother's friends during the first two weeks of returning home from Vietnam. A couple of them were at the pool hall that morning and wanted to go with us. Their names were Rusty and Paul, who would become pot my smoking buddies the following year.

Satsop Rock Festival and More Vietnam Experiences

The trip from Wenatchee to the state's western side is a beautiful drive. It takes you through the heart of the Cascade Mountain Range. It had been quite some time since I had been on that highway, so I was looking forward to the trip. However, driving along, Rusty began questioning whether I was ever involved in the Jesus thing. I thought this was rather strange as I hadn't shared with him or any of my friends about my experiences with Jesus in Vietnam. Yet, he had somehow picked up a vibe from me that Christ was a part of my life. At this point in my life, I wasn't sure where I stood on the issue, but I knew something was deposited into my spirit due to a vision I had while in Vietnam, which I will discuss in detail in a later chapter. So, John and I shared our Vietnam experiences and how we had gotten into Jesus for a while.

We were both assigned bunker guard positions at the second company where they sent me for rehabilitation—where John had already been for a while. Bunker duty meant we could sit in a bunker all day while smoking pot, reading, and studying our Bibles together.

I discovered that John had turned himself in as a heroin addict and had undergone treatment. By the time I arrived, John was out of treatment and into Jesus. During our days at the 539th, several of us got into Jesus, but John wasn't. We all knew he was getting addicted to heroin. Rusty and Paul both  listened with great interest as we shared many of our experiences in Vietnam. We shared stories of constantly thumbing our noses at the military authority and about Sgt. Cain, who was trying hard to bust potheads.

Sergeant Cain

On one occasion, Sergeant Cain grabbed five or six of us and had us marching all over the flight line while he lectured us about smoking pot and what useless soldiers we were. We took the opportunity to give him a taste of his own medicine. We began to call him every name in the book, telling him what a no-good lifer he was. It was pretty humorous to watch him react, knowing there was nothing he could do about it. This little episode did nothing more than to ignite the hatred between him and us further. A few days after the incident of him marching us all over the flight line, Sergeant Cain was coming out of the company office, and John happened to be just outside and said something to him that pushed his buttons. Sergeant Cain responded by punching John and knocking him to the ground. Well, that was the end of Sergeant Cain. The Company Commander shipped him out after that. We never saw him again.

The encounter with Sgt. Cain was one of the reasons John received an undesirable discharge rather than a general discharge. It wouldn't be the last time John got into a punching match with someone in authority. It also taught those in authority in our company—Don't mess with the heads; they will get you in the end. On one occasion, our company commander was trying to conspire with our First Sergeant in a campaign to bust all the heads. We later discovered our First Sergeant wouldn't go along with it because he had a better way of dealing with us. His method was to leave us alone and communicate on friendly terms. We all respected and liked him very much.

Earlier in the year, when we teargassed the lifers, the First Sergeant came to me and asked me, in an amenable sort of casual way, if I had anything to do with it. He knew I was responsible for throwing a smoke grenade in his barracks on another occasion because someone had reported that they had seen me running from his barracks after I threw the grenade. Though he knew it was me, it was never proven, so I never got in trouble. After the smoke grenade incident, the First Sergeant was smart enough to have his door sealed air-tight so that he would never be subject to that again. On another occasion, he came to me because he was concerned about one of his Spec-5 guys, who seemed addicted to heroin. He was genuinely asking me for advice on how to deal with it. Of course, I had to tell him that I had no idea. My implication to him was that, as far as I was concerned, this person was a pig because he was an E-5. He was one of my friends, and I knew he was getting addicted to heroin. He became Frank's roommate after I moved into a hooch with the other heads. He became Frank's heroin or "skag" buddy instead of me. I later went to him and told him about my conversation with the First Sergeant. I told him that the pigs were wise to him and that he had better be careful.

After a little over three hours of driving, we finally arrived at the festival grounds. Upon arrival, we found a place to camp for the next few days down by the river. We were ready to have three fun-filled days of drugs, rock and roll, and whatever else came our way. We saw Eric Burden, War, Delaney and Bonnie, and Wishbone Ash, among others, stoned out on acid. As John and I were making our rounds, I saw another friend I had recently met while staying with my friend, Jack, in the Bay area. He was wearing this colorful hat with the words LSD on it. As it turned out, he was selling acid. I convinced him to give us some LSD to enjoy the festival.

All in all, it was a great time, especially being reunited with John. On our way home, we dropped John off at the I-5 Intersection, where he hitchhiked back to his home in Eugene, Oregon. It was sad to see John go, but he had his life to get on with, and I had mine. That was the last time I ever saw or heard from him. It was pretty sad!

Readjusting to Civilian Life
Chapter Three

Once back home, I needed to figure out what to do next. I felt like I had worked out some restlessness and the need to experience freedom from my time in the army for almost two years. Before joining the military, I worked at a frozen food plant in Wenatchee and knew I could get my job back with my seniority intact as they honored those who had served in the military. It was also a union-based job, so I knew they had to accept me back. It seemed like a logical thing to do, so that is what I did.

Back at My Old Job

Upon returning to the job at the frozen food plant, I was put back in my previous position. It meant working in the hopper room where all the vegetables were mixed in big hoppers before going to the packaging machines. My job was to ensure I mixed them correctly according to the packaging ordered. Sometimes I would also work in the silos where the company stored corn and peas in below-freezing temperatures. I would have a giant vacuum hose that sucked all the vegetables as I walked on them. From there, they went to the packaging.

After a few weeks on the job, I was transferred to the ice plant at a different location but owned by the same company. The ice plant was in the railroad freight yard, where they put together trains. My job was to shove 300 lb. cakes of ice into the refrigerated cars. After working there for a couple of months, my foreman approached me one day and asked me about my plans. He wanted to know if I planned on becoming a permanent employee. It made me think about what I wanted to do with my life. I had no idea. One thing was sure! I wasn't ready to settle down into permanency, where every day was doing the same thing over and over.

It was well into September 1971, and the apple harvest season had begun. I thought I would rather pick apples with my father and uncles. Picking apples was a way to make fast money. I grew up in the apple orchards and knew I could make $40 to $50 a day, which was good money in the early 1970s. So that's what I did. I quit my job and drove to the apple orchard near Lake Chelan. I felt like I was making a good decision even though my family thought otherwise. Nobody could understand why I would quit what they considered a good job. I had just spent the last 13 months in Vietnam. I was just not ready to be tied down to a job when uncertain about what I wanted to do, so I headed to Chelan to pick apples.

Apple Picking and Paul Peters

Every year, most of my uncles and my dad would take their vacations and pick apples at Paul Peters' apple orchard near Lake Chelan. They had been doing this for as long as I could remember. In fact, on one occasion, the local Wenatchee paper put out an entire piece on my dad and my uncles called *"Reunion in an Apple Orchard,"* which ran this picture of all of them.

During my high school years, my brothers and I lived and worked in Manson during the summers. Paul's orchard had several cabins on the property. My brothers and I would stay in one while my uncles stayed in another one down the road. I have many fond memories of those days, working from the early morning until mid-afternoon. After working hard, we would head to the lake to spend the remainder of the afternoons swimming. One summer, we were even allowed to have a couple of our friends join us working there. It was a great summer. During my senior year in high school, I was allowed to take a week out of school to pick apples. I made almost $300 the week I took off, which was good money in 1967. These were some thoughts I had when I decided to quit my job with the Frozen Food Company and Ice Plant.

Following the apple harvest, I went to work in one of the Apple Sheds in Wenatchee, where my brother, Bob, was working. This job lasted well into February. My other brother, Dick, now called Junior, eventually got a couple of our friends, Bob, and me, positions on the steel gang in the early spring of 1972. Because Dick was still a teenager when he started working for the Railroad, they started calling him Junior, a name that has stuck with him through all these years. Junior was now an assistant foreman on a railroad steel gang, which enabled him to get us jobs. I enjoyed the variety of jobs I was doing in those days. It was easy to get employment when needed without feeling tied down to any permanency.

Working on the Railroad

The railroad had different types of crews. There was the "tie gang," whose job was replacing worn-out ties. I was a part of a crew called the "steel gang" because of the nature of the job. We traveled all over the State of Washington, putting down the new ¼-mile rail sections instead of the old, short sections. It was a great spring and summer job. We lived in railroad cars with a mess hall car and everything. It reminded me of my army life, with a bunch of guys living and working together and three meals a day provided. Even though the work was hard, it was an enjoyable time. I was hired as a laborer, pounding spikes and anchors into the new rail we laid down. We started in the Seattle area in Sedro Woolley and ended up near Spokane.

After a few months of working on the railroad, I was ready to move on again. Something within me wanted to seek more of an adventure out of life. I was still very unsettled and needed to get going and do something new. I thought about hitchhiking to the East Coast to visit another army buddy named Ed. I had become somewhat radical in my thinking, not wanting to be tied down to anything. As a result, I sold my car and the stereo system I had shipped home from Vietnam. I sold anything that represented being tied down. I then purchased an ounce of hashish and some China White Heroin, which I had just begun to use at the time but only snorted it. One of the guys I was working with on the railroad had an excellent connection for getting heroin and kept a few of us well-supplied. I also purchased a new backpack and an army-issued down sleeping bag. With all this, I got my last paycheck from the railroad and hit the road with my dog, Freak. I was headed for the East Coast, hoping to satisfy the longing for something different than what I had been experiencing since coming home from Vietnam.

East Coast Hitchhiking Adventure
Chapter Four

I was headed for Pennsylvania, where my friend Ed lived. During this trip, I lost my wallet, which contained all my money—about $350 and my ID. I was going through Wisconsin with another guy I had started hitchhiking with back in Idaho. A man in a pickup truck had given us a ride, and somehow, my wallet had fallen out of my pocket when he dropped us off. I would be without money for the remainder of the trip. When I eventually got home, I discovered the person who had found my wallet had mailed it back to me. All the money was intact except for a small amount he took out for postage.

Meeting up with Traveling Companions

Upon quitting the railroad to hitchhike across the country to Pennsylvania and purchasing the hashish and some of the Heroin, I was on my way. After passing through Idaho and entering Montana, I met up with four hippie-looking characters on their way to Connecticut. We decided to travel together since we were going in the same direction. They were happy to take up with me since I had plenty of drugs. Somewhere along the way, we all decided to take a detour and hitchhike up to Glacier National Park. I had never been there, so I was up for it and thought it would be a great adventure. Along the way, we stopped at a KOA campground and went into the Laundromat to get high on heroin. I didn't realize at first that I had taken up company with a bunch of junkies. As it turned out, these guys were hard-core junkies. I was just dabbling in it and snorting it, whereas they had needles and were ready to inject it. I warned them that it was probably much purer and more potent than they were accustomed to using. I didn't want them overdosing on me. In Nam, the heroin was so pure that we smoked it in cigarettes, although I occasionally snorted. I had only used a needle once before to shoot up our liquid speed in Vietnam. With my first experience with the needle, I overdosed on the speed, which caused me to be cautious of injecting anything again.

After sitting around for a while and enjoying the high from the heroin, we decided to hit the road before people started getting suspicious of our behavior. We realized that the four of us traveling together would make it difficult to get rides, so we split up. I also had my dog, Freak, with me. He was half Collie and half German shepherd— a beautiful dog very protective of me — a one-person dog. We decided to split up into pairs. Two of them took off in one direction, while two of us took off the other way. I was hitting it off with the guy named Norm. He and I decided to continue to Glacier National Park. I realized some time later that the other two had somehow stolen the rest of the heroin from me. I still had the hashish, so I wasn't too concerned. It was probably a good thing as it prevented me from using too much heroin and getting addicted. Had I stayed working on the railroad, I'm sure I would have gotten addicted as I was moving in that direction. Even though I dabbled in heroin occasionally, I never got strung out on it. I would go through mild withdrawals from time to time, but nothing serious like I had experienced some of my buddies going through in Nam. Watching them go through gut-wrenching cramps gave me a healthy regard for it. The thought of going through severe withdrawals scared the living daylights out of me.

Norm and I arrived at Glacier National Park in the early evening and headed to a restaurant. I had a few hundred dollars from my last paycheck from the railroad but didn't want to spend any of it, knowing I needed to stretch it out as far as possible. I also had my hashish. We were able to talk a couple of waitresses into giving us a free meal, and sure enough, they did. In return, we gave them some hashish. They were very grateful and said we could have ordered steaks for that. After leaving the restaurant, we found a nice campsite and hit the sack. My first day on the road turned out to be a great day, and now I had a friend to travel with for the remainder of my trip to the East Coast. I was one happy camper!

Hiking in Glacier National Park

We were in Glacier National Park and had no idea what to do. We had breakfast with the people camping next to us and began asking what there was to do. They suggested we go on a hike to a nearby lake. Taking their advice, we headed out for the lake, happy that we had something to do. It would be a nice hike that would end with a cabin. So off we went on another adventure with Freak tagging along. Before hitting the trail, we stopped by the store to get enough food to last a few days. The hike was exhilarating, with a good part of it going uphill. I was in surprisingly good shape from having worked on the railroad, so it wasn't too much of a physical challenge for me. Norm seemed to be huffing and puffing a bit, but he made it without too much trouble. We arrived late afternoon; sure enough, the cabin was just a couple hundred feet from the lake. We were excited and happy as we viewed it from a distance. We spent the next few days hanging out at the cabin, eating, sleeping, and smoking hashish. We wanted to go out on the lake, so we constructed a raft with rope, boards, and logs we had found. Norm and I were hitting it off well. It was good to have someone to travel with after spending part of my first day alone. We planned to continue to Pennsylvania, where I would stop, and he would continue to Connecticut. We planned to visit the other National Parks: Yellowstone, the Black Hills, and Mount Rushmore. I had seen these places as a kid with my parents on vacation, but that was a long time ago.

After a few days at the cabin, we were beginning to get bored, so we hightailed it back to the campground and restaurant area. We had another meal at the restaurant, spent another night at the campsite, and then decided we had seen enough of Glacier. So, we found a ride out, this time going a different way than we had come in on. The ride out was a very scenic drive, revealing the wonders of God's creation.

Hitchhiking Games

By this time, Norm and I were fast becoming good friends. As we were hitchhiking toward Yellowstone, we were constantly smoking hashish. Stoned out of our minds, we started making up games with the rides we were catching. We would dream about the perfect ride, and it would happen. Our dream rides went on for a couple of days. Finally, after smoking so much hashish, we were hungry and had the munchies. As we thought about what our first dream ride should look like, we came up with the idea of having them take us out for some fried chicken. For some reason, we were very hungry for chicken. Sure enough, it happened just as we had envisioned. After our first dream ride worked out so well, we decided our next ride would be a car with people who had some beer. Sure enough, it happened again. We were having the time of our lives as we were enjoying each other's company while dreaming up the perfect rides. It was now getting late into the evening. We needed a long ride that would allow us to sleep through the night and take us to Yellowstone. As if on cue, our next ride turned out to be a nice long ride through the night that dropped us off the following day just outside of Yellowstone National Park. These experiences seem rather strange, but that's what happened. They also instilled in me the confidence I needed for my journey. Even though I wasn't serving the Lord at this phase of my life, I sensed He was watching over and protecting me.

After spending a day or two in Yellowstone visiting *"Old Faithful"* and other sites, we were ready for our next adventure. Our next stop would be the Black Hills and Mt. Rushmore. We had a wonderful time getting rides through the Black Hills and the Badlands of South Dakota and then playing tourists at Mt. Rushmore. Leaving South Dakota and Mt Rushmore behind, we were now off to our final destinations: Pennsylvania and Connecticut. When Norm and I reached Pennsylvania, I called Ed and found out he was in jail for selling heroin. He wouldn't be out for another week, so I decided to go to Connecticut with Norm and spend more time with him and his friends.

A Week with Norm in Connecticut

The week with Norm went very well, except for the fact that my dog, Freak, was stolen. He wasn't doing well after being hit by a car in the Midwest. Norm and I had been on the other side of the *"Freeway Rest Stop"* having coffee with some people we had just met and had left our packs with Freak to guard. When we returned, he got excited and ran across the highway to meet us. He was then hit by a car. He probably had some internal injuries. However, he was an excellent hitchhiking companion. A car would stop, and he would jump in and sit next to the window, behaving very well. On one occasion, after being picked up, the driver finally realized I had a dog with me after we were down the road for quite a ways. He turned and said, "I didn't even realize you had a dog. He's so well-mannered."

While in Connecticut with Norm, we met up with the others who were with him when we first met back in Coeur d'Alene. They were still talking about how good the heroin I had shared with them back in Montana was. Of course, they never admitted to stealing the rest of it from me. I had decided to let it go since I was now on their turf. There was nothing to gain by making a big deal about it. Besides, they had told their friends how good it was, which caused them to welcome me into their band of friends. We all took some LSD together and had a great time.

I found it quite interesting; often, when tripping with others, I would be the one who ended up guiding the trip. In this case, we were all sitting around tripping on the LSD, and I fell into a meditation thing when I suddenly realized it was what we were all doing.

I remember saying something to the effect, "We can do something else. I was just getting carried away with my thoughts."

Their reply was, "No, we like this."

Partying with Ed and His Friends in Pennsylvania

After a week of parting with Norm and his friends, it was time to hit the road and go back to Pennsylvania to visit my buddy, Ed. During my time in Nam, I looked up to Ed. Out of all of us, he seemed to have it most together. Like Jack, Ed had experienced much in the drug and

hippie culture before joining the army. But, unfortunately, like many others, he, too, got addicted to heroin while in Nam.

I spent nearly three weeks with Ed and his friends, partying in the woods and doing crazy things. I was really into LSD during this phase of my life and took it whenever it came my way. We had a campground set up with people constantly coming and going. There were always lots of drugs, including LSD, and I still had some of my hashish left. By the time I left, my ounce of hashish was gone. It was a good thing because a policeman stopped and searched for me on my return trip to Wenatchee while waiting for a ride on the side of the road. It must have been before *"probable cause"* because there was no reason for being searched other than how I looked. I was waiting for a ride on the ramp when the policeman stopped and began scouring my body and backpack.

My return trip home was somewhat uneventful, except for meeting another person in Colorado who wanted to hitchhike with me for a while. At one point, I started getting tired of him and suggested we part ways. I let him have the first ride while I waited for another one. A day later, while passing through Oregon, we met up again. He didn't seem to have any destination in mind, so I let him tag along with me all the way home to Wenatchee. He stayed with me at my parent's home for a week until he got into a fistfight with one of my friends living in a trailer parked on their property. He was the guy from my railroad job who had the heroin connection. The railroad crew I had been working with before taking off to the East Coast was now working near Wenatchee. After the alteration with my friend, I had to tell him to leave. Now, back on my home turf, I wondered what would be next.

Jack and the Minnesota Group
Chapter Five

Once back in Wenatchee, I wasn't sure what to do. I spent a couple of weeks not doing much of anything. I then decided to go back to work on the railroad. The steel gang was now working along the Wenatchee River in the Leavenworth Cashmere area, so I decided to see if I could get my job back. Sure enough, they hired me back.

Jack Shows Up

After a few weeks of working on the steel gang again, my friend Jack showed up unannounced from Fremont. I was able to get him a job working on the railroad as well. We had a great time working together, although some of my friends on the railroad didn't take to him very well. Jack had a strong ego and clashed with others of the same temperament. My brother, the assistant foreman, tried to fire him on one occasion, but I interceded, and he kept him on.

After finishing up the work near Wenatchee, our crew was ready to move to its next job in Spokane. I no longer had a car, so Jack, I, and a few others elected to ride the train in our sleeping car to the new destination. We all began smoking pot while traveling along on the train. Jack and I got stoned and thought climbing onto the train's roof would be cool. I know this was stupid; nevertheless, we were very high and stoned people occasionally tend to do stupid things.

Fired from the Railroad

As we sat on top of the train, while speeding along, another train going the opposite way passed us. They saw us and radioed our train conductor. Before we knew it, the train stopped to deal with us. We knew we were in big trouble. When we arrived in Spokane, my brother, the assistant foreman, had been assigned to deal with us. He fired us on the spot and told us to pack our stuff and disappear quickly. My railroad days now come to a screeching halt. No more *"Gandy Dancing"* for me![3]

---

[3] **Gandy dancer** "Before machines were used to construct and maintain railroads, manual labor was used. The laborers who work on the railroads were called gandy

Jack and I found our way back to Wenatchee and temporarily settled in at my parents' home. We just hung out during the next few weeks, getting to know people in town. It was now apple harvest time. We decided to get a job at the apple packing shed where I had worked the previous year. We were both hired immediately and went to work. My brother, Bob, was working there as well. Since we didn't have a car, we moved into the old Columbia Hotel, a few short blocks away.

Hanging with New Friends

We had recently met a group of people who were new to the area and renting a home a few blocks from the hotel. We became very friendly with them and began hanging out together regularly. They were all from Minnesota and hoping to get some work picking apples. Jack and I continued to work at the packing shed until, one day, he got fired. He was always getting things mixed up, and they finally got tired of his mistakes and fired him. A few days later, I lost interest in the job and quit.

Jack and I were both using heroin during this time. A couple of guys working at the apple packing shed had an excellent connection to Mexican brown heroin. We would all go to one of their homes during lunch breaks, shoot up, and then return to work. I was now shooting it rather than snorting. I had started shooting it when Jack and I were working on the railroad. My friend from My first venture working for the railroad was still supplying some of us with good China white heroin. On one occasion, we even dropped acid while working. It is no wonder Jack got fired. Surprisingly, I could function reasonably well on drugs, even LSD.

We continued hanging out with the Minnesota group and even got a job picking apples together outside the city. Working with a bunch of hippies was different from working with my uncles. All they wanted to do was take one break after another, which doesn't work well when you're getting paid by how much you pick compared to getting paid by the hour. I was picking two to three times as much as them. I was at home in an apple orchard and knew what you had to do to make good money at it. They had no idea.

The Minnesota group was starting to get frustrated with the apple-picking thing and wanted to return to Minnesota. Jack and I had both become interested in the girls. Jack was interested in Paula, and I had

---

dancers. Though it is unclear how the word originated, this slang term started being used in the early 1900s."

taken an interest in Nancy. The four of us were always doing things together. They wanted Jack and me to go with them, which resulted in all of us planning to catch a freight train to Minnesota. There were six of us altogether. It would be my first experience riding a freight train. Little did I know I would become amazingly comfortable riding freight trains in the months ahead! Once we decided to go, we didn't waste time waiting around. With our packs packed and ready to go, we found our way to a good spot while waiting to catch the right freight train going East. When we realized what train we needed to catch, it was already moving about five miles an hour. We had to run alongside it, throwing our packs in and jumping aboard. We all made it without mishap.

Jack gets Arrested in Montana

Traveling through Montana, we stopped at one of the freight yards along the way for quite a while. While waiting for the train to continue, the Railroad Police detected us. They checked all our IDs and discovered Jack was a wanted man in California. He was then taken into custody and shipped back to California. We were allowed to continue our trek to Minnesota, but we were all a little depressed after losing Jack. We ended up spending a week or so in Minnesota, but it wasn't the same without Jack. We rode horses on a ranch that a relative of one of the gals owned and then returned to Minneapolis. We stayed at Nancy's mother's home for a couple of days before making plans to leave. They all wanted to return to Wenatchee, which I didn't desire to do. I felt my time with them was over, especially with Jack out of the picture. The thought of returning to Wenatchee didn't resonate with me. So, I followed my intuition, split with the Minnesota group, and struck out independently. I said my goodbyes to everyone, stuck out my thumb, and headed for Arizona.

Meeting Hobo
Chapter Six

With Jack out of the picture after getting arrested in Montana, I headed for Arizona. Because I didn't have a strong enough connection with Nancy, the gal I was with from the Minnesota group, nor did I want to go back to Wenatchee, I took off for Arizona on my own. I had no idea what I was getting myself into but was eager to discover what was yet ahead as I struck out alone on this crazy adventure.

I had come a long way since returning home from Vietnam but was still very much confused and lost while wondering what would become of my life. The trip to the East Coast gave me the courage to strike out alone in Phoenix. I was amazed at the bold steps I was taking to figure out who I was becoming. It was as if an internal force was pushing me forward. It all seemed so out of character with the person I had been while growing up. I had changed in many ways. The time in Vietnam and the drugs had definitely altered my personality.

A New Friend for New Adventures

After a week or so of hanging out with my new friends in Tempe, Arizona, a new friend appeared in our small group of vagabonds. He went by the name "Hobo." Both of us, being Vietnam Veterans, hit it off right away. He was a Marine who had recently completed his service in Vietnam and had just spent the last few months hitchhiking through Mexico. He was now passing through Arizona, and I was happy to meet up with him. For the next week or so, we continued to hang out with the others but also found ourselves taking off on our own, exploring the bars, and doing other things around Tempe while occasionally working odd jobs.

Before meeting Hobo, I had become very unsettled in my feelings, not knowing where I was headed or what I was doing. I didn't have much direction except for a desire to experience something different. I was very unsettled after returning from

Nam. I just felt the need to get away from all that was familiar and encounter what was out in the world. Growing up in a religious and confining environment, I lived a sheltered life. I was ready to experience what I perceived during this phase of my life: absolute freedom. So, I felt free but very unsettled, and then I met Hobo. He would eventually start calling me *"Space,"* which resulted in me being called *"Space"* for the next year while doing crazy things with him. He was about to invite me along on the adventure of a lifetime.

One night, after partying in a bar with some other guys, we stepped out the back door to smoke a joint with them. It was getting quite late, and one of the guys asked us where we planned on sleeping that night. We were both a little drunk and high from the pot, which meant trying to get back to our cave in our present condition seemed a little ridiculous. So, we decided right then that we would sleep in the alley. We crawled into a nearby car that appeared to be abandoned and went to sleep.

When we went back to our cave the following day, I discovered someone had stolen my down sleeping bag. I thought to myself, "Just great! What was I to do now without a good sleeping bag?" I found some blankets somewhere, but they weren't the same as having my nice bag.

In the next few days, Hobo said, "Hey, you want to go to New Orleans with me?"

His invitation was just the adventure I was looking for, so I said, "Sure, I'd love to."

That was all it took. We immediately began planning to leave Tempe and head out to New Orleans. Hobo was a guy who was always on the move and ready to explore new places, so I was more than happy to take up with someone who knew all the ropes of living on the road. In addition, he seemed to be offering me the kind of security I needed during this phase of my life. As mentioned earlier, I had been feeling very unsettled, and Hobo's offer to travel with him was now causing the feeling to dissipate.

Beg, Borrow, and Steal

We had arranged a ride to Tucson with someone we had just met, but I still needed a sleeping bag. So, we drove out to where we had all been camping, and I stole one of their excellent down bags. I figured I needed it more than he did, so I took it. Our motto for survival over the next several months while living on the road would be "beg, borrow, and steal." Later that afternoon, I ran into the person from whom I had stolen the sleeping bag on the street in downtown Tempe.

He said, "Someone stole my sleeping bag the same way yours was. All they took was the sleeping bag and nothing else."

I could tell he was a little suspicious that it was me because he wanted to know why my pack was so full. Fortunately, I had stashed the sleeping bag in the car's trunk and still had the blankets in my backpack. I showed him my gear, and he saw blankets, which convinced him it wasn't me. I felt guilty and nearly confessed that it was me but decided not to. So, after he left, I got into the car with Hobo. It was the last I ever saw of that group, even though we passed through Tempe a couple more times over the next several months.

After arriving in Tucson, we planned to catch a freight train, stay on it through Texas, and not get off until we arrived in New Orleans. I had hopped on a freight train for the first time in Washington with my friends when we left for Minnesota, so this wasn't a new experience. Also, in Tucson, I had my first experience selling my blood at a Blood-Bank to get drinking money. Hobo was quite accustomed to this and said it was easy to make a few bucks when needed. We would do this over and over the next few months in various places we visited.

As we walked around Tucson, Hobo said, "We should go hang out at the college campus. I've learned from experience that college girls are interested in people like us."

His words proved true because it wasn't long before we met a couple of gals living in the girls' dorm. We ended up staying with them in their dorm, partying with them and their friends for the next few days. I was beginning to settle into this new life of living on the road and enjoying the new adventures that were starting to come my way. Having a partner like Hobo was exciting and fun. He was a natural extrovert, while I was an introvert. It encouraged me to get out of my shell, learn to take advantage of situations and enjoy what was happening around me.

Freight Train to New Orleans

After a few days, we had worn out our welcome with the girls, so we decided it was time to hit the road again. I discovered that this would happen to us quite often over the next several months—we would party with people until we wore out our welcome and then move on to our next destination, wherever that might be. After leaving the girls, we headed towards the freight yard, hoping to catch a train going toward New Orleans. Upon locating the freight yard, we began to ask around if there was a train headed in the direction of New Orleans. One of the workers pointed us toward a train about to leave. When we reached the train, it had already started moving about 5-10 mph.

I yelled at Hobo, "Come on; we can do this!"

We had to run alongside the train and hop on while it was moving. We quickly found an empty car with open doors, threw our packs in, and jumped on. I'm not sure what would've happened if we had not made it with our packs already on, but we did. It had been quite an experience, but we managed it and were now on our way to New Orleans.

Hobo was quite taken aback by my bravado and said, "I'm not sure that we should have tried such a daring exploit."

But it all worked out. I had first done this when we all had to jump on the train leaving Wenatchee for Minnesota, which accounted for my bravado. After that, I knew we could do it. However, looking back, I realize that it was a foolish thing to do.

Our goal was to stay on the train through Texas. We had heard that Texas was a redneck state and didn't take kindly to hippies or freaks, as others were now calling hippies. We wanted to get through Texas as fast as possible. Unfortunately, our hunger pangs would get the best of us, and we would eventually get off the train when it stopped in San Antonio. The train ride was a lot of fun and a great way to see the country. We often would sit in front of the open doors and wave at people as the train sped down the tracks. We enjoyed watching people's expressions and the scenery as we sped along. I also discovered that riding freight trains was a good time to sit back and smoke a joint while meditating and contemplating many things, especially about my life and what I was doing.

Deep Reflections of 'Nam

As I mentioned earlier, I had a real spiritual awakening in Vietnam. Before arriving in Nam, I had only tried drugs a few times. I had smoked hashish a couple of times and had dropped LSD once. The first time I took LSD, I fell in love with it. On my first day in Vietnam, I began to smoke marijuana regularly and took LSD periodically. It wasn't as readily available as the other drugs were. It was usually only available when someone's friends back in the States sent it. Some of my buddies were now snorting heroin, but I held off for quite a while from doing that. After one of my friends, Larry returned from a drug rehab program from using heroin, I began to use it sparingly. He would have me hold his stuff so he wouldn't use it as much. It was during this time that I would take an occasional snort. It went on for a couple of weeks.

One day, upon returning from an unauthorized outing to Saigon, I realized I had contracted the clap.[4] As a result, I went to the military dispensary to get my penicillin shots. Unfortunately, on the second day of getting the penicillin shots, I went into severe convulsions before the doctor could even get the needle out of me. The penicillin must have reacted to all the drugs I had been taking.

The episode with the convulsions was the most frightening and terrible experience I had ever encountered! My body was totally out of control, with my legs and arms flailing wildly while simultaneously experiencing flashbacks from LSD. The medics eventually got me under control, and I seemed alright after that, but it left me with a sharp sense of how fragile one's life can be. As I was walking back to my company unit, I ran into one of my sergeants as I walked by the PX. I can remember mentioning to him that I had just come close to dying. I honestly felt like I had. Later that evening, I began to feel like I was going to go through convulsions again and was becoming quite frightened. I figured I had better get the orderly clerk to drive me to the dispensary to see if they would give me some tranquilizers to calm me down.

On the way, I began to pray, "Oh God! Get me out of this mess, and I'll give my life to You."

I was as serious as ever when I prayed that prayer. I had grown up in a good Christian home, so I knew what you were supposed to do when you were about to die, and I honestly felt like this was it for me. I had always known about God's plan for salvation but had rebelled against it because I wanted to experience more of what the world had to offer. But right then, I couldn't care less about the world. The only thing that mattered was God reaching out and saving me.

I made it to the dispensary, and they gave me a potent depressant, and I survived the immediate crisis. God was looking after me. He saw the direction my life was going and decided enough was enough! He decided it was time for the rock to come crashing down on me; that's precisely what happened. It woke me up to the reality of what was taking place in my life.

As I look back on this time in my life, I realize that I am truly fortunate to be alive and in a sane mind today. During those lost years, I

---

[4] **Gonorrhea** is a sexually transmitted infection that is often referred to as the clap.

abused my mind terribly with all the drugs I took. I am very thankful to the Lord Jesus Christ for saving me and giving me a sober mind that allows me to enjoy everything around me without the aid of mind-altering drugs.

Though I didn't fully commit my life to God at that time while riding along on the freight train and listening to the sounds it was making as it traveled towards San Antonio, I realized even though I wasn't following God or His ways now, He wasn't far from me. As a result, my thoughts would often drift back to Him, wondering how the pieces to the puzzle all would fit together.

As we continued on the train, my mind again flashed back to that night after getting some depressants. I got into my bunk and tried to sleep, but my mind was wide awake. Unknowingly, I was beginning to go through mild withdrawal symptoms from heroin and couldn't sleep. So, once again, I began to pray. I was becoming increasingly frightened as I kept thinking back about the convulsions I had gone through earlier in the day.

The Vision of Seeing My Life Flash before Me

As I began to pray, I saw my whole life flash before me. From my earliest memories, God showed me how He had been with me at each stage of my life. It was an amazing thing! I was experiencing a vision from God. There were so many things that He showed me in the vision. The experience with the vision would become one of the most significant defining moments of my life—an event that would typify other related events that would follow. God took me into the future as the vision progressed, revealing my calling. The calling He disclosed to me was indelibly stamped upon my soul to the degree that I couldn't shake it in the three years that followed. Over the next several months, I got into Jesus and the Bible along with some of my pot-smoking buddies.

After the convulsions and the vision incident while in Vietnam, I was a nervous wreck. I came close to having a complete breakdown. The experience caused me to begin to re-examine everything I had been doing. At times, it seemed like my mind had exploded entirely. It was as if it shattered into a thousand pieces; now, I had to try to put them all back together.

When God revealed my calling, I remember saying, "Yes, I will allow You to work Your will in my life, but You will have to take it slow and easy."

God Gets His Hook into Me

I wasn't ready to tackle what He had shown me in the vision all at once, but I was open to it with the realization that something extraordinary had happened to me. God had gotten His hook into me by planting the seed that would eventually cause me to turn to Him wholeheartedly. Even though I would spend the next three years trying to spit it out, I would discover I couldn't. I would discover many pieces to this puzzle that would take me years to figure out as they unfolded. Well, God was taking it slow and easy. So, there I was—two years later—on a freight train to New Orleans, and I still hadn't given in to what God wanted to do with my life. Though I was running from God and the vision, I found He wouldn't let me go. He had set the hook and was now very patient with me while slowly reeling me in. God is faithful and long-suffering with us even when we seem to give up on Him.

I remember what my mother said to me the day I left home on the freight train with Jack, our girl friends, and two others. She said, "Kenny, you're running from God."

I tried to convince her that what I was doing was somehow God's plan for my life. But unfortunately, I was deceived because of the drugs I was unwilling to give up then, which allowed Satan to get his deceptive hooks into me.

The Bible says, *"There is a way that seems right to a man, but its end is the way of death."*

I hadn't experienced death yet, but I sure was one lost puppy. I was hoping to find a way to connect with the vision I had while in Vietnam without having to give up drugs or the lifestyle I had now chosen. Talk about being deceived. I was very deceived but too lost in myself to know how deeply.

Getting a New Hippie Name

"Hey, Space!"

Hobo started calling me Space after a conversation we had one day. He was telling me that if I was going to be a road freak, I needed a different name. I had told him I had a similar conversation with another hippie, Yellow Dog, whom I worked with on the railroad, who gave me the name Space Cowboy. From then on, Hobo began to call me Space.

"Yeah, you can sure tell you used to do heroin. You nod off from time to time, just like the junkies."

He was referring to my time sitting there while my mind wandered back to my Vietnam days. As we were riding along the train, I was aware that even though I wasn't right with God, He hadn't abandoned me. Looking back, I now realize Hobo had come into my life at this juncture as part of His protection in watching over me. God is faithful even when we are not. He knows our future and the decisions we will eventually make and works with us accordingly.

Hobo then joined me, sitting by the open door as we talked about what we might expect once we got to New Orleans. It was nice just sitting there enjoying each other's company as the train sped down the tracks. Neither of us had ever been to New Orleans, so we weren't quite sure what to expect other than it being a fantastic partying place where lots of drugs and women were probably readily available. Nevertheless, we were both looking forward to it with much anticipation.

Texas: Surprise, Surprise
Chapter Seven

Our train was now rumbling through Texas, and we were famished. When it finally came to a screeching halt in the San Antonio freight yard, we had already decided to get off. Our hunger pangs had gotten the best of us. We then found our way downtown, where we began panhandling to earn enough money to eat. It didn't take long to get enough for a decent meal, so we headed for the nearest place to find something to eat.

Getting Comfortable with Panhandling

Panhandling was still something with which I wasn't comfortable. Fortunately, I recognized that it was the best way to come up with the money needed to survive in this present lifestyle I was acclimating to. However, as an introverted person raised with a strong work ethic, the idea of panhandling to support me was difficult to accept.

I remember a time in Tempe when we were panhandling outside a supermarket, and a pretty gal came up to me and said, "Why are you doing this?"

It made me think! I realized I needed to accept it as a necessary fact of life to survive in the lifestyle for this season of my life. I needed to come to grips with it by stepping outside of myself while learning to enjoy it. Otherwise, I wasn't going to succeed at it. I also discovered it was a way in which I learned to deal with the fears and obstacles that had the potential to hinder me in whatever process or endeavor I was involved in. Over the years, some of these early lessons have taught me to embrace the new things in my life that would catapult me forward into the destiny God has had for my life. Recognizing my fears and insecurities and then moving forward despite the fact has been a significant key to the victories God has granted me over the years.

There were always soup kitchens, the Salvation Army, and other places where you could get a free meal, but they weren't always available when you needed them. They had their time schedules, and we were hungry right then. So, panhandling was a great backup plan. Over the next several months, I discovered that living on the road would be relatively easy without having to work. Even though some aspects of living on the road went against the morals and work ethic I had grown up with, I recognized I was now on the adventure of a lifetime. I needed to embrace new things that didn't always agree with my upbringing.

A Change of Plans

While chatting with various people we were meeting on the streets of San Antonio, we began hearing about a Rock Festival that was to take place northeast of Austin, Texas, at Gatlin Creek. Even though we had planned to get through Texas as fast as possible, it couldn't be all that bad if they were having Rock Festivals.

Within an hour or so, we were on our way—hitchhiking to Austin. New Orleans would have to wait. Flowing with whatever was happening was an aspect of living on the road that I would come to love. We could drift with the flow and not worry about where we were supposed to be since there was nowhere, in particular, we were supposed to be—rolling stones with no direction home.

It should have only taken us a few hours to get to Austin, but it took a couple of days. As a result, we found ourselves waiting long periods between rides. During these long waits, I often thought and meditated about many things. Where am I going? What am I doing? Should I have taken up with Hobo? What kind of a person is he? I was unsure about any of these questions, but I was willing to keep on because things were going well. I was enjoying his company and the opportunities that came my way because of his extroverted personality.

On our way to Austin, we found ourselves in a small town with our hunger pangs getting the best of us. We didn't have any money and didn't want to spend time panhandling for it. We had spotted a church down the street, so we hit them up for a handout. This was our first experience with this type of begging. We told them we were stranded with no money and badly needed something to eat. To our surprise, they gave us about $30.00 cash—a lot of money for a couple of freaks not used to having money to spend. We then went to a grocery store and bought food and a fifth of whiskey. Drinking was never a big thing with me, but Hobo sometimes liked to indulge. He could always hold his liquor rather well. Later that evening, when it became clear that we wouldn't make it to Austin in one day, we found a secluded spot not too far away from the highway and made camp for the night. We made a fire, using the whiskey to help get it going, and then settled into the evening, drinking and eating the food we had purchased.

All in all, it had turned out to be a great day despite not getting good rides. We had gotten off the train early that morning with plans of getting back on and continuing our trip to New Orleans. Instead, we found ourselves on our way to a Rock Festival. Not bad for a couple of road freaks waiting for the next free ride to nowhere in particular. Texas was beginning to look better all the time.

Austin and the Rock Festival

We still had some food left the following day, so we finished it off and continued our hitchhiking adventure to Austin. After arriving, we soon discovered it was a college town, so we headed over to the college. Thanks to Hobo, I had already found that road freaks like us were a novelty with college students. Their curiosity about us caused them to be very friendly and welcoming. It wasn't long before a young female college student with beautiful red hair approached us and started a conversation. She was curious and wanted to know what we were up to and where we had just come. We told her about the Rock Festival at Gatlin Creek that was to take place and that we were a few days early and had time to kill with nowhere to go.

Melanie

After spending about an hour enjoying the company of our new friend, Melanie, she invited us to stay for a few days in her apartment. Hobo, being the extrovert, hit it off very well with her while I just tagged along. We had fun with her over the next few days, eating her food and partying with her and her friends.

Even though we were having a good time with Melanie and her friends, we were getting antsy. Finally, we were ready to head out for the Rock Festival, even though it was still a day early. The festival was 25 miles west of Austin, near Gatlin Creek in Dripping Springs. It only took us a couple of hours to hitchhike there.

The event was called *"A Concert at Gatlin Creek."* It occurred over three days, November 21-23, 1972, with about 78,000 people attending during the three days. The lineup included Freddie King, Bob Seeger, Foghat (formerly Savoy Brown), Bo Diddley, and others—many of whose names I didn't recognize. The Moody Blues were supposed to be there but canceled out at the last minute. Their cancellation was a bummer, as I would have loved to have heard them. On the first acid trip I ever took, I got into the Moody Blues while listening to their song, *"Ride my Seesaw,"* and the other songs from the Album *"In Search of the Lost Chord."* Since I had been to the Rock Festival in the Northwest in Satsop, Washington, in the summer of 1971, this wasn't a new experience for me. I knew there would be lots of drugs, rock and roll, and whatever else came our way.

We arrived at the festival grounds near Gatlin Creek late in the afternoon. It was still a day early, but we managed to get in by following some people who were part of the set-up crew. We joined them and became part of their crew, helping wherever possible. Using our street smarts, we could blend in as if we were just as much a part of getting things going as anyone else. Hobo was a natural at this. I just followed his cues. We made some new friends and made our campsite near them. Our goal was to meet people and start partying to get free drugs and food since we didn't have much money to buy anything. We still had a few bucks left from what the church had given us, but it didn't amount to much.

The following day, we woke up to a lot of commotion going on around us. People were arriving for the festival, and others were hastily putting together various booths for food and merchandise. We found our way to some free food being passed to those busily setting things up. Our day was off to a great start. The next item on our agenda was to score some drugs before the concert started later in the afternoon. Walking around the festival grounds, we soon realized getting drugs wouldn't be a problem. They were everywhere. We soon located a group of people who were sitting around smoking pot. We joined in and started toking along with them. Our day was moving right along. We were enjoying ourselves and exceptionally pleased with the way things were going.

By late afternoon, warmup bands were beginning to play, but Hobo and I were still hanging back in the camping area, enjoying ourselves as we wandered around, getting to know people. The only thing that seemed to dampen our spirits was that it looked like it was going to rain.

As we were hanging out and starting to get off on the LSD we had just scored, someone said, "Freddy King is beginning to play. We should wander down and see him."

We then made our way toward the stage and the crowd. It had now begun to rain. As we were sitting there listening to Freddy King and his band play, a fantastic thing began to occur right before our eyes. The stage was located at the bottom of a small hilly area with groups of people in clusters on the hilly slope. One by one, each group began to build campfires to keep warm. It was getting dark, and the whole slope was a beautiful site of hundreds of small campfires stretched around the entire arena from the top of the hill to the bottom. Our weekend was off to a stunning start. I have always been very touched by the beauty of nature. Seeing the site with all the campfires surrounding the arena while enjoying the music and atmosphere was a delight to my senses, especially with the LSD now having its full effect upon me.

A Key "Spiritual Connection."

The next day, as Hobo and I were making our rounds through the campgrounds looking for food and drugs, we met a group of people from Houston, Texas. Meeting this group would become a strategic relationship with us in the months ahead. They were a very warm and friendly bunch of people who invited us to hang out with them for the afternoon. On the outside, they all looked straight and normal. But here they were at a Rock Festival, getting high like everyone else. They didn't have long hair and beards like Hobo and me but were friendly and hospitable. We took an instant liking to them. They seemed delighted with us as we told them of some of our experiences.

Again, we were finding people took an interest in us because we were what they called *"Road Freaks."* As we began to get to know them, we soon discovered they were into God. Having grown up in a Christian family, I was familiar with Christianity and soon realized what they were into wasn't the same. They were more into everyone being god and connecting with the universal consciousness. Hobo and I played along with their game and got along very well with them. As a result, they invited us to spend a few days with them if we were ever in Houston.

Alternative Ideas to Christianity

Encountering groups with the appearance of Christianity wasn't my first encounter with groups that were somewhat different in their beliefs. I had met up with the cult group *"The Children of God"* on two separate occasions. The first time, some of my friends and I had hitchhiked to Seattle for the weekend from my hometown, Wenatchee. We ended up spending an evening with them. I knew something was different about them than what I had experienced growing up in a Christian family when I heard them swearing. Aside from that, we got a ride with a man on our way to Seattle. Then, on the way home, the same man came by and picked us up again. How strange was that? He had this photo of Jesus appearing in the clouds, which seemed authentic. Looking back on it, it was just another way the Lord was trying to get my attention to His reality. The other time I experienced *"The Children of God"* was on my way back from my first major hitchhiking trip to Pennsylvania. I was coming to St. Louis and had met someone hitchhiking in the same general direction. As it turned out, he was from this same cult. He invited me to spend the night at their *"colony,"* as they called their community houses. On both occasions, I discovered this group had morals different from those I had experienced in Christianity. Swearing was a part of their everyday vocabulary, and they thought nothing of having sex outside of marriage. The guy I was hitchhiking into St. Louis with was considered an older brother in the community and had bragged to me how easy it was to score with the younger sisters. At this point in my life, I wasn't a practicing Christian, but I knew what was right and wrong.

What I found fascinating about this group was that they had colonies all over the United States and Europe, enabling one to travel relatively freely with places to stay wherever one went. The problem was that leaving was difficult once you got into this group. When I was trying to leave the following morning to continue my trip back home, they tried extremely hard to intimidate me by giving me a hard time about going.

Over the next several months, I discovered that my beliefs in God and Jesus Christ were being tested and challenged to the degree that I wouldn't know for sure what I believed. I was about to encounter other belief systems that seemed fascinating and alluring but would lead to disillusionment and confusion. Even though I wasn't following Christ then, I remained a seeker at heart, which opened me up to the spiritual maze of all the beliefs espoused in the early 70s. Would I be able to navigate this spiritual maze without losing what I had begun to find while in Vietnam? Only time will tell. As I mentioned earlier, while in Vietnam, I had an enormous spiritual awakening that opened up my spiritual senses. Several of my buddies and I began getting into Jesus and the Bible. It was a wonderful time of discovery for me, with the seeds of Christianity further planted in my life. So, there I was in Gatlin Creek, Texas, at a Rock Festival, getting another dose of alternative ideas to Christianity. Again, the seeds of doubt were being planted.

The festival continued for a couple more days as Hobo and I hung out, got high, met many people, and listened to great bands like Foghat and Bo Diddley. At one point, we somehow got backstage and were snorting cocaine with some of the band members. Hobo was the type of guy who could talk himself into almost any situation. I was only too happy to tag along with him. I was having a blast! On the last day of the festival, an announcement came over the sound system, telling everybody to get rid of their drugs before they left the festival grounds. Of course, Hobo and I took full advantage of this opportunity by gladly taking drugs off whoever was willing to give them to us. We were able to score some mescaline and THC capsules for our trip back to Austin. The thing I remember about our ride back to Austin was the high from the mescaline was ruined because of the THC we took along with it.

Back in Austin with Melanie

When we returned to Austin, we quickly looked up our new friend, Melanie. She was nice enough to let us stay for a few days while we recuperated from the festival. After a couple of days, she got tired of us eating all her food. When we returned from wandering the streets one afternoon, we found our packs outside her door with a note saying she had had enough of us and it was time to move on. Over the next several months, we would discover that this type of thing would be typical for us and part of our survival mode. We would meet people and party with them, eating their food and using their drugs until they got tired of us and told us to leave. Once we had worn out our welcome, we would be on our way to the next destination, wherever it might be. It was quite an adventurous and carefree lifestyle in which every day was a new adventure with new experiences. We would often never know from one day to the next what city we would be in, or, for that matter, what state. We were traveling through our nation's cities, mooching off whatever people or resources came our way.

We had worn out our welcome in Austin, Texas, so it was time to move on. We then decided to take our new friends, whom we had met at the Rock Festival, up on their offer. So, we headed for Houston to see what new and exciting adventures awaited us there.

Onto Houston and the Aquarian Cult

We made it back to San Antonio in pretty-good time by getting a couple of good rides. Whereas it had taken us a couple of days to travel to Austin from San Antonio, it only took a few hours to get back to San Antonio. It was early evening, so we decided to find a mission or Salvation Army to spend the night and get a meal. Sure enough, we found a place and a nice warm dinner and bed. I discovered it was hard to starve while living on the road with so many people and businesses willing to give free handouts to people like us. With this in mind, we took full advantage of the situations as they came our way.

Visiting the Alamo and a Free Ride to Houston

The following day, we had a good breakfast and headed out to see what the day held. Since we were in San Antonio again, we decided we should see the Alamo. So off to the Alamo, we went. We had a great time playing tourist and learning all about the Alamo. While there, we met an older man with a beat-up old pickup headed in our direction. He didn't seem to have an actual destination in mind, so we talked him into giving us a ride to Houston. We told him we knew a lot of women there and could hook him up. With that said, he was more than willing to give us the ride. It was only about a three-hour drive to Houston, which would put us there in the late afternoon with plenty of time to hook up with our friends from the Rock Festival. Before taking off to Houston with the old guy, Hobo and I had devised a plan to ditch him once we had arrived. Unfortunately, we couldn't take him with us to meet our friends. Our goal was to tell him to drop us off on a street corner near a pay phone; while he drove around the block, we would make the call to our friends. Then, we would duck into a building and hide until we were sure he had given up looking for us. I know this doesn't seem nice, but this was just one more aspect of our living on the road with our survival mode: *"Beg, borrow, and steal."* We had begged for a ride with him but couldn't follow up on our promise.

As we were driving along in his pickup, people were passing us and pointing to the back of the truck. As we looked back, we realized the back of the truck was on fire. It was my backpack, which had somehow burst into flames. We immediately stopped the truck and put the fire out. Fortunately, it was just the top flap on my pack that had caught on fire. Unfortunately, my backpack was without a top flap and had all my stuff exposed. We figured the fire started by throwing a cigarette out the window, landing on my pack.

We arrived in Houston without further mishap and had the old guy drop us off as planned. Once we were sure he was gone, we found a pay phone and called our new friends. We saw him circle the block several times, and then that was it. Our friends were excited that we took them up on their offer and drove out from the suburbs into the city to meet and give us a ride to their home.

We stayed there for about ten days, meeting more of their friends. Their home was like Grand Central Station, with people coming and going. There was never a shortage of drugs and girls. I connected with one gal who became my constant companion during our time there. Unfortunately, a guy named Billy became very jealous of the attention we were getting from the group and tried to pick fights with us. He and Hobo got into it on one occasion, but Hobo—being the clever person he was—put him in his place without having to bloody him up.

One night, we all went to a concert near the Houston Astrodome to see the Rock Group, Traffic. It was an awesome concert, and a thrill to see them in action. Another time, we went to the zoo and watched the animals while stoned on pot. Again, it was a fascinating experience.

They were all into the God thing, with everybody being their own god and connecting with the universal consciousness. They were pretty emphatic about sharing their understanding of God to the extent they were giving us books to read. As I began to read and study the books they fed us, I realized what they were into was quite different from what I had been exposed to in my upbringing. As I mentioned earlier, I grew up in a fundamental Christian home with solid evangelical beliefs about who Jesus was and the eternal consequences of not accepting Jesus as my personal Savior. Although I wasn't a practicing Christian, I still believed in Jesus as the Son of God and the concept of heaven and hell.

Studying Alternative Ideas

As I was reading and studying, it became very apparent their concept of God didn't include Jesus as the manifestation of God in the flesh, nor the idea of Hell. They acknowledged Jesus as a great prophet and teacher but not as God. How could Jesus be a great prophet and teacher if they considered Him a liar since He said He was God?[5] What little spiritual foundation I had at this time prevented me from buying into this theory, but I played along. The other problem I had with what I was reading was that I wasn't finding the sense of purpose and destiny I had begun to discover when I was in Nam and getting into Jesus and the Bible. The seeker in me was interested in learning who I was concerning my purpose and destiny. When I had the defining moment with the vision of my life flashing before me in Vietnam, a strong sense of purpose and destiny was deposited into my spirit. I didn't sense this in the books I was reading. Despite all the indoctrination we were getting from our new friends, we enjoyed their company. They were getting a kick out of us,

---

[5] John 8:55-58 (NKJV) Yet you have not known Him, but I know Him. And if I say, 'I do not know Him,' I shall be a liar like you; but I do know Him and keep His word. Your father Abraham rejoiced to see My day, and he saw it and was glad." Then the Jews said to Him, "You are not yet fifty years old, and have You seen Abraham?" Jesus said to them, "Most assuredly, I say to you, before Abraham was, I AM."

John 10:31-33 (NKJV) Then the Jews took up stones again to stone Him. Jesus answered them, "Many good works I have shown you from My Father. For which of those works do you stone Me?" The Jews answered Him, saying, "For a good work we do not stone You, but for blasphemy, and because You, being a Man, make Yourself God."

especially Hobo. He could be quite charming at times. He knew how to play the game, but I showed little interest.

As the saying goes, *"A rolling stone gathers no moss."* It was getting time for us to move on again. We hadn't worn out our welcome yet, but we were getting anxious to get to New Orleans. It had been almost three weeks since we had arrived in Texas. So much for just getting through Texas as fast as we could, as we initially planned! We packed what little belongings we had in our backpacks and headed out. One of the gals had even taken the time to repair my backpack with a new flap. She had done an excellent job with it as it lasted over the next several months, as Hobo and I continued to travel together.

Our friends sent us on our way by giving each of us a book to take along. They gave me a devotional book called *"The Impersonal Life"* and Hobo the *"Aquarian Gospel."* They were kind enough to provide us with a ride to the freight yard where we could catch a freight train to New Orleans.

We found our way to the freight yard and asked when the next train would be leaving for New Orleans. Other road freaks we had met during our travels warned us that we had to be careful in the Houston yard. The railroad bulls didn't take kindly to people like us. You could land in jail if you weren't careful. We were still learning the ropes of riding freight trains, which caused us to ask questions concerning the various ways freight yards operated. Whenever we would run into others doing what we were doing, we would learn from them by asking questions.

We were able to find our train and get away without being detected. So, there we were, finally on our way to New Orleans. We left with fond memories of Texas and our first few weeks of traveling together. Everyone was now calling me *"Space."* Hobo and I had become terrific friends and enjoyed each other's company as we traveled from place to place with no specific destinations in mind. I had come to understand Bob Dylan's song, *"Like a Rolling Stone,"* especially the parts where it said:

"You used to laugh about
Everybody that was hanging out
Now you don't talk so loud
Now you don't seem so proud,
About having to be scrounging your next meal.
How does it feel, how does it feel?
To be without a home – *Bob Dylan*

New Orleans and Places Unknown
Chapter Eight

Our adventures through Texas had been an excellent experience for both of us, but we were thankful to be on our way to New Orleans and wherever our adventures might take us. Our first few weeks of traveling together gave me the confidence and assurance to *"Keep on Truckin"* in this new lifestyle I was discovering. I didn't know where our adventures would take us, but I was content to go along for the ride and let each day take care of itself. So far, this philosophy and way of life has worked quite well. I was enjoying the ride!

Wrong Train, Wrong Direction

Even though the railroad bulls didn't detect us in the Houston yard, we soon discovered we had made a critical mistake when we jumped on the freight train. We were headed in the wrong direction. The workers in the Houston yard must have deliberately pointed us in the wrong direction, thinking, *"We'll fix those stupid hippies."*

We thought, "If that's the worst that happened to us in Texas, we did fairly well." We knew from experience that trains had to stop periodically to allow the trains from the other direction to pass. We figured as soon as the train had to stop, we would get off and wait for the next one coming from the opposite direction. Within an hour or so, our train had to stop. We jumped off, sat, and waited. It took a couple of hours before another train coming in the direction we wanted to go appeared. Fortunately, it was the one designated to pull over and stop. We found an empty car, hopped on, and were finally on our way to New Orleans. Our only concern was whether this train would travel right through Houston rather than it being the end of the line. When trains arrive in a big yard, they are either disassembled or continue, depending on each train. Those dispersed are assigned a new train towards where their merchandise was intended or stay for its intended purpose.

More Reflections

As we rode along, my mind began reverting to my time in Vietnam. I was thinking about where I was at that moment. I thought about the changes I had experienced in the past couple of years that brought me to the place of now riding on a freight train to New Orleans. Vietnam and the drugs had opened a whole new perspective of life for me. I felt a restlessness that prompted me to catch up on what I had missed in my upbringing. Before leaving Nam, we had begun listening to the Rolling Stones' Album, *"Get Yer Ya-Yas Out,"* which I was now doing before getting ready to settle down. Growing up in a very sheltered and protective environment, I hadn't experienced much before joining the army. Currently out of the military, I wanted to encounter as much as possible. As stated earlier, I grew up as a child in a country setting on the outskirts of a small town. Because I grew up in a restrictive religious environment, my brothers and I were kept in check until we were old enough to drive and get out and about.

As mentioned earlier, our family went to church every Sunday morning and evening. It was a church that focused more on the do's and don'ts rather than the grace and mercy of Jesus Christ. We were never allowed to go to movies, dances, or other things. As a result, we were never socially accepted in the cliques at school. Not being socially accepted caused me to develop a rejection complex. The fact that I was timid didn't help either. My junior and high school years were painful and lonely times in my life. In my senior year, I began to date and ended up in a steady relationship, which brought me much happiness and joy. Unfortunately, the experiences of my childhood had already been imprinted on my soul, and I had become a very lonely soul with a rejection complex. The rejection complex caused me to fall in with the drug culture, where acceptance came easily. Even though my need for acceptance approval had dissipated, I felt restless and wanted to experience as much as possible. Traveling along on the train helped me to bring these thoughts into focus. There was nothing else to do but sit and think until Hobo abruptly brought me back to reality.

Snapping me out of my thoughts with excitement in his voice, he said, "Space! I think we're getting close to New Orleans!"

I got excited as well. We had now been on the train for about 10 hours, part of it sleeping the time away. Fortunately, our train went straight through Houston without having to stop. We figured we'd be arriving in New Orleans in less than an hour, so we began to talk excitably about our plans. But, of course, the first thing we needed to do was to find some food. We were getting hungrier by the minute and needed something to eat before making our way toward the French Quarter.

It was late afternoon when the train finally rolled into the New Orleans freight yard. We got off as fast as possible and out of the yard without being detected by the railroad bulls. We began to find our way in the direction of the French Quarter. We didn't know where we were going but discovered the general direction, so off we went. As we were walking along, we spotted a donut shop about to close and decided to go in and ask if they had any donuts they were going to throw away. Sure enough, they did. They gave us a big sack of donuts. Not much food value, but they filled the empty spot in our stomachs until we could find something more nourishing, so we were grateful.

The French Quarter and the Hare Krishna's

An hour or so later, we finally found our way into the French Quarter. What a fantastic place! I had never experienced anything quite like it. By now, it was evening, and the streets were barricaded, which produced one big party-like atmosphere. We spent a couple of hours walking around, taking it all in when our hunger began to get the best of us. The long walk had worked up our appetites once again. We started to ask around where we could get a free meal, and someone told us the Hare Krishnas would probably give us something to eat. Even though it was our first night in the city, we knew we would be there for a few days, so we headed in the direction given to fill our stomachs and find a place to sleep.

We then made our way and found ourselves, once again, walking several blocks before we found the place. Sure enough, they had some food for us. They came out with two small bowls of stuff I couldn't recognize. I began complaining that the little amount they gave me wouldn't be enough. They got angry with me but gave in and brought me a big bowl.

Then one of the Hare Krishna guys says to the other, "Stay there with him and make sure he eats every bite of it."

I took one bite and almost barfed right there on the spot. It was the most awful, foul-tasting stuff I had ever tasted. As hungry as I was, I couldn't eat another bite. Hobo managed to get his down, but I wasn't going to eat this stuff. With darkness settling in, we decided to go and find a place to camp for the night. We eventually found a secluded spot in a park not too far from the Krishna Temple. Unfortunately, I went to bed hungry that night. It wasn't the first time, nor would it be the last.

The following day, we headed to the closest grocery store and began panhandling to get enough money for breakfast and whatever might come our way. We had a good time meeting others while panhandling and, within a couple of hours, had enough to get breakfast and get through the day.

The Beans and Rice Place

Once our hunger pangs were satisfied, we headed back to the French Quarter. It was much different during the day, with traffic and such—slow compared to the evening. We found some other road freaks involved in the same lifestyle we were and began to hang with them. They had been hanging out for a week or so and told us about a place a few blocks away where we could get a plate of beans and rice every day at noon for only 35 cents. With that in mind, we all set out for the beans and rice place. It was an excellent place with many other hippies just hanging out and enjoying a cheap meal. Visiting the Beans and Rice place would become part of our daily routine for the next few days. It was a great place to meet people and get the needed drugs. It was nice to hang out with other freaks with the same lifestyle as we shared stories and experiences.

Neither Hobo nor I were doing hard drugs such as heroin, speed, or cocaine. Hobo never did heroin. He was very much opposed to it. I had used heroin periodically since coming home from Vietnam, but it had never become a habit. Had I stayed working for the Railroad, it probably would have. As mentioned earlier, one of the guys on the Steel Gang I was working on had a good connection for good China White Heroin. He kept a small number of us supplied. It seemed like every time I started using heroin; something would happen within a few weeks that would change my circumstances drastically to take me away from it. In Vietnam, the situation was convulsions. Before leaving Washington at the beginning of this adventure, I worked in an apple packing plant, and several of us were using heroin. Again, within a few weeks, I quit and took off on the freight train to Minnesota. Looking back, it is obvious to me that the hand of God was upon my life, protecting me from myself. I believe because He knew my future, He was protecting and watching out for me.

Hobo and I kept our drug appetite primarily with marijuana and would use LSD on occasion. It was always easy to come up with a joint or enter in with others while smoking. We very seldom ever paid for drugs. At the Beans and Rice Place, we found the necessary connections we needed for pot and LSD, as well as other people like us. At this stage of my life, I was very much into using drugs, mainly pot and LSD. I immensely enjoyed getting high. There would come a time a couple of years later when I would experience total burnout from them and even regret the fact that I had been so heavily involved with them. I was fortunate to get away from them before they destroyed my life because I know they would have destroyed me if I hadn't. But that would come later, not at this point in my life. I am so grateful to be alive and in a sane mind today after all the drugs I took and the way I abused my mind.

Hobo and I spent the rest of the afternoon in the French Quarter, panhandling here and there, hoping to get enough money to go bar hopping in the evening. It was nice hanging outside of the various bars. They all had outside speakers, so there was music to listen to wherever you went. As evening was upon us, we found ourselves hitting the bars and having a great time drinking and smoking pot. At one point, we almost got busted for being drunk in public because we were very obnoxious and singing the Rolling Stones song *"Sweet Virginia"* very loudly from the *"Exile on Main Street Album."* The part that says, "You have to scrape the sh__t right off your shoes." When the policeman stopped us, he searched us and found the little New Testament Bible I carried in the leather pouch I had attached to my belt. Hobo had encouraged me to keep it there, thinking it might come in handy sometimes. However, when the cop discovered it, he couldn't understand how we could be drunk and use such vulgarity if we were Bible believers. The upshot was he let us go. We then decided to cut our losses and head back to where we had slept the night before. For the next several days in New Orleans, we ate, slept, found drugs, panhandled, and then drank in the evenings. We met new friends and shared our adventures all the time. We had a great time. Thanks to Hobo, I enjoyed myself immensely as I acclimated to my new surroundings. He was always good at BS'ing his way into situations. I was only too happy to tag along.

What's Next? Destinations Unknown!

After being in New Orleans for several days, we started getting a little bored. We had seen and done all we wanted and were ready to move on. We had never discussed what or where we were going beyond New Orleans. It was getting late into the fall of the year. Thanksgiving time had come and gone, and the weather was starting to cool, so we decided on Florida. Why not spend the winter in Florida, where it was always warm?

When Hobo and I began traveling together, I wasn't sure how this partnership would work out. Then, while still in Tempe and partying in one of the bars, someone who had been in a long conversation with Hobo began to warn me about him.

He said, "You should stay away from this guy because he's trouble."

I had no idea what he was talking about but filed it away. So far, my relationship with Hobo is working out great. I was experiencing things with Hobo that I would never have had the opportunity to do otherwise. He was a great guy, and I enjoyed his company and the adventures we were experiencing. I had never met anyone quite like him, and these first few weeks of our travels gave me a foretaste of what was to come. I was full of anticipation and excitement as we contemplated what we would discover as we headed towards Florida.

On our last evening in New Orleans, we ended up at a real honky tonk type of bar on the outer perimeters of the French Quarter. We pulled our usual routine, scouting the place to see who we could start a conversation with and help them drink their beer. As it turned out, a group of people seemed to be having a great time, so we wandered over and began to chat with them. Before we knew it, we were sharing their beer and having a great time. It was a wonderful evening to close out or stay in New Orleans. I ended up meeting a gal and dancing with her quite a bit. We hit it off very well, and she invited me to spend the night. She let Hobo come along as well. Whichever one of us would end up with a girl for the night, we ensured the other came along so that we both had a place to sleep for the night without getting separated. In those days, we didn't have cell phones to stay in contact.

When we woke up the following day, the gal I was with informed me that she had to go to work but was hoping we would be there when she returned. I didn't have the heart to tell her we were leaving for Florida. Later in the morning, after she had gone and we had gotten ready to leave, we noticed mushrooms growing in one of the rooms. An older lady was also living there, so we asked her if we could have some. We, of course, knew right away what they were. They were magic mushrooms, as some would call them. They gave you a similar effect to LSD but not as dramatic when eaten. On our way out of town, we ate the mushrooms. Much to our chagrin, they didn't give us much of a high.

We decided to hitchhike this time rather than hop on a freight train. It didn't take long to get our first ride. We were on our way to Florida, and our destinations were unknown, with an expectation of whatever would come our way. What will happen tomorrow? Or, for that matter, what would happen next week? We never knew, and that's what I enjoyed about this adventurous lifestyle. I was beginning to find my way, but deep inside, I was still empty and lost and wasn't sure how I would end up. I was enjoying each day, trying not to overthink the complexities of life. Deep down, I knew I would probably be a follower of Jesus Christ and discover His calling for me someday. But not now! I was too busy making up for the lost time. The Bible does say that sin is pleasurable for a season, and I was still in the season where it was very gratifying. I was having the time of my life and wasn't ready for it to come to an end any time soon. My day of reckoning was still yet to come.

Gulf Coast Hitchhiking Experiences
Chapter Nine

As we were leaving New Orleans, we weren't sure what to expect as we hitchhiked our way through the Gulf Coast and into Florida. Besides a few short stints, we had been continually riding freight trains since leaving Arizona. We were now heading into unfamiliar territory and adventures unknown, which is what I found extremely exciting as I anticipated what would happen next. Because we seldom stayed in any one place for more than a week, each day was a new adventure.

Our first two rides out of New Orleans were uneventful, especially since the mushrooms we had eaten were not giving us the desired effect we had hoped they would. Nevertheless, we were on our way to the warm sunshine of Florida. It was a great day for a new adventure.

We were about a third of the way through the State of Mississippi when our next ride came along. It was always interesting to see what kind of people would pick up a couple of long-haired freaks like us. Hobo looked kind of scary. He sported a messy beard and long, curly black hair down to his shoulders. He wore a black cowboy hat with a chain of big silver buttons around the rim and a buckskin shirt with leather tie strings loosely threaded at the top, which allowed his hairy chest to show. He also had a necklace made of tiger teeth. I overheard comments about him from time to time, such as, "That Hobo guy looks like a warlock." The tiger teeth necklace he wore only reinforced their suspicions.

I had two pairs of jeans and a pair of coveralls I traded off from time to time. I usually wore a vest over my shirt. My hair was shoulder length as well, and I had a scraggly-looking beard. Of course, neither one of us smelled that great. We made it a habit to sleep in our skivvies so our clothes wouldn't smell as bad. We showered and cleaned up as much as possible. We even stopped at Laundromats occasionally to clean our clothes, but that wasn't always sufficient.

63

This ride happened to be a hippie couple headed for their home near Biloxi, Mississippi. We were riding along, and it was getting into early evening as we began sharing our adventures with them over the past few weeks. They seemed intrigued by our carefree and adventurous lifestyle and wanted to know more about us, so they invited us to spend the evening with them. We arrived at their home within the hour, and the hippie lady began preparing something for all of us to eat. As we were eating dinner, they started quizzing us about our adventures and what we believed. Of course, Hobo began telling them about our recent experiences with our friends in Houston and how we are all gods. I pretty much kept my mouth shut and just listened.

New and Weird Ideas

As it turned out, they had some strange views. They were trying to convince us the earth was flat and not round. I reminded them about the astronauts who had been to outer space and sent pictures of our planet and how round it was.

Their response to this was. "NASA is just feeding us a big lie. There were never any astronauts or spaceships that had gone to outer space or the moon. So, it was all a big lie."

It was unbelievable that someone could believe something like that, but what can you expect from hippies? We all had weird ideas. They also introduced us to the books by Carlos Castaneda, *"The Teachings of Don Juan"* and *"Separate Reality."*[6] These books were supposedly the religion behind peyote buttons, which was also a hallucinogenic experience when digested.[7] They gave us a copy of the first book, *"The Teachings of Don Juan,"* which we added to our growing arsenal of reading material. Sitting beside the road waiting for a ride, it was often good to have some reading material. I was looking forward to reading the book. As for the stuff about the world being flat, I immediately discarded it as nonsense. We spent the next couple of hours smoking pot and just chatting about various things and listening to the Rolling Stones'

---

[6] The teachings of Don Juan were from a series of books that Carlos Castaneda wrote in the late 1960s and early 1970s. They described the use of peyote and mescaline in relationship to a god called Mescalito.

[7] Peyote is found in small, spineless cactus native to southwestern Texas and throughout Mexico. It has psychoactive properties that are very similar to mescaline. It was used by many of the native Indians in those areas in their spiritual worship, which explains the Mescalito Spirit.

newest album, *"Exile on Main Street."* We first heard this album back in Houston with our friends. *"Exile on Main Street"* would become our favorite album to listen to over the next several months every time we got the opportunity to do so. I have no memory of what the sleeping arrangements were, except I'm sure it must have been inside and not outside. We probably slept under the stars 85% of the time, so it was nice to have the chance to sleep comfortably inside at times.

The following day, they sent us on our way with a hearty breakfast. Our travels would take us through Mobile, Alabama, where we arrived mid-afternoon after an uneventful day of hitchhiking. There were no great conversations to speak of, just a couple of boring rides with boring people. Nevertheless, we reached our destination and took off to see if there was a local mission or Salvation Army where we could get a hot meal and spend the night. As it turned out, a Salvation Army church put people up for the night and provided a good meal. What do you know? Three nights in a row with dinner and a bed—life doesn't get much better than when you're on the road.

The Bread Truck from Heaven—A Day of Surprises

Our next day began with breakfast and then hitting the road with great anticipation of what the day would hold for us. We knew we would probably make it into Florida if all went well. As we traveled through Alabama and entered Florida, we were somewhere near Pensacola when we started getting hungry. We had a jar of peanut butter we had picked up along the way and wished we had some bread to go along with it. While contemplating our dilemma, I thought back to the hitchhiking experience with Norm when I took off for the East Coast. I began to tell Hobo the story about how Norm and I would dream up rides, and they would happen.

I told Hobo the whole story, and he got amazingly excited and said, "Well, let us try it! Our next ride will be a car that has some bread to go along with the peanut butter."

As we were standing there alongside the road waiting for our next ride, we spied a station wagon coming down the road, so we stuck out our thumbs, and, sure enough, he stopped. To our surprise, he was a bread salesman, and his whole car was full of bread he was delivering. We were able to talk him out of a couple of loaves. Don't ask me how this happens. I don't know. It just did. Since coming home from Vietnam the previous year, I developed a metaphysical mindset. Maybe that had something to do with it. I don't know! Or maybe God was answering our simple prayer and showing us His ability to respond to our needs despite ourselves. Whatever the reason, we were grateful and surprisingly blown away by the experience. In our eyes, it was very supernatural.

Free Cigarettes from a Broken Machine

We were now well into Florida and had gotten a good ride that was taking us further south down the Gulf side of the coast. As we were driving along, the driver decided to stop for gas. At the gas station, we all got out. Hobo and I were nosing around when Hobo spied something.

He says, "Hey, Space, do you see what I see?"

He had spied a cigarette machine with a long piece of tape spread across all the handles you pull on to get your pack of cigarettes after depositing the money. We could see the machine was full of cigarettes, so there was probably only one reason for the tape. The device was broken.

Seeing he was probably right in his assessment, I said, "Well, let's see if we can get some free cigarettes."

No one seemed to be paying attention to us, so we pulled the tape off and started pulling on all the handles. Sure enough, we were getting free cigarettes. What a score! It turned out to be quite a day of unexpected surprises, and we got a big kick out of it. We were both smokers. Most of the time, we resorted to bugler tobacco and rolling our own, so this was quite a score for us. As we returned to the car and continued our journey into Florida, I noticed Hobo chain-smoking one cigarette after another. He was enjoying the smokes.

We made it as far as Lake City, Florida, and decided to find a place on the side of the road to sleep for the night. There were places in the bushes along the sides of roads where you could get out of sight to sleep. I remember my first experience doing this. When I returned from the East Coast on my first hitchhiking adventure, I would sleep at rest areas and in the bushes next to an on-ramp. Our day had been full of surprises, and now we were ready for a good night's sleep under the stars. We woke up the following day to peanut butter sandwiches for breakfast. We were now well on our way to Florida with a couple of great hitchhiking days behind us. Finally, we were ready to explore Florida and the adventures that were to come. So far, we were off to a good start. We had several good rides, plenty of cigarettes to last us for a couple more days, and, of course, bread to go with our peanut butter. What more could a couple of road freaks want? Somebody was watching out for us!

Florida Gulf Coast Adventures
Chapter Ten

It was mid-December 1972. We were on our second day in Florida and were traveling down the highway when we spotted an orange grove. Thinking this would be a great place to stop, we asked the driver to stop the car and drop us off. We said our goodbyes, thanking him for the ride, and then headed for the orange grove. We sat there for a good hour just eating those delicious oranges and then filled our backpacks. For the next couple of days, that's all we ate! I must say, my system was utterly flushed after that.

We headed for the ocean, hoping to find a place to camp and enjoy the Florida Gulf Coast for a few days. We ended up at an ocean beach near Clearwater, where we spent the late afternoon and evening smoking pot and hanging out with some other hippie-looking characters. As the evening wore on, we found a nice, secluded spot, made camp, and went to sleep. It was a great day! Florid looked promising.

Caught in the Rain

We were both awakened in the middle of the night to a miserable experience. We were drenched and cold. It had been raining hard during the night. We, along with our sleeping bags, were thoroughly drenched. We were desperate, which meant doing something desperate. One of the people we had hung out with the previous afternoon was parked close by in his camper trailer. Realizing we needed to do something drastic, we knocked on his door to see if we could spend the remainder of the night with him. He was kind enough to let us in where it was nice and dry, although we were still thoroughly soaked. So far, we hadn't encountered any hazards of living on the road. When it rained at the Rock Festival, we stayed in someone's tent to keep dry. Hopefully, this wasn't an indication of what we would be experiencing in Florida.

By the time we woke up, the rain had stopped, and the wonderful Florida sun began to shine. So, we laid all our stuff out in the warm sunshine to dry out as much as possible. Unfortunately, they were still a little damp when we were ready to crash that evening. We spent the next few days hanging out, eating our oranges, and generally having a good time. It was a very refreshing and relaxing time for us. After taking it easy on the beach for a few days, we were itching for some city life, so we headed east toward Tampa for a few days. It was a short trip–about 30 miles. So, we stuck out our thumbs, and away we went.

I was also anxious to check my mail. I had lost my ID card and had called my mom to send me my birth certificate. We would use General Delivery boxes in whatever city we expected to visit. Hobo had told me about using General Delivery boxes back in Arizona, so I had already started using them. Sometimes, it didn't always work out, and we would have to put a forwarding address to the next place we thought we might be. I still corresponded with the gal from Minnesota and always enjoyed getting a letter from her. When we were in New Orleans, a letter from her awaited me.

Tampa, Florida, and the Furry Freak Brothers

Upon arriving in Tampa, we began to look for a park to hang out in and meet people—other freaky-looking hippie characters like us. Often, this would be our mode of meeting people and finding out what was happening. There was usually plenty of free dope floating around. Sometimes, we would find a spot on a street corner and keep our eyes open to what was happening around us, or we'd find a bar frequented by hippie-looking characters. Most of these places almost always provided avenues for getting to know people and getting invited wherever they were partying and getting high. We would then become a part of their band of friends, floating from one house to another until we knew we were on the verge of losing our welcome. And then we would be on our way to another city doing the same thing all over again. It was amazing how often people would just come up to us and begin chatting, wanting to know what we were all about, where we were going, and what we were doing. Again, Hobo could talk himself into almost any situation, and I would be more than happy to tag along. I could never master the art of bull as he did. He was great at it.

Over the next few days, we met a few people, which led to meeting their friends and partying with them. However, we always seemed to end up at the park late at night with nowhere else to sleep. Although, we did find a nice, secluded area in some bushes near the park's outskirts, which worked quite well for a camp. We had been in Tampa for about four or five days, just hanging out with no hurry to be anywhere in particular. We'd found a couple of good spots to panhandle that netted us enough money each day for coffee, food, and cigarettes. It wasn't the best time, but we enjoyed ourselves as we hit the streets each day and even scored a joint now and then. We were blending in and becoming a regular part of the street scene. People were getting used to seeing us around as we got accustomed to the same familiar faces.

As we were hanging out on the street panhandling one day, we met a couple of grungy, hippie-looking dudes who reminded us of the Fabulous Furry Freak Brothers from the comic books we read at times.[8] They seemed genuinely interested in us as we began to exchange stories about being on the road. As it turned out, they had also hitchhiked around quite a bit. We mentioned we were staying near the park down the street and looking for a place to get showered and cleaned up. After chatting with them for an hour or so, they invited us to their pad and said we could crash there if we wanted. We took them up on their offer, with both of us needing a shower. We spent the evening smoking pot and telling stories. Unfortunately, their pad wasn't much. It was dirty, grimy, and smelly. It didn't look like they had washed dishes for days on end. Dirty dishes were piled up everywhere. We also noticed there were cockroaches everywhere, especially in the cupboards. If we didn't know better, we would have thought we were hanging out with the Fabulous Furry Freak Brothers. When morning rolled around, we were ready to leave. The filth was just too much for us. We decided that we had had enough of Tampa and then hit the road again. After stopping by our favorite grocery store and panhandling for breakfast, we found our way to the freeway onramp to wait for our first ride. We didn't have much of a destination other than working toward Miami. If the ride was headed in that general direction, we were content.

As we settled into waiting for our ride, we began to pull out the reading material our friends back in Houston had given us. The furry freak brothers from the night before had given us a couple of joints, so we lit up and settled into reading while waiting for a ride. I was reading the little devotional book on *"The Impersonal Life,"* and Hobo was

---

[8] The Fabulous Furry Freak Brothers are a trio of underground comic strip hippie characters that were available in comic books during the 1970s.

reading the *"Aquarian Gospel."*[9] I hadn't given up on Christianity, but I was exploring other avenues of spirituality while trying to discover my life and purpose. I hadn't come to a place where I had firm convictions about anything other than partying and getting high, even though Christianity had been a part of my life growing up and exploring it further in Nam.

Still Lost and Looking for Answers

In Vietnam, my buddies and I would sit around for hours and read the Bible while smoking pot. I believe we were learning with God planting His seeds of truth. However, true conversion hadn't occurred during that stage of my life, so I was still trying to discover who God was and how He would fit into my life. The vision of seeing my life flash passing before me with the calling that God had indelibly stamped upon my soul and spirit was continually in my thoughts. I had been given pieces to a puzzle but was unable to connect them. So, my search continued, and this little book was just one more place I was looking for the answers to my life and purpose. At this point, I was still one lost individual looking for answers while enjoying the ride simultaneously. I knew I hadn't found what I was searching for because of the lack of peace that continually gnawed at me. The crazy thing was that while in Vietnam and going through the discovery process of getting acquainted with the Bible and Jesus Christ, I was beginning to find the peace for which I was longing. However, I was unwilling to submit to the process at that time—kind of like the seed that fell by the wayside. As a result, I began losing what I started to find and began to look elsewhere, which is where I now found myself.

Once again, we were sitting on the side of the road, waiting for someone to give us a ride, and Hobo nudged me, "Hey, Space! It looks like that car is going to stop."

The car initially passed us but stopped and pulled over to the side of the road about 100 yards ahead. We quickly put out the joint we were smoking, grabbed our packs, and jogged toward the car. The couple in this car was a middle-aged husband and wife headed to St. Petersburg. They took us back across the bay and south for about 25 miles. We weren't on a time clock and didn't have a particular destination. If we were headed south towards Miami, we were good and welcomed the ride.

---

[9] *The Impersonal Life* is one of the books written on the topic of self-discovery and leading a spiritual life by Author Joseph Benner.

We soon arrived in St. Petersburg and decided to hang out for a while and see if anything was happening. It wasn't long before we discovered it was a retirement community with not much going on. We panhandled a bit, then hit the road again. We still had the best part of the day ahead of us, and it was only another 120 miles to Ft. Myers, which would be an excellent place to make it to by the end of the day.

It took us several rides and most of the day to make it to Ft. Myers, but we arrived early enough to check things out. We were hoping to find a nice place to sleep. Still somewhat burned out from our adventures in Tampa, we decided to take it easy and focus on getting something to eat and a place to crash for the night. Within a couple of hours, we found both. We made enough panhandling for a bottle of wine and some cheese. We both had come to enjoy a good bottle of Hearty Burgundy with a hunk of cheese. We then settled in for the night at a park with plenty of shrubs to keep us out of sight of the local authorities.

The following day, we woke up, finished the cheese, found a restroom, and cleaned up the best we could. We then set out for an onramp to wait for our day's first ride. It was about 150 miles to Miami, our destination for the day. We carried a map I was constantly looking at so we would know where we were going and the best places to stop. I saw that we would be going through the Everglades on the way to Miami, which was exciting. As much as I enjoyed our hitchhiking adventures, I also enjoyed sightseeing and discovering all the cool places our country had to offer. On this day, we were on our way to Alligator Alley and the Everglades Parkway. We had been sitting in the same spot for over an hour. It was one of those days when we spent more time waiting for rides than getting rides. Oh well! That's the way it goes. It was just part of the adventure. We had our reading material and enough cigarettes to keep us happy, so we were content to sit and wait.

More about Nam and what I did there

While sitting there, Hobo asked me, "Hey, Space, what did you do while you were in Nam?"

I began to tell him, starting with the landing at Cam Ranh Bay. Cam Ranh Air Base was one of three aerial ports where the United States military personnel entered or departed South Vietnam for their 12-month tour. Cam Ranh Bay is where I landed in May of 1970 after completing 16 weeks of Advanced Individual

Training at Ft. Eustis, Virginia, following Basic Training at Ft. Lewis, Washington. From Cam Ranh Bay, we received orders regarding our place of duty for the following 12 months. The military sent me to the 539th Transportation Unit in Phu Loi, about 30 miles Northeast of Saigon.

As mentioned earlier, I enlisted in the U.S. Army because I didn't want to be drafted and end up as a grunt and possibly get killed. One of the reasons for joining the army was you only had to serve three years as an enlisted soldier rather than four in the other branches.

The Army trained me as a Chinook helicopter mechanic and door gunner. My tour of duty took me to a non-combat unit—a general support company whose mission was to repair helicopters.

My recruiter had pointed me in the right direction. The Phu Loi base was a heliport where Chinooks, Hueys, and—of course—the deadly Cobras flew out for their many missions. It was always interesting towards the end of the day when they returned from their missions. If they had made a confirmed kill that day, they would have red smoke coming out of their copter to brag about their kill. Many of the companies on our base were fighter units, which we supported by keeping the helicopters in the air. Our company slogan was *"Keep 'Em Flying."*

Being in a non-combat unit didn't necessarily mean I was exempt from danger. Our post would get hit by rockets and mortars at least once a month. Whenever this happened, we would run for a bunker. In my case, we had a huge one just several feet from my sleeping quarters, which was in the middle of our company area. We used the top of it as a sun deck to hang out when we were off duty.

Our sleeping quarters also had revetments in front, and the back to supposedly block mortars and rockets from getting to us. However, they were only about four feet high, so they wouldn't have been much help if the mortar round had scored a direct hit on the

building. Aside from the big bunker with the sundeck on top, we also had several others spread throughout the company area, where we would run for safety whenever the sirens would go off.

When I first arrived at the 539th Company Unit, I was a mechanic assigned to the maintenance squad for the Ch47 Chinook helicopters. Being a helicopter mechanic was my M.O.S. *(Military Occupational Specialty)*. I soon discovered, however, that most of the other guys assigned to this squad were drinkers, whom we called juicers. Juicers were very much opposed to potheads, which made it difficult for me as I was trying to find my place. I would hang out with the potheads in the evening and work with the juicers during the day. Unfortunately, the sergeant in charge of the crew had a vendetta against potheads. Before I had arrived, one of his crew members had been a speed freak and went berserk one night and almost killed himself. He then took on the responsibility of getting the guy straightened out and, thus, was constantly trying to catch the potheads in action and bust them.

At the bottom end of our flight line was a pond where the potheads would go to smoke in the evenings. It was far from the company area, where they were unnoticed. The maintenance shack was also located near the pond as well. One day, shortly after I had become part of this squad, the sergeant took our whole crew to the pond and began dumping oil and junk into the pond. I asked why we were doing this.

He responded, "Because those stupid potheads swim in here, I want to mess with them."

I knew then my days were numbered, and I would never make it with this squad. It would only be a matter of time before the sergeant figured out I was a pothead; therefore, I decided, even if it was going to hurt my military career by not working in my M.O.S., I was going to try to change jobs with someone. I wasn't planning on making the military my career, so I didn't care. I found someone in the ground handling crew who wanted to work as a mechanic, so we went to the NCOs in charge and asked for a change. After much discussion about how it would affect our standing in the military, especially after we returned stateside and the brass realized we hadn't been working our assigned M.O.S., they agreed we could make the change.

My new job was working with the ground handling crew. It was a great job. I loved everything about it! It included driving a tow truck for towing helicopters that needed repair from one place on the post to another.  I also drove the fuel truck and filled the helicopters with fuel. As the fuel truck driver, I also had fun burning human excrement. Thankfully, I wasn't the one that had to collect it. Instead, my job was to thoroughly spray it with JP4 Jet fuel and set it on fire. Burning the crap was a daily thing.

The best part of my job was driving the Maintenance Truck. I cared for a 2½-ton truck and went on little missions to pick up parts or other items for the Maintenance Dept. The fun part of this job was that I got to be the courier driver for the Battalion once a month. As the courier driver, I would  make daily trips to Saigon, Long Binh, Bien Hoa, and other places. I would take a load of people, dump them off at a given location in the morning, and then pick them up late afternoon. The rest of the day, I could do whatever I wanted. These daily trips enabled me to be the one who would score the pot for all of us. A pound of weed would only cost a couple of cartons of cigarettes. Purchasing weed was relatively easy.

While driving along, there would be little roadside stands that were nothing more than simple shelters with a Vietnamese person selling Coca-Cola. The Cokes were just a front for the pot they had hidden nearby. I would say, *"GI want Caànsa,"* and they would get it from the hiding place, and I would pay for it with a couple of cartons of cigarettes and be on my way. I often drove through the main gate, returning to my post with a load of people and a pound of weed hidden in the truck. The cool thing was that if I ever got caught, I could say, "It's not mine." Fortunately, I never got caught. I had a few close calls, but not with the truck.

As I told Hobo about my Vietnam jobs, he interrupted me, saying, "Hey, Space, I think this car is going to stop."

We had been sitting in the same place for about two hours, and it looked like we would finally get a ride. We were Miami-bound! This ride took us to Bonita Springs, where we stopped and found a grocery store to panhandle. It was well past lunchtime, and we were getting hungry. After getting a bite to eat, we still had plenty of time to make it to Miami before evening set in, so off we went, with our thumbs out, waiting for another ride. Fortunately, we got a ride right away, which took us across Alligator Alley. It was a great ride and sightseeing adventure. We arrived in Miami early in the evening, so we took off to see what we could find.

Nothing Happening in Miami

We ended up spending a few days in Miami but didn't like it because it was so crowded with people. It turned out to be relatively uneventful. However, as we began to talk with people, we began to develop the idea of going to Key West for Christmas. Christmas was just around the corner, and we wanted to be somewhere fun for the holidays. Once we decided, we were in a hurry to head over to Key West. Why wait around? Especially since things weren't going that well in Miami. So off we went to the Florida Keys. It was supposedly about a four-hour drive. The good thing was, in all probability, we'd get one nice long ride since most people going that way were headed toward Key West.

Christmas in Jail
Chapter Eleven

We arrived in Key West around mid-afternoon and spent the next few hours getting acquainted with the place. Key West was a cool place. I immediately fell in love with it.

There was a spot where you could go, and it said you were standing on the most southern point of the continental United States. The town was quaint and kind of like the party atmosphere we had experienced in the New Orleans French Quarter. It appeared like it was going to be a good time for us.

Key West was everything we hoped to find. Many locals gathered at the pier on the edge of town each evening to watch the sunset. In addition, many freaks or hippies were there wandering around. We immediately realized this was the place to meet people and score drugs. The only problem we found with Key West was that there were very few places where we could sleep at night out in the open. Locating a place to sleep each night was a constant challenge for us while there. We often had to sleep in someone's yard and then get up early before they noticed us.

Over the next few days, we established a routine. We hung out on the streets during the day, panhandling for food and cigarettes while trying to meet people so we could find out where they hung out in the evenings. We thought we would be spending quite a few days there, so we signed up for food stamps one day. The only problem was that it would be a few days before they would be issued to us. We also spent part of our days watching the filming of a movie called Key West, which starred Stephen Boyd. It was about a former CIA agent and his friend. They operated a boat service in Florida only to find themselves the target of an eccentric millionaire with a score to settle. It came out in 1973 as a made-for-TV movie.

One day, after hanging out at different places, including the pier, we had a decent day of panhandling. With a bit of money in our pockets, we wanted to score some LSD. It had been quite a while since we had taken it, so we hoped to score some. The last time we had LSD was at the Rock Festival in Texas, so we were more than ready for another trip. There seemed to be quite a bit floating around, so it wasn't long before we found someone and hit them for a couple of hits. After hanging out at the pier for a while, we took off with some other freaks we had just met.

They knew about a party where others were tripping, smoking pot, and drinking wine. It turned out to be a great evening. Much later that evening or early morning, after the party, as we were coming down off the acid, we wandered back to the area where we had slept the night before and found another yard a few blocks down the road. We didn't want to stay in the same place each night for fear someone had seen us and would be watching for us. So, we were constantly on the lookout for new places to sleep. We woke up the following day soaking wet, as it had rained most of the night. There wasn't much we could do about it, so we just slept in the rain. Thankfully, it wasn't too cold. Once again, the hazards of living on the road had struck. But the carefree, adventurous lifestyle we were experiencing was well worth the minor difficulties we experienced periodically. However, we realized we needed to purchase army-issued ponchos and a plastic tarp to cover our sleeping bags when it rained. As it was, we had no choice but to pack our wet stuff and head into town, knowing we would have to spend most of the day getting our sleeping bags dried out.

Busted for Panhandling

Having established our routine, we were having a great time just wandering the streets, panhandling, and getting high whenever the opportunity struck. Then, one day, the unforeseen happened. We got busted for panhandling. Evidently, the city wanted to clean up the streets of our kind for the holidays, and we found ourselves in handcuffs on our way to jail. It was my fault. I was getting too aggressive at it and was hitting up middle-class tourists. The cop told us if we were going to panhandle, we needed to stick to hitting up our kind. Unfortunately, he didn't have any mercy on us and hauled us to jail. Our arrest happened on a Friday morning, with Christmas just around the corner on Monday. Since we had no money to bail ourselves out, we were stuck there for the weekend—spending Christmas in jail.

Jail turned out to be a nice respite from constantly hustling for everything. We got three squares daily, showers, and a good bed to sleep in every night. Hobo and I ended up in a cell together. Our cell consisted of a bunk bed, a sink, and a latrine. The cells were all connected so we could carry on conversations freely enough. During the day, the jailer escorted us to a larger cell, where we hung out with all the other jailmates. Most of them were road freaks, just like us. We spent our days playing cards, watching TV, and sharing stories. During this time, I began to see things I didn't necessarily like about Hobo. As I continually observed him with others, I noticed he was somewhat of an egomaniac. No matter what the conversation was, he always had to outdo others to the point of extreme exaggeration. One night, we were all lying in our bunks telling stories, and a couple of guys had an incredible, shared experience in which Hobo couldn't participate, causing him to feel left out. Suddenly, he blurted out what it was like in Nam, and they had no way of knowing what it was like to be a marine in the middle of a battle with bullets flying everywhere. All the attention turned to him, but it was somewhat awkward. I was embarrassed for him. But he was my partner, and I put up with his quirks just as he had to put up with mine.

Almost Busted in Saigon

Hobo was always trying to get me to tell stories from my Vietnam experiences that would get a rise out of the guys. On one occasion, when we were all playing cards and telling stories, Hobo said, "Hey, Space, tell them about the time you almost got busted in Saigon."

So, I began to tell the story.

It started one day when John, Ed, and I wanted to sneak off to Saigon for the day. We had the day off, so we were up for some action. Our first order of business was to find someone to get passes and then forge them. We found J.R., one of our buddies, who worked as a clerk in the orderly room to get the passes and forge them. Our base was about 30 miles from Saigon. We could either hitch a ride on a Huey helicopter from the company next door or go to the main gate and hitch a ride on a truck or jeep. We decided to hitch a ride rather than take a helicopter ride. By taking a helicopter ride, we would have to show our passes. Because our passes were forged, we didn't want to show them unless we had to. Once we arrived in Saigon, our first order of business was to find a place where we could hook up with some Vietnamese women. Hooking up with these types of girls was never too difficult since the young boy-sans constantly came up to G.I.'s and said, "G.I. want girl? G.I. want coke?"[10] We had our fling and realized we were also in an opium den. We proceeded to get

---

[10] Coke was the term used by the boy-sans for heroin. When many of the G.I.'s started using it, they actually thought they were using cocaine and not heroin. This is how many G.I.'s got hooked on heroin. Many of them had never used either heroin or coke and didn't know the difference in the highs. The popular term for heroin eventually came to be known as skag.

high on opium and the weed we had. Later in the day, when walking through the streets of Saigon, we spotted a military PX store. We had noticed there were two Military Policemen (M.P.) standing at the door checking for passes, but we decided to go in anyway. As soon as we showed one of them our forged passes, they immediately started reading us our rights. It appeared we had forgotten to put the date on them. So, we were in deep trouble–not just because we were AWOL (Absent without Leave), but knowing we were holding dope, we knew they would search us in all probability. John was the one who was carrying the dope in his pockets.

The M.P. told us to follow him into the store. As he turned, John had the foresight to empty his pockets of all the dope and lay it on top of one of the cement barrels. We all went inside, and the M.P. made a phone call and then took us back outside. When we returned, he saw all the dope on the barrel and went ballistic on us. He was so mad he hit his fist against the wall. He then searched each of us while we were laughing and taking pictures of each other as they searched us. You must understand we were stoned out of our minds when this happened.

When they searched me, they discovered rolling papers. Thinking I was the culprit who had put the dope on the barrel, they thoroughly searched me, looking for the slightest crumb of marijuana. Luckily, they didn't find any. We always kept our weed in little film canisters, so it was doubtful they would find traces of it. They then handcuffed us and got us ready to be hauled to the M.P. Headquarters in Saigon. Another M.P. had now arrived to take us away. As we got in the jeep, the M.P. took each of our hats and pulled them down over our eyes to be mean. When we got to Headquarters, they called our First Sergeant and asked him what they should do with us.

He said, "Send them back to the base, and I will deal with them."

The MPs couldn't prove the drugs were ours, so that's all they could do. We were all given a week of extra duty working in the motor pool for our little escapade. We didn't even get an Article 15 for being AWOL. I almost got busted on another occasion, but that is another story.

Monkey Tom

One of the freaks we met in jail was a guy named *"Monkey Tom."* He had a deep, gravelly voice and had some of the best stories to tell out of all of us. He told us about all the cool places to hang out in Florida where you could survive relatively easily. He mentioned a Jesus freak community in Bonita Springs where they would let you stay for quite a while. He said they were a great bunch of people despite being Jesus freaks. We filed it in the back of our minds in case we ended up over that way again. He also told us about a place in Boca Raton with a cool bushy area where you could live and camp for days on end, located just a few yards from the beautiful beach. We filed that away as well. He also said the best place to hang out in Miami was Coconut Grove, which was good information because we still wanted to give Miami another chance.

A public defender came to talk to us about our charges and what would likely happen to us. He told us that if we agreed to leave Key West immediately, they would release us on Tuesday following our court appearance. We accepted the terms but weren't in a hurry to go anywhere. We were enjoying ourselves in jail. The Salvation Army people brought us all turkey dinners on Christmas day, which was nice. We also got along well with the jailer. He seemed like a nice guy who just accepted us for who we were. I would discover later that our easy-going relationship with the jailer would pay off.

Kangaroo Court

Tuesday finally rolled around, and the jailer took us into the courtroom to await our sentencing. It was interesting to listen to some of our jailmates' charges. One guy was charged for eating scraps off people's plates at restaurants. He would sit down and finish their leftovers when people got up from their meals. I guess that didn't go over too well.

As they called my name, I went before the judge, and he said, "I understand you have agreed to leave town immediately if you are released."

"That's right."

"You're free to go with time served as your punishment."

Hobo was next, and the judge asked him the same question.

Hobo said, "I signed up for food stamps and need to pick them up before leaving."

The judge said to him, "Seven more days."

That was it. I was free, and Hobo was back in jail for another seven days. The judge had no mercy on him.

Getting Hobo Released from Jail into My Custody

As my new buddies and I gathered outside the courthouse following our short trial, they started getting on my case about being willing to take off without Hobo.

They said, "You can't just leave Hobo here. You're his partner; you need to go and talk to the jailer and tell him that you've been traveling together for several months and can't just leave town without him."

I decided they were right. So, I proceeded to go and talk to the jailer. I told him the whole story, and—believe it or not—he let Hobo out if we would leave town immediately. Once again, we had worn out our welcome and were on our way to a new destination that fate and our instincts would lead us to.

Florida East Coast Adventures
Chapter Twelve

Following our experience in jail and getting Hobo released into my custody (after promising the jailer I would get him out of Key West,) we headed to Miami once again. Hobo and I had decided to take Monkey Tom's advice and check out Coconut Grove. Hobo was now talking in a deep, gravelly voice, trying to imitate Monkey Tom. His phoniness irritated and embarrassed me because it was so blatantly phony. Anybody with half a mind could pick up on the phoniness he was conveying. He seemed to go to great lengths to appear cool to others. Maybe this was what the guy back in Tempe was trying to warn me about him. I don't know. The sad thing was Hobo was an incredible person with a great personality just the way he was. He didn't need to put on an act. He always told people he was from Tombstone, Arizona, instead of British Columbia.

He would give me this line of bull, saying, "Space, you can't keep telling people you are from Washington because Washington isn't a cool place to be from. It would help if you told people you're from Texas."

Irritated, I often responded to him, saying, "It's pretty hard to tell people you're from Texas when you don't have a Texas drawl or a big belt buckle."

I decided to leave it at that, knowing I wouldn't convince him or change his ways, but I was determined not to go along with him.

Adventures in Coconut Grove

We arrived in Coconut Grove early afternoon and spotted some people hanging out on a sidewalk, leaning against their cars. There happened to be a pay phone nearby, and Hobo immediately made a phone call without saying anything to me. He got on the phone and started talking to someone in his new gravelly voice, loud enough for everyone to hear what he was saying. Hobo was carrying on a phony conversation with someone about buying a kilo of weed. When he finished the conversation, everyone listened to the dime drop into the coin return and immediately knew he was trying to impress them. I was embarrassed for him and myself. Someone commented on what an idiot he was and what great lengths some people go to impress others.

Because Hobo's phony conversation didn't go over well, we took off down the street to a park just around the corner. We ended up hanging out there until we could get our bearings to figure out our next move. Meanwhile, I started getting on his case about his phony way of talking and what he had just done.

He responded, "Space it's necessary if we want to meet cool people and be accepted."

"Well, we've been doing fairly well so far without having to resort to that kind of bull," I said back at him with a lot of irritation before letting the matter drop.

As we sat in the park, collecting our thoughts and taking things in, we noticed a shopping area up the street with a coffee shop where many people seemed to be hanging out. Sighting a likely place to meet more people, we headed to the area. We discovered right away this was the place to be. There were Hare Krishna's, Jesus freaks, plain freaks, and hippies all hanging out together. They all seemed to be getting along, but it was interesting to hear the Krishna guys and the Jesus freaks get into it with each other about who was right and wrong.

I overheard one of the Krishna guys say to one of the Jesus freaks, "You just lost your reward because you told everyone you were fasting."

As we were hanging out and getting to know some of them, they invited us to the park, where we had just come from, to smoke pot. Hobo must have taken to heart some of the things I had said to him, or maybe he was humiliated enough by what had just happened to drop his fake voice. The upshot was that he was now toning down his rhetoric.

Our new friends were some of the most interesting freaks we had met. I sensed a real spiritual vibe coming from them. They seemed to be in tune with the spiritual forces around them. Because of my spiritual background, I was attracted to these kinds of hippies. They were heavy dudes. As we began to get off on the pot and the way the conversation was flowing, there was an intensity to what we were experiencing. There was an understanding that some were on the side of evil and others on the side of good. One conversation was about wars and fighting. And we, as freaks, were supposed to be removed from all that. The conversation then shifted to the fact that there was an understanding of good and evil, but freaks handled it differently. It was all somewhat confusing to me. I was still trying to process things through my view and understanding of Christianity versus the devil. What they were talking about was on a whole different level.

When you mix pot and other drugs with religion, it can get bizarre at times. I had been mixing drugs with spiritual experiences since my

Vietnam days. As a result, spiritual deception and confusion began to settle into the fiber of my being and thinking.

For the next few days, we continued to hang out at the coffee shop and in the park with the same people we met the first day. We had found a nice place to sleep in a secluded area near the park and were making enough money each day, panhandling to supply us with food and cigarettes. Despite Hobo's initial blunder, we were fitting into the scene. Hobo had given up the gravelly voice and was acting normal again. I think he realized he had made a blunder and cooled it.

Another LSD Trip

One day, we all dropped some acid, and things started to get weird. The acid had speed mixed with it, which made it strange. I was on this trip where I would be just within reach of discovering the missing pieces to my vision in Vietnam, only to see them disappear beyond my reach. It was very frustrating. We were still in the middle of the acid trip when someone suggested we take off for another place one of the guys had mentioned. It was an adventure that would lead us to a place where we could discover the truth and the missing pieces we were all seeking. It was interesting because we were all on this trip together, trying to find the missing pieces of our lives. Yet, individually, each person was looking for something different.

Getting Fed up with Hobo

Hobo and I got into a big argument about this. I wanted to go, and he didn't.

I told him, "I'm going whether you come or not."

He got mad and said sarcastically, "Go ahead! See if I care. It's your loss."

Because I was getting fed up with him, I just took off without him. Incredibly intrigued with my new friends and the trip we were on, I was happy to accompany them. However, the adventure turned out to be another dead end, ending in someone's backyard as we were coming down from the psychedelic, laced speed trip. Hobo had somehow found his way to where we were, and we made our peace with each other and took off the following day together. When he realized I was serious, he came looking for me. I'm not sure how he ended up finding us, but somehow, he did.

Even though the acid trip was enjoyable in many ways, it once again left me feeling empty and unfulfilled. I felt like the spiritual forces were messing with my mind. While trying to navigate the spiritual maze and connect the missing pieces of the puzzle to my life, I was feeling empty time and time again.

It appeared that it was time to move on once again. Hobo and I then decided we were through with Coconut Grove. As fun as it had been, it was time for a change in scenery to whatever that might be. Later in the day, we ended up in another part of Miami, where we hooked up with a couple of gals we had met while panhandling. As the day wore on and we were enjoying each other's company, they began to tell us about a party several miles south of Miami, off Highway 1. They had a friend who had a car and said we were welcome to come along. It sounded like a reasonably good plan, so we were happy to oblige them. One of the gals sat in the front seat with the driver, while Hobo and I ended up in the back seat with the other gal. She and I had already been hitting it off, so we snuggled up and made out the whole way to the party while Hobo stared out the window.

Shortly after arriving and meeting their friends, we could hear the girls in another room getting into an argument with the guys whose house it was. The upshot was the girls coming back and telling us we had to leave. Her friends somehow concluded we were junkies and didn't want anything to do with us. They told the girls to get rid of us. The real problem was that I think they were jealous that I was hitting it off with the gal I had been having fun with on the ride to the party. The girls had led us to believe we would be spending the night there. The other two guys in the car must have informed them what was happening in the car. Obviously, I was highly disappointed, thinking I was going to spend the night with her since I had been making out with her during the ride there.

The problem was we were about 45 miles south of Miami with no car, and it was about 1:30 AM. So, we just left, walked a few hundred yards, and found a place to sleep on the side of the road. Some adventure that turned out to be!

The following day, we started hitchhiking back to Miami and caught a ride with a redneck driving a pickup truck with a fifth of whiskey lying on the front seat next to him.

When he picked us up, he said, "Hello, hippies!"

He kept a running conversation as we drove towards Miami. We were enjoying his company as we sipped whiskey with him. He was a real redneck but enjoyed meeting other people and learning about them. He quizzed us quite a bit on what we had been doing. As we told him about some of our adventures, he was getting a big kick out of us. It turned out to be a great start to our day despite the mishap from the previous evening. Upon arriving back in Miami, we were ready for whatever the day had in store for us. We had learned to take the bad with the good, so we didn't allow what had happened the previous evening to dampen our spirits.

New Year's Eve—Getting Caught up in a Riot

It was now New Year's Eve, and we were looking for somewhere to party for the evening. We had met up with a couple of hippie gals earlier in the day, who had told us about a significant event at a place called *"The Castaways."* So, as the evening wore on, we made our way to the event. Unfortunately, by the time we got there, something had happened to provoke a riot. Police officers were everywhere, chasing people away. As we were leaving with the two girls, we were walking down the street; two cops came up and started beating us on our backs with their clubs.

They yelled at us, "You're not walking fast enough. Get a move on."

We had no idea what had happened to provoke a riot but were determined to get away after being beaten with clubs by the cops. Somehow, amid all the confusion, the girls got scared and took off. I'm not sure what happened to them. Having just gotten out of jail and not wanting to end up there again, we got out of the area as fast as we could, especially when we had no idea what was happening. Unfortunately, we had a lousy New Year's Eve. Finally, after two disastrous evenings, we decided to cut our losses and get out of Miami.

The next day, New Year's Day, we set out for Ft. Lauderdale, about 30 miles away. We arrived early in the afternoon and started walking along the beach. We couldn't believe how crowded it was. We knew from experience we did better in places that were a little less crowded and where we were more of a novelty. Here we were, just another face in the crowd. We didn't like it, so we decided to continue north up the coast.

Fun Times in Boca Raton

Monkey Tom had told us about Boca Raton, which was only another 25 miles up the road. So, we set out again in search of a great place where we could settle in and hang out for a while—a place where we could kick back, take it easy, and have some fun. Boca Raton turned out to be the perfect place for us. Upon arriving there, we found a nice beach area with a pavilion where high school and college kids would come to party and have a good time. A few yards from the beach, we discovered an area full of bushes and shrubs. Many campsites were already there in the bushes where others had camped. We were called the *"bush people."* There were a couple of outside showers at the pavilion, which was helpful, and just a couple of blocks down the street was a 7-11 store where we could panhandle when needed. So, we decided to settle in and take advantage of this beautiful spot. We soon discovered how remarkable this spot was as we had all these high school and college chicks bringing us food from their homes every day. We were quite the celebrities. Everyone was getting a kick out of us, and we were enjoying it and playing it for all it was worth.

New Friends—Logan and Curly

We spent the days swimming in the ocean and learning how to body surf. Many other people were doing the same thing we were doing—living in the bushes and hanging out. We hit it off well with a couple of guys named Logan and Curly. Curly had long, curly hair, which was why he went by that name. They had been hitchhiking around Florida and would later travel to the other side of the state with us. We would all make our afternoon trips to the store down the street to panhandle and shoplift as much as we could. One day, we decided to steal several bottles of wine to party with the following evening. Only one person was attending the store, and he was behind the cash register, so it was relatively easy to shoplift. We ended up with several bottles of wine and food for the evening. We had a great time partying with all the locals who came to the pavilion in the evening. Hobo and I got pretty well intoxicated, along with our new friends, Logan and Curly.

Overdosing on Quaaludes

The next day was even more eventful. The night before, we met a young college gal who took a genuine interest in us and invited the four of us to her home to hang out for the afternoon. She let us take real showers and get cleaned up, and then we sat around and smoked pot with her all afternoon. Towards evening, we all headed back to the beach and the pavilion. Out of the four of us, she seemed interested in me. I guess she liked the shy and quiet type. She also had a bunch of Quaaludes, and we all took them. Unfortunately, I took more than anybody else for some reason and overdosed.[11] I had never experienced anything like this before. I had taken downers many times before, especially when I was in Vietnam, but I had never experienced this effect. I was so out of it that I became paralyzed. My mind seemed to function all right, but I couldn't get my legs to respond. I thought if I could get to the outside shower, I could maybe sober up a bit, and my legs would start working, but that wasn't to be. I was still paralyzed.

As I mentioned earlier, I realize without a doubt that I am incredibly fortunate to be alive and in a sane mind today. I could have ended up dead from the overdose. I was lucky I made it through the night and that phase of my life alive without doing too much damage to my mind. I am so thankful that God never gave up on me but finally delivered me from the drugs to the extent that I now have a sober mind that allows me to enjoy everything around me without the aid of mind-altering drugs.

After the failed shower attempt, I crawled on my hands and knees back to our bush fort and crashed for the night with the help of my new companion, the gal who had taken an interest in me and supplied all of us with the quaaludes. Thankfully, my arms were still functional, but my legs were completely paralyzed. The following day, when I woke up, I was fine, just a little hungover and groggy. I was very relieved. It could have been much worse. The gal spent the night with me, but nothing happened because I was too wasted.

With our routine well established, we stayed in Boca Raton for about ten days. Boca Raton was the best place we had been to up until then. I immensely enjoyed myself there. We were hanging out on the beach daily without having to hustle too much for food since we had all these girls bringing us food from their homes. It was a very relaxing time.

Escorted Out of Town by the Police

On our last day, a policeman found us at the pavilion and said, "I know you guys have been shoplifting at the 7-11 store down the street. Several complaints were filed against you, and I will give you all a choice to either go to jail or be escorted out of town. Which will it be?"

The four of us chose to leave town. The Policeman was relaxed about the whole thing, saying, "If I were in your shoes, I'd probably be

---

[11] Quaaludes or methaqualone was a prescription drug used in the treatment of anxiety, called an anxiolytic, or to promote sleep. Methaqualone is a sedative drug which is similar in effect to barbiturates, a general CNS depressant.

doing the same thing, but I have no choice but to escort you out of town because of all the complaints."

Once again, we had worn out our welcome, and it was time to move on and *'keep on truckin',* which was the common slogan of the day. He then gave us a ride to the edge of town, and the four of us headed to the west coast of Florida.

Jesus Freaks
Chapter Thirteen

Once again, we found ourselves following Monkey Tom's advice. We were headed back across the Alligator Alley highway to check out the Jesus freak community in Bonita Springs on the Gulf side of Florida. Only now, there were four of us traveling together. We had been hanging out with Logan and Curly the whole time we were in Boca Raton. After being escorted out of town with us, they wanted to tag along for a while.

Spiritual Dilemma

I was unsure about staying with the Jesus Freaks because I knew what would happen. At this point in my journey, I had pushed the whole Jesus thing to the back of my mind. It wasn't that I had quit believing; I just wasn't at a place where I wanted to be committed to anything spiritual. I enjoyed exploring other ideas about God and who He was while having the time of my life. I also enjoyed the carefree, hippie lifestyle and didn't see it ending anytime soon. I knew that going to a Jesus commune would put pressure on me to come to a commitment—something I didn't want to do. As I mentioned earlier, the Bible does say that sin is pleasurable for a season. You might say I was still in the season where I was having too much fun enjoying sinful living. Even though I often felt empty inside with a lack of true peace and contentment, I was unwilling to come to a place of surrender at this time. After giving it some thought, I gave in to the others. I just decided to harden my heart and not allow the conviction of the Holy Spirit to sway me.

We arrived at the Jesus Freak's community house in the early evening. They welcomed us with open arms. They were all very friendly and seemed genuinely excited we were there. We spent the next few days simply attending Bible studies, eating at community meals, working odd jobs with them, and getting to know everyone. Surprisingly, it was a very relaxing time without putting too much pressure on us. It was much like what Monkey Tom had told us. They were simply great people with a lot of love for other people. The leader's name was Alan. He was warm-hearted, caring, and genuinely interested in our well-being. Hobo asked him one day if he remembered Monkey Tom. He said that he did but encouraged us not to get involved with him as he wouldn't be a good influence on us.

After a few days, they suggested that Hobo and I move to another one of their other community houses in a nearby town to get more of a feel for their lifestyle. Curly and Logan stayed there while Hobo and I moved on. I am not sure why they didn't come with us. It may have been that Alan wanted to split us up intentionally so that they would have a better chance of getting us converted. Our days at the new community house were similar to Bonita Springs. The main difference was that we had more freedom to roam around as long as we were back for meals and Bible studies in the evening. Another fact that made this house more interesting and enjoyable was a beautiful gal named Kelly, whom I enjoyed being around. As I became increasingly infatuated with her, I chose to hang out with her and others during the day rather than take off on adventures with Hobo.

Hobo Gets Fired Up

During one of the evening Bible studies, the leader and a couple of others started getting a little aggressive in trying to convert us. They were telling us that God had sent us there so that they could share the gospel with us. Well, this got Hobo going.

He said, "Maybe God sent us here to enlighten you guys further."

I was thinking to myself, "Hobo, just shut up."

He then proceeded to share the Aquarian Gospel with them. Well, that went over like a lead balloon, and the discussion quickly ended.

Bible Studies and a Pretty Girl

While others roamed during the day, I hung back at the house because I wanted to be around Kelly. Hanging back with Kelly also meant being more influenced than I had intended. One day, while Hobo was out and about, he ran into our two friends—Logan and Curley. They had since left the other house and were roaming around the area. They all showed up together at the new community house and couldn't understand why I was starting to get into the whole Jesus thing. After they met Kelly and saw how pretty she was and that I was interested in her, they understood and quit giving me a hard time. As the day wore on, Logan and Curley decided to take off rather than join us for the evening meal and Bible study. We never saw Logan and Curly again. They were not interested in spending any more time with Jesus Freaks.

Eventually, things began to grow cold with me. Hobo confided in me one day that he had been committing adultery with the leader's wife. She had told him she had come to the community about six months back, stoned on a bad LSD trip. They took her in, and everything happened so fast. Without getting grounded in the faith, she found herself getting married to the leader. She woke up one day and began to wonder what she was doing. By the time Hobo and I entered the scene, she was in a very vulnerable state of mind. I also noticed Kelly, who I had become infatuated with, was more interested in the leader than me. I would see them flirting and often taking off together on his motorcycle. It was apparent that something was happening between them and that he knew his wife was playing games with him.

Caught Smoking Pot at Church

Sunday rolled around, which meant it was church day. We all packed into cars and went to church. To our surprise, all the friends we had met at the first community house were there. It was good to see everyone again. Hobo and I sat through a good part of the service. But halfway through the sermon, we decided to go out to the car and smoke a joint. While toking on a joint in the car, our house leader got suspicious and came looking for us. Unfortunately, He found us smoking the joint and demanded we put it out and give him all the pot we had. I am not sure why we gave in to him, but we did. Maybe it was because we were not ready to leave.

Time to Move On

When we got back to the house, we were given the third degree and told it was time to move on, that it was apparent we weren't making much of an effort at being converted. The leader was also somewhat aware of what was happening between Hobo and his wife. So, I figured he was looking for an excuse to get rid of us.

I had heard him asking one of the other members, on one occasion, "Where's my wife at?"

Someone said, "She's with Hobo."

Expressing extreme displeasure, he said, "What's she doing with him?"

Again, we had worn out our welcome, and it was time to move on. Only this time, we were not sure where to go, so we just started heading north. Who knew where our next adventure would take us? We sure didn't. And that is what was so great about what we were doing. Every day was a new adventure full of surprises. We enjoyed ourselves as we traveled from one place to another, meeting all kinds of people who were more than willing to let us mooch off them. It was a carefree life with no responsibilities. I loved it!

Leaving Florida
Chapter Fourteen

We had been in Florida for over a month, and it was almost the end of January. We decided to head north—up the Gulf Coast side of Florida. We were thinking of revisiting Clearwater, which was only about 150 miles from where we were. Even though it had rained when we first came to Florida, we liked the place. So again, we stuck our thumbs out and waited for a ride to take us to our next destination. It took us until noon the next day to get there. Unsuccessful at getting rides, we had to camp that night on the side of the road in some bushes near an onramp. We had a little food with us as the Jesus freaks were kind enough to send us on our way with some sandwiches.

After being with the Jesus freaks for a week, I was very unsettled in my emotions and thoughts. At one point, I was almost ready to give in to the Lord, even though I was partially motivated by my infatuation with such a pretty girl as Kelly. If things had turned out differently, I would have been willing to let Hobo go his way while staying with the Jesus freaks. Upon experiencing the vision of my life that flashed before me while in Nam, I had this overwhelming sense that God was pushing me forward into an unknown destiny. Attending Bible studies with the Jesus freaks awakened me—once again—to the truth of the Scriptures. It also brought back many memories of what I had experienced with Jesus and the Bible in Nam.

Reflections: Spiritual Awakening in 'Nam

I remember one morning—while in Nam—I was standing in front of my wall locker. I noticed the two New Testament Bibles that had been lying there on the shelf since the first day that I had arrived. One of them was a Bible a family friend had given to me. It had belonged to her son, a Green Beret, who had been killed in action while serving in Vietnam. The other was a Living New Testament my mother had given to me. They had both been on the shelf untouched for the first six months I had been in Vietnam.

For some reason, I decided to pick up the Living Bible and take it with me that day. At this point, during my tour, I spent most of my days in the Bone Yard with my pothead buddies. It was the place where all the wrecked helicopters were stored. Although I was still the

Maintenance truck driver, I and others who were known potheads were relegated to the Bone Yard. I would get my truck from the motor pool daily and park it near the Bone Yard until I was told to go somewhere.

Vietnam Reflections: The Boneyard and Explosives

Since the Bone Yard was now our principal place of duty, we made ourselves comfortable with hammocks strung up. We had also put together makeshift awnings with tarps to keep the sun and the rain off us. We would sit out there and smoke pot all day long. The lifers, as we called them, would leave us alone for the most part. By now, they knew better than to mess with us too much. We had tear-gassed them in the night on more than one occasion. They also knew we had hand grenades and C4 explosives. At one point, we figured out that they  didn't post guards at the ammo dump at lunchtime, which was standard throughout the base, from noon to 1:30 pm. They were having their lunch during that time as well. So, on occasion, we would all jump in my truck, head over to the ammo dump, and avail ourselves of all kinds of explosives, including tear gas and smoke grenades.

 At one point, someone suggested putting a swimming pool together in the middle of our company area, but for whatever reason, it was unsuccessful. All the parts ended up in the Bone Yard with us. Some parts were long tubular poles, out of which we made firebombs. We would take the C4 explosive pieces attached to a blasting cap with a long wire running out, which would be connected to the clicker in our hands. We would then jam a couple of quarts of oil down the tube and ignite the C4. A huge firebomb would shoot into the air several hundred feet or so. It was quite a sight for everyone to see. As a result of our fire bombs, the Company NCOs decided to do a thorough search and found several hand grenades, tear gas, and C4 explosives. They couldn't prove who they belonged to, so we didn't get into trouble. However, they now knew and

were somewhat afraid of us. Our intention was never to hurt anyone. We just wanted to scare them into leaving us alone.

The Beginning of the Jesus Movement in our Company

The Boneyard environment was where I found myself on this day. I made myself comfortable, rolled a joint, and began reading the story of Jesus in the New Testament. To my surprise, another one of my buddies had brought a Bible with him and started reading. That was the beginning of the Jesus revolution in our company. It wasn't long before I was writing home about what was happening, and my mother began sending me Bibles to give away to all my buddies. Of course, everyone wanted the Living New Testament like I had.

I had recently returned from a two-week leave over the Christmas holidays and brought back George Harrison's new album *"All Things Must Pass."* His album was full of spiritual overtones, including the song *"My Sweet Lord."* Even though the song was about Krishna, we didn't pay much attention to the fact as we immersed ourselves in his lyrics. Over the next few months, I and some of my other pot-smoking buddies were constantly reading the Bible and witnessing to others. We would smoke pot and read the Bible at the same time. It was an incredible period of discovery and enlightenment. The gospel seeds were planted into my heart, even though I didn't wholly repent and surrender to what Jesus wanted to do in my life.

These thoughts and memories filled my mind as I sat on the side of the road, waiting for our next ride toward Clearwater. Once again, I had to reconcile these thoughts and emotions as they stirred within me. I would always come to the same conclusion: someday, I would probably surrender my life to the Lord completely—but not now. Somehow, that would give me the peace I needed to keep going and enjoy the journey I was currently experiencing.

We arrived in Clearwater around noon the day after leaving Bonita Springs. We immediately headed to the beach where we had been when we first came to Florida about a month earlier. Several people were hanging out, so we joined them. They had built a fire and were roasting hot dogs, which they offered us.

Wheels and a New Friend to Travel With

As we chatted and got to know one another, we met another guy named Randy. We soon discovered he had just come from Indiana and was traveling around the country in his Volkswagen Bug. He seemed to take a genuine interest in Hobo and me and began asking us questions about our travels. We began to share with him our adventures starting from Tempe, Arizona, and how cool it was to catch rides on freight trains. He was pretty intrigued by the idea of riding on a freight train but didn't see how it would be possible since he was stuck with his car. Over the next few days, we continued hanging out with Randy and the others at the beach. We would take off with him, periodically, in his VW Bug to check out places around town. It was nice having someone around with wheels and not having to walk or hitchhike everywhere. Randy was genuinely interested and continued to quiz us about our travels and how we got by without any money. We told him how we survived by panhandling, hitting up missions or the Salvation Army, and finding party houses where we could hang out until we wore out our welcome. We told him how we even stayed with Jesus freaks. We also told him about our friends in Houston and how they had let us stay with them for over a week and had invited us back anytime.

One day, after sensing Randy was wishing he could do what we were doing without being strapped to a car, we suggested he come with us to Houston, where we could drop his car off at our friend's home and then hit the rails for L.A. He was overly excited about the idea, so we planned to leave for Houston the next day or so. It would be about a 1,000-mile trip, which we would try to do in two days. Hobo and I were extremely excited! With a free ride with wheels, we would have a relatively easy trip to Houston, where we could hang out for a week and then take off for L.A. riding freight trains with Randy.

Anxious to start a new adventure, we headed out of Florida with Randy in his VW Bug. Florida had been good for us despite a short stay in jail over Christmas and being escorted out of Boca Raton by the local police. We had enjoyed our time in Florida, but it was time to move on. This time, we had a ride to Houston. We planned to drive as far as Mobile, Alabama, and stay at the Salvation Army, where we had previously visited. We would then go straight to Houston the next day. We would skip New Orleans, knowing we would return for Mardi Gras in February. Randy and I would take turns driving. I already discovered Hobo didn't enjoy driving.

As we were driving towards Mobile, I began to think back over the months that had passed since leaving my friends in Minnesota. I had come a long way and had changed a lot. I had adjusted very well to life on the road. I wondered when it would end and questioned whether I wanted it to end. Only time will tell. I was enjoying this life, for the most part. I was experiencing things that most people never get the opportunity to do because they're too chained to their day-to-day lives. I also saw our country from a unique perspective while discovering who I was. In addition, I was meeting all kinds of interesting people.

Finding My Way through the Spiritual Maze

I was still in the process of finding my way through the spiritual maze I found myself in. I was no longer feeling lost and insecure about my life and its direction. However, even though I had made peace with the life I was now living, I knew deep down in my heart there was still a sense of emptiness. I still had a hunger and a thirst for God that left me unfulfilled. I knew deep down in my heart that it wouldn't be filled until I fully surrendered to Him and His purpose for my life, but I was unwilling to come to that place at this juncture. I still wanted to taste and see what the world and this lifestyle had to offer. I enjoyed getting high and experiencing this exciting and carefree lifestyle. I just wasn't ready to give it up.

Having arrived in Mobile, we spent the night as planned at the Salvation Army, where we got a good meal and a good night's sleep with a hearty breakfast to get us on our way the following day. By evening, we would be with our Houston friends, getting high if everything went well.

Just as planned, we arrived in Houston as it was getting dark. We called our friends, who couldn't wait to see us and hear what we had been doing. In just a short while, we would be reunited with them and enjoy a week of getting high, relaxing, and having fun without having to hustle for food, drugs, and shelter. Life was good, and I was enjoying it immensely.

Houston and on to Los Angeles
Chapter Fifteen

Our friend, Carol, whom we had met at the Rock Festival and who owned the home in Houston, gave us directions. We then headed out to the suburbs and found the house quite quickly. They were happy to see us again and welcomed us with open arms. We introduced them to our new friend, Randy, and explained our plan to leave for L.A. in a few days, hoping we could leave Randy's car with them while we traveled by freight train. They were all good with this but were in no hurry for us to go. They were excited to see us and wanted to hear about our adventures. We spent the evening drinking wine and smoking pot while sharing our stories with them.

Back in Houston at Carol's Home

We spent about a week with Carol and her friends, enjoying our time with them. Somehow, Randy hit it off with Carol and ended up in her bedroom the whole time we were there. So, we spent plenty of time sitting around playing their god games with them.

We would be sitting around listening to music and getting high, and all of a sudden, Hobo would yell out, "Hi, Carol god!"

Carol would respond, "Hi, Hobo god!"

It was pretty amusing. The Houston people called it "Playing the Game."

One of the things we liked about hanging out in Houston at Carol's home was the opportunity to sit around and listen to music. Listening to music was something we never got enough of while traveling. In those days, there were no iPhones or iPods yet. You couldn't pull one out and listen to music. Our favorite album then was the Rolling Stones' *"Exile on Main Street."* We would make sure it got played whenever we were at a party house. Hobo and I had dug it ever since we first heard it at Carol's home back in November.

Carol's home was still like Grand Central Station, with people constantly coming and going. Then, one night, a couple of gals we hadn't met before came over. They found their way to Hobo and me, having heard about us, and began seducing us. Before the night was over, I found myself with one of them in her apartment and Hobo with the other gal in a separate apartment.

On another occasion, Carol's friend, Billy, who Hobo had the confrontation with the last time we were in Houston, ended up in the emergency room after trying to commit suicide by knifing himself. He required several stitches, but other than that, he was ok. He later told us he had taken LSD and was making a sacrifice to the devil. Over the years, I have noticed people who are unstable emotionally and mentally do not do very well with LSD. It can be hazardous for them. Billy had a lot of instability in his life.

LSD Experiences

I probably took LSD at least 60 times or more over four years, from 1969 to 1974, and I never had a bad trip. When I first got home from Vietnam, during my trip to the Bay Area in California to visit my buddy, Jack, we went to Yosemite National Park one weekend and took LSD. I had my dog, Freak, with me. As I was beginning to get off the acid, I walked across a bridge and pondered whether I should jump into the water. It was stupid, but I did it, throwing Freak off the bridge before me. Luckily, we both survived the jump. When I came up out of the water, I was hallucinating like crazy. We were sitting in a meadow with a line of trees about 300 yards away. As I came out of the water, the trees began to sing, weaving back and forth and clapping their hands.

Years later, I found this Scripture in the Book of Isaiah that described to a tee what I was hallucinating. It is located in the Book of Isaiah the Prophet. *"For you shall go out with joy and be led out with peace; the mountains and the hills shall break forth into singing before you, and all the trees of the field shall clap their hands." Isaiah 55:12* This was just one example of my trips on LSD. Another time  during this same trip to the Bay Area, some friends and I went to the Billy Graham Crusade in Oakland, California, stoned on acid. We even went forward for the altar call at the end but were so stoned we didn't know what we were doing. On another occasion, while taking LSD in Nam, I was on guard duty at one of the towers and hallucinated that the heavens were opening before my eyes. I say all this simply to reveal that many of my LSD trips had spiritual overtones because that is where my head was. Unfortunately, as described before, Billy's mind was much more fragile, and his LSD trip proved disastrous.

Even though drinking wasn't our thing, there were occasions when we would indulge. One of those occasions was during our time in Houston. We spent an afternoon drinking 150 Proof Bacardi Rum, and all got very drunk. Randy was concerned about us and wondered whether Hobo was an alcoholic. After having been with him for several months, I knew he wasn't. He just liked to "tie one on" occasionally.

Freight Train to Los Angeles with Randy

After about a week in Houston, we were itching to get on the road again. This time, we will be heading for LA and taking Randy with us. Even though he was having a great time with Carol, he was itching to go. Carol gave us a ride to the freight yard, where we said our goodbyes. We headed out to find a train headed in the direction of LA. Sometimes, when trying to find the right train, we would find out that it wouldn't be leaving for a few hours, which is what we had discovered concerning the train we were about to hop. We were concerned about being detected by the railroad bulls and didn't want to get caught, so we found an empty boxcar, got in, and waited. We parked ourselves in the far back corner so as not to be detected.

In all my travels on freight trains, I only got caught once. It was on my first trip from Washington to Minnesota. Jack, my army buddy from the Bay Area, was with me, our girlfriends, and two other people. The girls were from Minnesota, and we were going to visit one of their uncles, who had a farm in Northern Minnesota, where we spent time riding horses and other things. Our train had stopped in Montana somewhere, and while we were waiting for it to continue, the railroad bulls spotted us. As I mentioned earlier, they checked all our IDs and discovered my friend Jack from the Bay Area had a warrant for his arrest. He was taken into custody and shipped back to California, but they let the rest of us continue.

Now, several months later, I was in the Houston yard sitting in an empty boxcar, hoping not to get caught and thrown in jail. Several road freaks we had met on our travels warned us that the Houston bulls would haul you off to jail if they saw you. So, when our train took off towards Los Angeles, Randy got excited that we were on the way. In his mind, he was finally doing something fascinating and daring. Hobo and I were relieved we were on our way without being detected.

Randy was a clean-cut kid. He wasn't like Hobo or me in many ways—he wasn't a freak. He was simply a young guy wanting to experience different things. When he met us, he realized he could experience something he would never have had the opportunity to do. We all settled in to enjoy our free ride across Texas. This time, we were determined to stay on the train until we reached El Paso. Our friends from Houston had packed us a great lunch and bag of goodies, so our hunger wouldn't be an excuse for getting off in San Antonio. We wanted to get to LA as quickly as possible. El Paso would be at least a 14-hour trip, depending on how many stops the train would make. After that, we would be ready for a break after a long ride. Our train didn't leave Houston until early evening, which meant we would be traveling through the night. On long trips like this, we would roll out our sleeping bags and sleep through the night, which didn't always work out, as we would find out later when we were coming back through Houston. We arrived in El Paso the following morning and set out to find a place to eat. Randy seemed to have plenty of money, so we were happy to let him buy.

Drunk in Juarez, Mexico

After getting something to eat, we thought it would be a good idea to walk around and check things out to see what was happening. We quickly discovered it was relatively easy to cross the border into Juarez, Mexico. Wanting to give Randy a good experience, we thought it would be a good idea to go to Juarez, find a bar, and drink Mexican tequila. This trip was about showing Randy a great time with some experiences he would have to share with everyone back home. He was game, and we were willing to show him a great time since he was willing to pay. We found a bar right away and made ourselves comfortable. We ordered a fifth of tequila and beer chasers. We spent the next hour or so drinking. At one point, I became extremely sick and puked. I was never a great drinker. I preferred getting high on drugs. That was our queue, that it was time to leave. Hobo and I were drunk but still had enough wits to find our way back across the border with Randy's help.

As we made our way back across the border, we were suddenly apprehended by the authorities and handcuffed. *(I'm sure Randy had fun telling that story when he returned home.)* They thought we were on drugs and proceeded to strip-search us completely. We tried to explain to them we were drunk, but they searched us anyway. Luckily, we didn't have any drugs on us. Who knows what would have happened? We could've been locked up in a Mexican jail for who knows how long. They finally let us go after being convinced we had no drugs. We then figured we'd better sober up if we wanted a good place to stay for the night. Salvation Armies and Missions usually won't let you stay if you're drunk. However, it was still early in the day, so we had time to sober up. Randy hadn't been drinking as much as us and hoped we would sober up quickly. By the time evening rolled around, we were mostly sober. We were able to find the local mission without too much trouble, get a hot meal, and settle in for the evening.

We left the mission the following day, probably eating something like oatmeal, toast, and juice, which wasn't much, but enough to get us on our way. Our goal was to return to the railroad yard and find a train headed west. Often, the railroad workers would let us know what was up. They would let us know if we needed to be watchful of the bulls or not and what direction trains were going. Hopefully, they wouldn't steer us in the wrong direction as they did during our first trip to Houston. If everything went right, it would be an eight-hour ride to Tucson. We would most likely get there by late evening, provided there was a train. Fortunately, we found a train that would be leaving within the hour. It was heading for Tucson and had an empty car, so we jumped on with great expectations. Sometimes, it could be challenging to find an empty car, and the only thing available to ride would be a Sea-Land trailer or "piggybacks," as they called them. When this happened, you would be exposed to the cold, wind, and whatever the weather was bringing, which made for an extremely uncomfortable ride. Later in our travels, we ended up in such a situation.

On this trip, as we were traveling through the mountains, it was so cold the water in our canteens began to freeze with a film of ice forming on them. When our train stopped to allow another train to pass, we had some unexpected company. A couple of Mexicans had just crossed the border illegally and hopped into our boxcar. This was one of the hazards of train hopping. You never knew what kind of situations or people you might meet along the way. Thankfully, they were not banditos or a threat, so we got along fine even though we couldn't communicate effectively with them.

Near Death Experience in Tucson

We arrived in Tucson late, so there was no chance of getting a good place to stay for the night. As the train slowed down through the downtown area, we jumped off. We knew, from experience, that the railroad yard was a distance from town, and we wanted to explore the area and find a place to eat. Thankfully, we wouldn't have to panhandle since Randy was with us. He was doing a great job taking care of us while we showed him the experience of a lifetime. After getting a good meal, we set out to find a decent place to sleep for the night. Finding the right place meant looking for a park with lots of shrubbery. It didn't take long to find one, so we bedded down for the night to await the next day's adventure, whatever that might be.

The following day, we found a place to get a quick bite to eat. Then, because we were getting anxious about getting back on a train and continuing to L.A., we headed back to where we had jumped off the train. Our thinking was if another one happened to come by, we could run and jump on and catch a ride into the switching yard.

It wasn't long before a train came by and slowed down enough for us to run and jump on easily enough. The problem was, as I was running alongside the train, focusing on the train, I didn't see the sign right in front of me. As a result, I crashed hard into it, with my knee hitting it with full force. I was hurt quite badly and fell hard right next to the train as it was going by. It was a very frightening experience. The train would have hit me if I had dropped more to the left. God must have been looking after me. Almost getting myself killed wasn't the adventure I was looking for on this day, but it taught me a valuable lesson. *"Be careful; trains can be dangerous."* After this mishap, we all decided it would be better if we just walked the mile to the yard as there probably wouldn't be another train coming by for a while. Even though I was limping, we eventually found our way into the yard and located a train headed towards LA, thanks to the workers. Within an hour or so, we were on our way.

We got as far as Phoenix and noticed our train had stopped longer than anticipated. The workers in the yard informed us this was the end of the line for the train. A railroad yard is used to disassemble trains and put trains together. The train we had just come in on was going to be dismantled. Train hopping can be frustrating at times. But you have to learn to go with the flow. Otherwise, you get disillusioned.

Back in Tempe

As long as we were in Phoenix, we decided to hitchhike over to Tempe and show Randy around where Hobo and I first met. We showed him the park where we had all hung out and some of the bars we had frequented. We ended up at our favorite one, had a couple of beers and hamburgers, and then returned to the park.

Tempe held a special place in my heart as it was the beginning of my experience as a road freak. Even though I had been to other exciting cities and towns, Tempe was where I developed my bearings and where things began to jell for me. Returning to Tempe was like returning to your hometown after being gone for a long time. You notice how things have changed. People you once knew are no longer around or have moved on to other circles of friends. This is what we found upon arriving in Temple. The friends we had met the first time were nowhere to be seen.

We bedded down for the night in the park and woke up the next morning anxious to continue to LA. We then hitched a ride back to Phoenix, just a few miles down the road, and headed to the freight yard. It took us about an hour or so, but we finally found a train going to LA.

Los Angles, Here We Come

It looked like it was going to be another 8 to10 hour train ride. But we were up for it and anxious to be on our way. The ride was uneventful, with us arriving in the LA freight yard late at night. We found our way to a cafe down the street from the yard with Randy, who was again treating us to a hearty meal. After taking care of our hunger pangs, we found a place to sleep for the night and wondered what we would see in Los Angeles. The first thing we did upon waking up was to find a restroom where we could get cleaned up. It had been a while since we had cleaned up, so we did the best we could at the restroom. None of us had taken a shower since leaving Houston, so we needed one, but that would have to wait.

Randy was starting to voice his displeasure with the adventure. He wasn't used to being unclean for such a long period. Hobo and I were used to it and had learned to take advantage of situations as they came up. Getting washed and cleaned up was fine for us but not for Randy. He wanted a shower. We found our way back to the cafe from the night before, had a good breakfast, and headed into downtown LA. It was still quite a distance into the downtown area from the freight yard, so it took us a while to get there. None of us had ever been to LA, so we were unsure what to expect. We realized right away we were like small fish in a large pond. Whereas in smaller towns and out of the way, people treated us with curiosity and interest. No one had any interest in us here. Randy was getting disillusioned with the whole adventure.

We ended up just spending the day wandering the streets and taking in the sights, and we did not accomplish much. We were not meeting anyone, nor were there any drugs floating around. It just wasn't happening. We were now at a loss as to what we should be doing. We were hanging out with hopes that something would work out for us.

Narrow Escape

As the day wore on and early evening was upon us, some Jesus freaks approached us and started a conversation. They wanted to know what we were up to and where we were going. Also, they seemed interested in whether we had somewhere to stay. As it turned out, they were from a commune in the country outside of LA. They all came into the city on a bus to share the gospel with people. They looked at us as likely victims since we needed both showers and a place to sleep for the night. They informed us that a bus would be coming soon to pick them up and take them back to the commune. Because we mentioned we needed showers and a place to sleep, they jumped on this and invited us to come along. They said we could get a good meal and even take a shower. The prospect of taking showers was very inviting to us, especially Randy. We decided to take them up on their offer and had no sooner agreed than the bus appeared. We all jumped on and were ready to head out to their commune for a free meal, showers, and a good night's sleep. For some reason, just before we were about to take off, Hobo and I looked at each other with questioning eyes.

Hobo says to me, "Space! Do you think this is a good idea? I have a bad feeling about this."

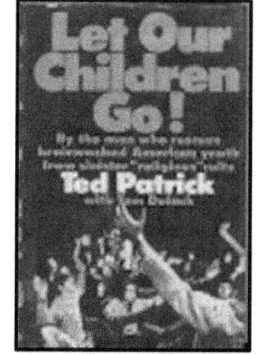

I agreed with him and yelled at Randy, "We're getting off the bus. Come on!"

We jumped off just as they shut the doors, barely making it time. So much for the free meal and shower!

Many years later, I read a book by a man named Ted Patrick titled, *"Let Our Children Go!"* He was a deprogrammer who kidnapped people from cults and then deprogrammed them. My wife's cousin was involved with the cult *"Love Israel."* Her parents hired Ted Patrick to kidnap her from the cult and deprogram her. Her story was one of the featured stories in the book, which was why we were reading it. As I was reading the book, I came across a chapter on the *"Children of God"* cult near the LA area. The book described how they would pick people up on the streets of LA, load them on a bus, and take them to their community outside of the city. It described how they would deprive the new people coming into the community of sleep and food until they memorized Scripture and made other adjustments to their lifestyle. Looking back, I realized it was the Lord who urged us to get off the bus. He was still watching over me even though I was running from Him.

It was too late to find a mission or Salvation Army, so we again resorted to finding a secluded area to sleep for the night. Unfortunately, LA wasn't working out, so we decided to cut our losses and head back to Arizona the following morning. Randy was getting more and more disillusioned with what was going on. We were not sure how long he would continue traveling with us.

Randy Has Enough

The following day, after grabbing a quick bite to eat, we headed towards the freight yard. As we began to get closer, Randy was getting very apprehensive.

He finally said, "Listen, guys! I have had about as much as I can take. This adventure is just not working for me. So, I'm going to catch a bus back to Houston and cut my losses."

Hobo and I wanted to catch a freight train back to Arizona, but Randy wanted no part of it, so we split company with him. He took off to find a bus station while we headed towards the freight yard. We had enjoyed Randy's company and were sad he was going but realized it was probably the best thing. Our lifestyle was just a little too much for him. We returned to the freight yard and immediately caught a train to Phoenix. We decided to go back to Tempe, hang out for a while, and figure out where we would go next. We eventually wanted to return to New Orleans for Mardi Gras, but it was still too early. It was early February, and Mardi Gras was still a month away.

Discovering More of Arizona
Chapter Sixteen

When we arrived in Phoenix, we made our way as quickly as possible to the mission so that we could get a shower and get a good night's sleep. We had already missed dinner, so we would have to go without food. Still, getting a shower and a good night's sleep would be worth it. We started the next day with a good breakfast and then headed out for Tempe, just a few miles down the road.

Randy Shows up Again

Once back in Tempe, we needed to find a Laundromat and wash our clothes. The last time we washed clothes was back in Houston. Later in the day, we returned to our favorite bar. As we were sitting there having a beer, guess who walked in? Our friend, Randy! He had taken the bus, and we had taken the freight train and arrived before him.

We were not sure why he was there, but it was good to see him. We later found out his bus had a layover, and he had a couple of hours to kill before heading back to Houston. So, we all shared a beer and talked about our trip. He was glad he had come along, but it was too much for him. He then left on good terms, but we never saw nor heard from him again.

We spent the next few days just hanging out around Tempe. The trip to L.A. from Houston and then back to Tempe had taken a lot out of us. So, we just wanted to take it easy for a few days doing nothing. We made a few new friends from hanging out in the bars and on the street. They kept us supplied with enough pot to keep us happy and free. We also met some people who had a party house and were kind enough to give us a place to store our backpacks and crash every night.

One night, when we were all sitting around smoking pot, we told them about all our travels. We mentioned we were a little unsure where to go next. Finally, someone told us about a ghost town near Prescott Valley called Jerome. Apparently, many empty, abandoned houses were sitting there for the taking. Jerome was a place that was fast becoming a haven for hippies. It sounded like just the place for us to check out, especially since we had time to kill. We still had time to spend a few more days in Tempe since we had a decent place to sleep each night. It was always amazing to me how things worked out for us as we traveled from one place to another without too much care as to where we were going. We were a couple of road freaks, looking for a free ride to nowhere in particular while mooching off whatever resources or people happening to come our way.

Jerome Arizona

As the idea of going up north to Jerome began to take shape in our minds, we began to get excited for the next phase of our adventures. We liked the idea of getting to experience more of Arizona. So, we opted to spend the next day doing some serious panhandling to have cash, food, and wine to take with us. One of our favorite things besides smoking pot was getting a bottle of hearty burgundy wine and a big hunk of cheese to go with it. It was a nice snack while sitting on the side of the road, waiting for a ride.

On our final day in Tempe, besides panhandling and preparing for our next adventure, we went to the Laundromat, once again, to make sure we had clean clothes. We wanted to start as fresh as possible, as we didn't know what the next few days would hold. When the next morning arrived, we were itching to get started. We said our goodbyes to our new friends, with whom we had been crashing for the last week, and headed for Jerome, Arizona. It was a beautiful February morning filled with lots of promise and anticipation for the day. Jerome was only about a hundred miles north—a three or four-hour journey.

We discovered that during the 1960s and 1970s, Jerome was a hillside haven that appealed to counter-culture types. Many people would come to Jerome, buying houses for relatively cheap or sometimes just taking over the more neglected homes. The town was building its reputation as an artists' colony, a ghost town, and an excellent place to hang out undetected.

Once we had our clothes washed and panhandled enough to get what we needed, we hit the road with great expectations. Our first ride was an indication that we were off to a great start. We got a great ride as soon as we got started. A guy named Bill stopped to pick us up. He was returning from the Phoenix Airport after dropping his wife off. She was going to be gone for a couple of weeks or so. He was a naturally talkative guy and had picked us up so that he would have someone to talk to. He took a genuine interest in us as we began to tell him about all our recent adventures. We told him we were going to Jerome for a week or so. As it turned out, he had a small farm just northeast of Jerome and would be going right by the Jerome turn-off. He was afraid he would be lonely with his wife away for a couple of weeks and wanted us to come and stay with him to keep him company. We told him we wanted to go to Jerome but might drop by after we had worn out our welcome. He even gave us a map and directions if we decided to take him up on his offer.

Upon arriving at the Jerome turn-off, we said our goodbyes to our new friend, letting him know we might see him in a few days, depending on how things went in Jerome. He reiterated he wanted us to come and see him if possible.

In no time at all, we had another ride, this time with an old man in a pickup. He wasn't as talkative as Bill, but we had a nice ride with him up the hill to Jerome. We arrived around mid-afternoon. It was a relatively small community, so there was little to see. However, a bar was located on the corner where we got dropped off. It had a park bench just outside the bar, so we sat there for about half an hour or so, checking out the people coming and going. As we sat there, our attention drifted to the rows of abandoned houses up along the hill on the other side of the street. Finally, we decided to take off and see if we could find a place to stash our packs and camp out for the next few days.

We were amazed at how many empty houses there were. They were all in bad shape; some were severely run down, and others not so bad. It wasn't long before we found the perfect house. It would serve as a place to crash and store our packs so that we could have the freedom to move around without our cumbersome packs. Obviously, there was no running water, electricity, or other comforts a home could offer. However, it was good enough for us, as our needs were quite simple.

Once we settled in and felt safe about leaving our packs, we headed back to the main street to explore more of the town. We met a few people, but nobody seemed to be taking much interest in us. We were a little surprised since this was such an out-of-the-way place. Jerome wasn't a place you just passed through. You got there because it was a specific destination.

We did notice other hippie-like characters wandering around, but they seemed much cleaner-cut than us. They weren't grungy hippie freaks. The original excitement we had about coming to Jerome was beginning to wane as we observed what was happening around us. We were a little bewildered by the lack of attention we were getting. It was getting late in the afternoon, so we walked back to the bar where we had started earlier. We thought we might as well try our luck at panhandling in front of the bar. We wanted to go in and have a few beers but had no money.

Not Welcome in Jerome

As we were panhandling from our corner in front of the bar, people would give us funny looks as if to say, "What do you think you are doing?" It was like an unexpected scene for them. It wasn't long before we realized just how surprising it was. Another person we approached for spare change responded very belligerently to us, saying, "What do you think you're doing? Why don't you go back to LA, where you and your kind belong?"

Well, that put a damper on our afternoon with hopes of making enough money for a couple of beers.

Another person said, "Why don't you guys get a job?"

"This is our job—this is what we do!" I replied to him with an attitude.

He laughed at us and went on.

Hobo started to get upset and said to me, "This is getting weird. Let's take off down the street and see what we find. I don't think these people like us."

Having had enough of their snide remarks, we took off down the street toward the residential area of town. It wasn't long before we ran into some hippie-looking characters who looked a little more like us. Walking along with them, we expressed our misgivings about coming to Jerome. Feeling sorry for us, they invited us to hang out with them for a while, letting us know they had a good stash of weed.

They said, "We've got some weed, so let's go get high. We'd love to hear about your travels and what you guys have been up to."

Those were great-sounding words, so off we went, taking them up on their offer. At their pad, others were hanging out as well. So, we spent the next few hours smoking pot, listening to music, sharing stories, and munching away. Unfortunately, they let us know that Jerome wasn't where people like us did very well.

They said, "Don't worry about it. Jerome caters more to hippie types who are there with a purpose besides just hanging out."

As the evening wore on, we headed back to the house where we had stashed our packs and crashed for the night. The next morning, we were unsure what to do or expect from the day. We still had food we'd purchased before leaving the Phoenix area, so we had enough to ward off hunger attacks. About mid-morning, we were back on Main Street to see what was happening. We were beginning to think Bill's offer to spend a week with him sounded like a good idea.

Visit from the Local Sheriff

As we were sitting in front of the bar, the local sheriff came over and began questioning us. He wanted to know what we were all about and why we were in Jerome. We told him we were traveling around the country and thought Jerome would be a great place to check out. He was a big, jolly, easy-going guy who reminded me of Hoss Cartwright from the Bonanza television series. Although he let us know in his easygoing manner, he had his eye on us.

Well, that was enough for Hobo. So, he turned to me and said, "I don't know about you, Space, but I've had about as much as I care to take from this town. So, let's get out of here while the getting is good."

I agreed, and within the next few minutes, we made our way back to the house where our packs were stashed and headed back down the hill with our thumbs out, waiting for another ride. It was time for our boot heels to be wandering again. After wearing out our welcome in Jerome rather quickly, Bill's offer now seemed particularly good. We still had the map and address he had given us; now, we needed a ride down the hill. For the most part, we had done rather well visiting places off the beaten trail, but it looked like Jerome was too far off the path. We just chalked it up as an adventure gone awry, knowing there were plenty ahead that would be more to our liking while others wouldn't. We had to learn to take the bad with the good and know when to cut our losses. In this case, we were cutting our losses and heading back down the hill to visit a new friend we had just met. The positive side was that we were seeing and getting to know Arizona.

It didn't take long to get a ride down the hill to the junction where Bill had dropped us off. We were headed northeast while our ride was headed back toward the Phoenix area. Bill's place was just an hour or so away, so we hoped to be there by mid-afternoon. We weren't sure what to expect but were up for whatever he had in mind. He seemed like a likable guy who wouldn't mind us mooching off him for a while. We had nowhere to be or go, so why not spend a few days taking it easy: not having to hustle for food or drugs while having a place to sleep?

Hanging Out with Bill, Our New Friend

As expected, we arrived at Bill's house around mid-afternoon. It only took a couple of good rides, with the second one dropping us at his driveway. We knocked on the door, feeling a little apprehensive. Sometimes, people say things, thinking they'll never see you again. We were unsure if that had been the case with Bill, but he seemed sincere when asking us to stay with him. After our experience in Jerome, we were a little gun-shy but willing to take a chance. His offer seemed sincere, and we had nothing to lose.

Bill opened the door, somewhat surprised to see us but happy and excited we were there.

The first words out of his mouth put us at ease right away when he said excitedly, "Wow! I wasn't sure whether I would ever see you guys again or not, but I'm sure glad you opted to come."

We were relieved and expressed our appreciation for inviting us to spend a few days with him. He asked us in, and we all sat around while telling him about our Jerome experiences. He felt bad for us, but we assured him we had taken it all in stride and wouldn't let it affect us. He pulled out his pot stash, and we all got high together. If that wasn't enough, he told us he would cook us a great dinner. We had meat, potatoes, vegetables, and goat's milk. It was a great dinner. Again, we felt welcomed and appreciated—what a relief!

We even learned to drink goat's milk while we were there. Bill had a couple of goats he milked daily, which we learned to do. The following day, after our showers, Bill took us outside to see his little farm. He had a wonderful garden he was working on, as well as goats and chickens. Bill also had a couple of dogs and cats. He had us milk the goats and proceeded to show us how.

Milking Goats and Other Chores

Milking a goat wasn't new to me. Having grown up in the country, we had small farms all around us. Our neighbors had cows, pigs, and chickens. One of our neighbors even had horses that we would ride. I also had a friend who lived about half a mile up the street from me who had all kinds of farm animals, including goats and cows. Our dads both worked at the same place and were somewhat friendly. One time, when his family went on vacation, our family took care of their animals, which was when I learned about milking goats and cows.

After milking the goats, we all returned to the house, and Bill cooked us a hearty breakfast of bacon and eggs. We spent the rest of the morning doing things outside on his farm. Bill wasn't shy about putting us to work on various tasks and feeding the chickens and goats. It was all good; we didn't mind doing a little work now and then, though we didn't want to make a habit out of it. At noon, we went back into the house and had a nice lunch. After that, we just hung out for a while before returning and finishing up the projects we were all doing. In the evening, after dinner, he would bring out his stash of pot, and we would all get high once again while just hanging out and listening to music or watching television. By the end of the second day, we had an established routine for the next several days while we were there. *(I'm sure there was more to his little farm than I mentioned. I don't remember that much aside from the goats. He didn't seem to have a job other than working on his farm.)* We were all getting along very well and enjoying each other's company.

Bill was very appreciative of having us there to keep him company while his wife was away. After about five days, Hobo and I were anxious to get our boot heels wandering again. It was mid-February, and we wanted to go to Houston and then New Orleans for Mardi Gras. Time was starting to slip away. Besides, we didn't want to wear out our welcome. Bill was a nice guy who had been incredibly good to us even though he had us working all the time. We had been at Bill's place for five days, and it was time to go to Mardi Gras. We let him know we were very thankful for the time spent but needed to get moving if we were going to make it to Mardi Gras on time. He understood and was grateful we had taken him up on his offer.

Back to Tempe, Once Again

We wanted to return to Tempe for a couple of days before heading to Houston and then to New Orleans and Mardi Gras. Once again, with our thumbs out, we were waiting for our next free ride to whatever adventures awaited us in Tempe. We left Bill's place full of anticipation and excitement, knowing we would be able to stay at the party house in Tempe again. We made it back to Tempe in good time and set out to look up our friends at the party house. The party house afforded us a place to stash our packs and get cleaned up before a night on the town. It had been a while since we were with girls, so we hoped to meet a couple of gals to keep us company for a day or so. There were always college girls hanging out at the local bars in Tempe, looking for a good time.

We were able to get back in plenty of time to get cleaned up before heading out to the bars. We had panhandled earlier in the day to make just enough money for a couple of beers each. Usually, that was all it took. Once we had a glass of beer in our hands, we could always refill them from whoever was chatting with us.

We had only been in the bar for a short while when a couple of college gals came over and started talking with us. They were both juniors in college and immediately took a liking to us. They were interested in where we had been and what we had been doing. We spent the next hour or so telling them about our adventures. The next thing we knew, we were invited back to their dorm to spend the night. We spent a couple of days with them, just hanging out and having a good time. Finally, we let them know it was time to leave on the third day as we needed to catch a train and head out for Houston and New Orleans. We then returned to the party house to pick up our packs, which we had stashed since returning to Tempe. We had so much fun with the girls that we only needed to stop a couple of times to get what we needed from our packs.

With our packs on our backs, we once again hitched a ride to Phoenix to catch the next freight train going east. It didn't take long to locate a train, as the workers in the yard helped point us in the right direction and let us know approximately when a train would be leaving. Unfortunately, we discovered the train wouldn't be going for a couple of hours, so we set our minds to panhandling by the grocery store down the street, hoping to get enough money to have some food for the trip.

Within an hour, we had scored enough for a loaf of bread, a jar of peanut butter and jelly. We then quickly returned to our train and got situated with plenty of time to spare before it took off. Peanut butter and jelly sandwiches were our staples when riding freight trains. We had learned from past experiences that these rides could be exceptionally long, especially if you didn't have anything to eat.

When I landed in Tempe several months earlier, I had no direction as to what I was doing. I just knew I wanted to get out and taste something different than what I had experienced. I was enjoying this carefree, adventurous lifestyle even though I still had an empty ache in my heart from time to time. I knew I wasn't submitting to God and what He wanted to do in my life. I was still searching and trying to figure out how God was supposed to fit into my life, but I hadn't come to any firm conclusions yet. It seemed like I was farther along the path than when I had started. I had encountered differing views of God but hadn't bought into them, though intrigued. Even though I was confused about my spirituality, I hadn't discarded my beliefs in Jesus Christ. I was still a believer in Jesus and believed someday, this chapter would come to an end. I felt—most likely—I would be a full-fledged follower of Jesus Christ sometime in the future. Even though I wasn't walking with the Lord, I had an overwhelming sense that He was still guiding me along this path, protecting me from natural and philosophical dangers.

On To Mardi Gras
Chapter Seventeen

Mardi Gras was still a few days away, and we were on a freight train to New Orleans. We would have a long ride ahead of us, meaning we would have to take a break somewhere between Phoenix and Houston. We planned to go to Houston and hang out with our friends for a day or two before continuing to New Orleans. We were both looking forward to returning to New Orleans for Mardi Gras. We enjoyed ourselves immensely when we were there earlier. With Mardi Gras, we expected it would be even more exciting.

As the train sped along, listening to the clacking wheels, I began to reflect on all I had been through in the previous months. When I first met Hobo after landing in Tempe in October, I was very green and insecure while feeling lost. I didn't have much direction regarding what I was doing or where I was going. However, I was now a seasoned road freak, acclimated to life on the road, thanks to a great companion like Hobo. Despite our peculiarities, we became great friends who genuinely enjoyed each other's company.

Short Break in El Paso and onto Houston—Well, Maybe!

Hobo had been sleeping while I was lost in my thoughts. Now awakened, he told me that El Paso, Texas, should be coming up.

"What do you think? Should we get off the train and take a break?"

Remembering what had happened the last time we were in El Paso, I said, "Yeah, let us do it, but let's not get drunk this time. Instead, let's find our way to the mission, get a good meal and night's sleep, and get back on a train first thing in the morning."

As the train halted, we jumped off and headed into town. Having been to El Paso recently, we knew our way around and quickly headed toward the mission. It was still early enough that we wouldn't miss the evening meal. It had been a long ride, and we were ready to chow down! The following day, we woke up, had a good breakfast, and prepared to continue our trip to New Orleans via Houston. We planned to stop in Houston and see our friends before continuing to New Orleans. We were hoping to see them once again by that evening.

Unfortunately, it was late afternoon before our train left the freight yard in El Paso, so getting into Houston would be exceptionally late.

That was the thing about riding freight trains—we were entirely at their mercy and schedule. Yet, it was a free ride from one end of Texas to the other. As our habit was, once darkness was upon us, we crawled into our sleeping bags and slept while the train cruised down the line to its destination. Falling fast asleep, we didn't wake up until the following morning after the train stopped. I'm not sure how long we continued to sleep after the train stopped. Unfortunately, we soon realized we had missed our stop in Houston. Oh well!

Fate as our Guide and a Free Ride to Nowhere in Particular

We had no idea where we were until we got off the train and asked one of the workers in the yard.

To our surprise, he said, "You're in Pine Bluff, Arkansas."

Talk about being in the middle of nowhere! This was one of the hazards of riding freight trains, but we had learned to adjust to our circumstances and see where the next adventure would take us. We were still on our way to New Orleans and Mardi Gras but now detoured. Our attitude was, "Well, we might as well enjoy the detour and see where it takes us."

Enjoying the detours was the thing Hobo and I had learned to thrive upon—going into situations utterly unknown to us yet being extremely comfortable. It was simply a matter of allowing fate to be our guide as we used our wits and street knowledge to hustle our way into whatever situations or opportunities came our way. We were a couple of freaks traveling through our nation's cities as vagabonds or rolling stones, looking for our next free ride to nowhere in particular. We would mooch off whatever resources or people came our way as we traveled from one place to another.

We soon discovered it was only about 35 miles to Little Rock, where we could catch another freight train to Memphis, Tennessee. We had never been to Memphis, so we were looking forward to the trip. It was another 140 miles or so from Little Rock to Memphis. If all went well, we would be in Memphis by early evening. It was still early morning, so we had a good chance of making it.

Freight Train from Little Rock to Memphis

We took off hitchhiking to Little Rock. We were there in less than three hours. By early afternoon, we had quickly spotted a train headed for Memphis. The only problem was there were no open box cars to ride in. We then found a part of the train with Sea-Land trailers on it. We realized it would be a cold ride in the open air, but we had our down bags, which we could crawl into as soon as the train was on its way. We had never tried this before, but we were game and decided to go for it. By mid-afternoon, we were on our way. We had only been traveling for about half an hour when we realized it was too cold. Because of the wind factor, we were freezing cold!

Hobo said, "Space, I know this sounds crazy, but I think we ought to try and make a mad dash for the third engine when the train stops."

I thought about it for a minute and said, "Let us do it! What have we got to lose?"

We then quickly rolled our bags and packed so we would be ready the next time the train stopped to let another train pass. With our decision made, we waited in anticipation, and sure enough, our train was the one designated to stop and let the other train speeding toward us pass. When it came to a halt, we both jumped off and ran like crazy for the third engine, hoping we wouldn't get caught. We had never done this before, but we were willing to try it, considering there seemed to be only two other options—either continue to freeze or get off the train in the middle of nowhere—stranded.

We made it unscathed and undetected. It was great! We were now comfortable and warm, riding in comfort toward Memphis, Tennessee. It was a beautiful sight coming into Memphis just as it was getting dark, with all the city lights in full view as we entered the city.

What had started as a fateful morning turned into a great day with the promise of a warm place to sleep upon reaching Memphis! What more could a couple of Road Freaks ask for as we allowed fate to lead us? Taking each day as it came and making the best of it was how we continually adjusted to whatever was happening to us. It seemed to be working for the most part, so we had no complaints. It was what made what we were doing exciting and fun.

Memphis, Tennessee

Once we were off the train, we quickly found out where the Salvation Army was located and headed there as fast as we could. We knew it was getting late and needed to get there before they closed for the evening. Also, we wanted a nice warm bed to sleep in after the long ride on the freight train the night before. Thankfully, we were able to make it with time to spare.

As we were hanging out and getting to know the others there for the night, we discovered a couple of guys with plenty of money. They were also headed for Mardi Gras and had been hitchhiking from somewhere in the Midwest. Realizing that this could be an excellent opportunity to hook up with a couple of guys we could mooch off for a few days, we began to share with them about riding freight trains and how cool it was. Besides, occasionally, it was always good to have company beside ourselves. The more they listened to us and our stories, the more they seemed excited about riding a freight train rather than hitchhiking.

New Traveling Companions, Bill & Joe

The following day, after a good breakfast, our new friends, Bill and Joe, decided to travel with us via freight train to New Orleans. We had done an excellent job convincing them. I am now humiliated to say this, but as we left the Salvation Army, we peeked into the storage room where they kept all the food. We spied a big ham—one of those that comes in a can. We decided right then and there to steal it along with a loaf of bread. I never got over feeling guilty about doing things like this, but I learned to live with the guilt as part of the *"beg, borrow, and steal"* code while living on the road. It was all about survival and what you had to do while traveling as a vagabond and mooching off whatever resources or people came your way. So, with the ham and bread to go with it, we talked our new friends into buying some wine to make the trip more enjoyable. They were more than happy to do so.

When we got to the freight yard, the train engineer who would be driving the train spotted us and came over to chat. We thought, at first, we were in trouble and wondered if he was going to tell us to get lost. But it was just the opposite. He was probably in his 30s and very intrigued with us. So, he invited all of us to ride in one of the engines. But, he said, we would have to duck down through towns. How cool! Two times in two days, we got to ride in the engine, and this time, we didn't even have to worry about getting caught.

We figured it would be a good idea to locate a boxcar that wasn't too far from the engine so that we would have a place to sleep when it got dark. We stashed our packs and stuff in an empty boxcar close to the engine and found our seats in the third engine. Our new friends were excited about this. We were off to a great start, and they were reasonably impressed and excited with how things were going. We had bottles of wine, ham, and bread. Everything was looking great. We were all excited about our present situation. What more could a bunch of freaks want? Traveling in this manner was promising to be a great day. Our little mishap of sleeping through Houston and ending up in the middle of nowhere proved to be a blessing in disguise—another great adventure as we allowed fate to guide us.

Next Stop, New Orleans, and Mardi Gras

It would be a 400-mile train ride from Memphis to New Orleans. It was early afternoon before the train finally took off, which meant it would probably be midnight or later when we arrived in New Orleans. As we were riding along in the third engine, I couldn't help but think of the lyrics of the song *"City of New Orleans"* sung by Arlo Guthrie, written by Steve Goodman. We were living the song, especially the part that says, *"Changing cars in Memphis, Tennessee, Halfway home—we'll be there by morning."* We had a great time sipping wine and munching on sandwiches as the train continued to rumble down the tracks toward New Orleans. Our new friends were getting a kick out of it. They were very appreciative that we invited them along. As the evening wore on, the wine began to take its toll on us. We were all a little drunk and getting sleepy. We decided the next time the train stopped, we would make a mad dash for the boxcar where we had stashed our stuff. Trains stop quite a few times to allow the trains coming from the other direction to pass. Sometimes, a train would have to wait for quite a while for the other train to come, as the passing areas were only at specific locations. The train finally stopped. We made it in plenty of time before it took off again. Once we were all settled in, we began to get very thirsty from drinking the wine and realized we had left our water in the engine.

For whatever reason, Bill and I were elected to retrieve our water the next time the train stopped. When the train finally stopped, we took off, making it to the engine just in time before it took off again. Unfortunately, this meant Bill and I would have to wait until it stopped again before we could return to the boxcar.

I could tell Bill wasn't feeling that great.

He said, "I'm not feeling so great. I'll stay here when the train stops and meet up with you guys when the train stops in the freight yard."

I told him, "I don't think that's a good idea."

He shot back, saying, "I don't care. I'm not feeling good, and I'm staying here whether you like it or not."

"Ok, but I'm going back."

I wasn't happy with his decision, but I didn't think I had much choice, so I left him. I was very sleepy, and Joe and Hobo were waiting for me to get back with the water. Once the train stopped again, I was back with Joe and Hobo, and they wanted to know what had happened to Bill. I told them he wasn't feeling well and was adamant about staying in the warm engine. None of us were happy with his decision, but there wasn't much we could do about it now. We were tired and sleepy from drinking the wine, so we crashed hard.

We Lose Bill

The thing about riding freight trains is that you always have to be prepared for the unexpected. We woke up the following day in a freight yard in the middle of Louisiana. Our train stopped in the freight yard in the middle of the night. We were all sleeping so heavily we didn't realize the train had stopped. The problem was our engines were gone. Sometime during the night, they unhooked the train engine from the train, which meant Bill was gone, and we had no idea where he was. We were very troubled by the loss of our friend. Joe was incredibly distraught. Unfortunately, we never saw Bill again; we still had his pack and sleeping bag.

We were now less than 100 miles from New Orleans, so we decided to hitchhike the remainder of the way. We got two rides taking us about 35 miles before being dropped off in the middle of nowhere. It was raining extremely hard, so Hobo and I put on our army-issue ponchos, but Joe didn't have anything to keep him dry.

We had been in this spot for about a half hour suffering through the rain when Hobo said, "I think we should build a shelter in the woods over there while it's still light. We'll get drenched sitting here waiting for a car that's probably not coming anyway, and it won't be much fun trying to build a shelter in the dark."

I said, "Ok, we can use the ponchos and rope we purchased a while back to put up a shelter. So, let's go for it."

After getting drenched in Florida twice, we purchased ponchos and some rope for situations like this. Then, Hobo and I took off for the woods, about 25 yards away, to build the shelter while Joe remained by the side of the road with hopes of still getting us a ride.

As we were about to finish the shelter, we heard Joe yelling, "I've got a ride. Hurry up! They're not going to wait forever."

We quickly tore the shelter down and hustled back to where Joe awaited the ride. By the time we got there, we were all drenched but happy to be in a warm car. Unfortunately, we had gotten soaked because we had taken the ponchos off to build the shelter.

The adventure with Joe and Bill, which had started so well the previous day, had gone awry. Events such as getting soaked by the rain and other mishaps were the things about being road freaks that sometimes made it uncomfortable. Like most things in life, there are ups and downs. Losing Bill was a real disappointment to the three of us. We felt terrible for him. Who knows where he ended up? We hoped we would see him in New Orleans, but that just wasn't to be. I could tell Joe was having a tough time with the turn of events. Hobo and I had learned to accept the good and the bad. Otherwise, we would have gotten disillusioned from time to time. You had to look at each day as an adventure full of new opportunities, no matter what happened the day before. We now had a ride into New Orleans and were ready for whatever opportunities were awaiting us.

New Orleans and Mardi Gras

We arrived in New Orleans around early evening. Our first objectives were to get something to eat and find a place to sleep. Joe had a little money, but Bill was the one with most of the money between the two of them. With that in mind, we set out for something to eat and bed down for the night. Once we found a place to get some food, we headed towards the place Hobo and I had used on our previous trip to sleep. Tomorrow would be another day full of new adventures.

The following day, we still had some food left over from the night before, so we finished it off and headed for the *"French Quarter,"* where the action was. We were still lugging Bill's stuff around, which was becoming a burden. We wanted to score some LSD or mescaline to enjoy the Mardi Gras celebration from a psychedelic perspective, so we began asking around, trying to score some. It didn't take long to find someone selling mescaline. We had used what money Joe had the night before when we bought food, so we were hoping to trade Bill's stuff for drugs. We talked him into trading enough mescaline for the three of us for our friend's pack, which he was willing to do after some coaxing. For the rest of our stay, we'd have to resort back to panhandling.

As we were walking around the French Quarter, taking it all in, and starting to get off on the mescaline, I spotted some friends Hobo and I had met when we were in Key West.

I said, "Hey, Hobo, look at those guys across the street. They're the same guys we hung out with in Key West."

He got excited and said, "You're right! I remember them. They were the guys we were with when we took the LSD that night."

We immediately took off across the street to catch up with them; sure enough, it was them, and they remembered us as well. We had a great time reminiscing and found out they had been doing the same thing we were doing, only just hitchhiking—no freight trains. They were road freaks who were traveling the circuit like we were doing.

Over the next few days, we enjoyed ourselves. Joe also enjoyed himself and had a good time. We watched the daily parades, wandering around while taking everything in and getting high when the opportunities struck. Joe had somewhat recovered from losing his traveling companion and seemed content to hang with us since he no longer had his partner, Bill, with Him. I could tell he missed having his partner around. They were good friends who had started together from their home in the Midwest. I kept thinking I should have insisted on Bill coming with me instead of staying in the engine. But the problem was he was insistent on staying, and I was too drunk and tired to force him.

Having been to New Orleans a few months back, we went back to the same park each evening to sleep. Getting to experience Mardi Gras was a trip, but Hobo and I had concluded we had enjoyed New Orleans much more on our previous trip. There were just too many people during Mardi Gras. Also, there were too many heads like us who were hustling in the same way we were. It was almost too much. After three days, Hobo and I had enough and decided to head back to Houston. We then split up from Joe. He went his way while we went our way. I felt bad for Joe and a little guilty as he was now without his partner and had to travel alone. If Hobo and I hadn't tried to coax them into coming with us, they would probably still be together and having a great time.

Heading North
Chapter Eighteen

We had been back in Houston for a couple of days when we began thinking about where we wanted to go. We had been to Florida, Los Angeles, Arizona, and New Orleans; we didn't want to return to those places. We were ready for something new. It was still early March, and we were not sure what the weather would be like if we were to head north. The weather forecast wasn't readily available like it is today. There were no cell phones with weather apps to see if the weather was to your liking. You had to take your chances. Once you did, you were stuck with your decision.

Hobo wanted to go to Canada, but it was too early. With that in mind, we planned to start heading north and take our time. We had decided against riding the freight trains for the simple reason we were in no hurry to travel long distances. There was still much to explore in Texas, and we had a lot of time to kill before getting too far north. As usual, we got antsy to go once we had an idea of what we wanted to do.

We had now been to Houston three times within the last few months to visit with our friends, whom we had met at the Gatlin Creek Rock Festival. They were wonderful people we had come to appreciate and enjoy very much despite playing their god games. They were always excited to see us and provided us with plenty of good times and fun. Our time with them was always a nice respite from having to hustle for our basic needs. We let them know we probably wouldn't see them again as we headed north and eventually into Canada. They were sad to see us go but understood by now our lifestyle as vagabonds.

The following day, our friends from Houston packed us a couple of lunches and gave us a ride to the nearest highway on-ramp, which would take us to the Dallas-Fort Worth area. We both had clean clothes and had taken showers that morning, so we were suitable for a few days. We would pass through Austin again but decided we'd seen enough of it. We wanted to try to make it to Dallas for our first major stop. It was only a little over 200 miles, so we hoped to make it there in one day.

It didn't take us long to get our first ride; it took us to San Antonio, which meant we would probably make it to Dallas if all went well. Arriving in San Antonio, we asked our ride to drop us off on the freeway exit ramp rather than go into the city. Since we had been there twice, we didn't need to go into the city and had food to munch on while waiting for our next ride. Our friends in Houston had supplied us with some food and a few joints, so we were in good shape. It took us about three good rides to get to the Dallas-Fort Worth area, which enabled us to make it there by early evening. We first needed to look for a mission or Salvation Army to spend the night and get a hot meal and breakfast to start the next day. After asking around, we were able to locate one that served hot meals and a bed for the night.

Nothing Happening in Dallas

We spent the next few days just wandering around downtown Dallas, but there wasn't much going on—at least not for us. No one seemed to be taking much of an interest in us. We continued hanging out and staying at the mission because we were killing time. Hobo commented to me at one point that he had noticed pretty girls were always looking me over, but nothing ever came of it.

Finally, bored with Dallas, we continued North once again. Big cities never seemed to work for us. We did much better in the smaller towns, a little off the beaten path. Our ride took us to a much smaller town called Denton. It seemed like a cool place where we might be able to meet some people and have a good time, so we hung out rather than spend the rest of the day hitchhiking. Meeting people was always our goal when coming to a new place so that we could have a good time hanging out with them until we either wore out our welcome or wanted to move on.

Good Times in Denton, Texas

It didn't take long to discover that we had made an excellent choice to stop in Denton. Fate, once again, dealt us a good hand as we traveled through Texas. Our first trip through Texas dissolved all our fears about Texas. We found it a warm and inviting place for us, except for the workers in the Houston yard who had deliberately pointed us in the wrong direction, causing us to get on the wrong train. In Denton, we found this to be true again. It wasn't long before we began to meet people showing great interest in us as we just hung out on the street corners with our packs. A couple of long-haired freaks hanging out on the streets with backpacks was of interest to people in these small towns, whereas, in big cities like Dallas, we would draw little attention. It wasn't long before we met a couple of gals who were sisters. Their names were Sandi and Jenni. Another guy named Jay, whom we had met earlier, seemed content to hang with us. He didn't seem to have anywhere in particular to be, so when the gals invited us to a nearby café for lunch, he came along. As we were enjoying lunch, Hobo commented on someone he had just seen walking out the door.

"Hey, Space, look at that guy walking out the door. He looks just like you. He could be your twin. Do you have a twin you don't know?"

"Not that I know of, but you're right. He sure does look like me. Do you know what they say? Everyone has a twin somewhere."

Sure enough, he looked like me, enough to be my twin. How often does that happen? Then, a few years later, it happened again when I was living in Anchorage, Alaska.

A year or so after I had left Alaska, one of my Bible teachers was walking down one of the church halls, spotted him, and said, "Ken, what are you doing back in Alaska?"

Obviously, he discovered it wasn't me.

Sitting there chatting with Sandi, Jenni, and Jay, they began telling us that Denton was part of a dry county, meaning no liquor was to be had. If they wanted alcohol, they had to go to the next county to buy it. They also told us about the nightclubs with good bands playing and suggested we all go to one of the clubs later that evening. It all sounded good to us. We were always up for a good time. Hobo and I looked at each other with a twinkle in our eyes, thinking the same thing, "This is just the kind of situation we had hoped to find. Let's make the best of it."

After eating lunch, Sandi and Jenni drove us around town and took us to meet some of their friends. We hit it off well with their friends while sitting around and smoking pot with them. We made plans to meet again at the nightclub later. Unfortunately, we would have to drive to the next town, another county, to buy the liquor. Nevertheless, this was turning out to be a good day. The only problem was there were two girls and three guys. By now, Jay had become a permanent fixture with all the plans we were making, about which I wasn't too excited. I noticed Hobo getting friendly with Jenni, whom I was becoming attracted to, and Jay was hitting it off with Sandi. Jenni was the quiet and shy type, so it didn't make much sense to me why Hobo was taking an interest in her. He usually went for Sandi's type, who was more outgoing and the more voluptuous of the two. I felt like the third wheel and didn't like it.

After leaving Sandi and Jenni's friends, we all ended up back at their apartment, where we got cleaned up for a night out in town. Unfortunately, Jay was still with us. We spent the rest of the afternoon just hanging out, smoking pot, and getting to know one another more.

Hobo and I told story after story about our adventures over the last few months. The evening was now upon us, so we all loaded up in Sandi's car to pick up a case of malt liquor and then head over to the club. We planned to find a secluded place in the parking lot to park where we could drink without being detected.

Once at the club, we found an excellent place to park, along with Sandi and Jenni's other friends. They had done this many times before, as we were to discover. Partying in this manner was their way of enjoying the clubs despite being dry. We had a great party right there in the parking lot. After downing a couple of Colt 45s each, we all headed to the nightclub to dance and have a good time. We would make several trips back to the parking lot for more drinking throughout the evening.

By evening's end, I was drunk to the extent that I was making a fool of myself on the dance floor. I was never a good dancer. Being intoxicated, I was all over the place and even fell on the floor once. It wasn't one of my better moments. We somehow made it back to the gals' apartment later that evening, with Hobo hooking up with Jenni and Jay hooking up with Sandi. I ended up in the living room on the sofa by myself. I was too drunk anyway, so it didn't matter.

The following morning, we all had breakfast together and talked about what a great time we had had the night before. Then, Jay said he had to go. It was Saturday, and he had a bunch of stuff to do. With Jay out of the picture, I was hoping Hobo would turn his attention to Sandi rather than Jenni, to whom I was attracted to. We spent the day just hanging out. To my dismay, Jay returned later in the afternoon. So much for him being out of the picture! As the evening wore on, we all sat around smoking pot, drinking wine, and watching television. I noticed Jenni was starting to pay attention to me. Hobo wouldn't like it, but I didn't care. I thought she was beginning to realize Hobo wasn't her type and was starting to get fed up with his egotism. However, sleeping arrangements remained the same that night, much to my chagrin.

The following morning was Sunday, and Jenni was the first one up and was messing around in the kitchen, looking for something to eat, but couldn't find anything interesting.

She saw me lying on the sofa and said, "Hey, Space, would you like to go to the store with me so we can get some stuff for breakfast?"

"Sure, just give me a couple of minutes, and I'll be ready."

The store was just a few blocks away, so we chose to walk and enjoy the beautiful morning.

As we walked along, I thought I might as well take the bull by the horns, so I said, "How are you and Hobo getting along?"

Responding in a way indicating she wasn't too excited about him, she said, "At first, I thought he was cool, and he is in so many ways, but he's just a little too much for me."

I took that as my cue to reinforce what she was saying and said, "I can see how that can be. I get a little put out with Hobo from time to time, too. He's a great guy, but he can sometimes be a little overwhelming."

We finally arrived at the store, which was too soon for me. I enjoyed the walk and getting to know Jenni a little more. We ended up getting some pastries and orange juice. On our way back, we came to a nice grassy spot and decided to sit down, enjoy the warmth of the sunlight, and eat some of the pastries. We had a pleasant conversation and were hitting it off very nicely. I could tell that she was warming up to me. As we got up to leave, I took her hand and helped her up, and to my surprise, she didn't let go as we began to walk to the apartment.

As we walked along, Jenni said, "What do you think Hobo will do when he sees the two of us together?"

I told her, "Don't worry about it. He'll get over it."

They were all in the front room when we entered and wondered what had happened to us. Hobo gave me a quizzical look, but I ignored him and said, "We went out and got everyone donuts and pastries."

After breakfast, Jay again said he had other things to do, so he took off, leaving the four of us to figure out what we would do the rest of the day. The girls had to return to work on Monday, so Hobo and I would probably be leaving and continuing our trek north. We wanted to make the most of the day as it would most likely be our last day together. We had a great afternoon, walking around town and then back to the café for a late lunch. Jenni and I were enjoying each other's company, while Hobo and Sandi seemed to get along well. After lunch, we returned to the apartment and got ready to settle into a quiet evening of listening to music and watching a movie. I think Hobo had pretty much accepted that Jenni was now with me. He seemed content to be watching the movie with us without getting any more involved with anyone. Knowing Hobo, he probably thought we were all splitting up tomorrow, so why not let things be? I ended up with Jenni that night, and Hobo ended up on the sofa.

The following morning, we all got up and had a quick breakfast. After that, the girls had to go to work, and we were ready to hit the road again. We talked extensively with them about our lifestyle, which meant we weren't committed to staying in one place for any length of time. Denton was a pleasant surprise, but we were ready to hit the road again. Hobo and I didn't have an opportunity to talk about where we were going next, so we headed to the coffee shop we frequented and began talking about what had happened over the past few days and our next destination. First, we cleared the air about Jenni. He was cool about what had happened but not happy about it. His ego was bruised a bit as he reminded me of a situation in Florida when I had pulled a similar stunt. I wasn't sure who he was referring to unless it was the gal from Boca Ratan.

Onto Kansas City

According to the maps I constantly carried, it looked like Kansas City would be our next destination. We would be traveling through Oklahoma, but there wasn't much on our path that looked like it offered much. It was at least 500 miles to Kansas City, so it was unlikely we would make it in one day. It appeared we would be sleeping on the side of the road somewhere in Oklahoma. Once we had resolved what had taken place over the weekend and had a plan, we hit the road and stuck out our thumbs as we waited for a ride to our next adventure, wherever that might be.

One thing was sure: we saw a lot of our country in a remarkable way—a way in which most people never get the opportunity to do so. We were able to experience Texas by hanging out with people in San Antonio, Austin, the Rock Festival, Houston, and now Denton. It was much the same everywhere we went. It wasn't just about the places but the people as well. The rides we would get also gave us insight into people, their ways, and what they thought.

Once again, we were waiting on the side of the road, thinking about our next ride. What kind of people would pick us up next, how far would we go, and where would it take us? The different types of people who picked us up always amazed us. You would think it would only be our kind, but that wasn't the case. Older people, middle-aged people, hippies, college students, people in business, and others were a part of the parade of people we experienced as we traveled from one place to another. We realized that no matter who we got rides from, they were all interested in hearing about our travels and what we were experiencing. Living on the road proved to be quite an unforgettable experience. Some people would pick us up out of curiosity.

Our next ride took us several hundred miles into the heart of Oklahoma. It was a middle-aged couple heading back home after spending the weekend in Dallas visiting family. They were immensely interested in us and picked us up because they had a son who had taken to the hippie lifestyle. They were curious, wanting to know more about what we were experiencing. After about 100 miles, they dropped us off, going in a different direction than we were. Our next ride took us close to Oklahoma City, but we decided to stay on the road rather than take the time to see what was happening there. It was still early afternoon, and we wanted to get as far as we could. We then lucked out with a ride, which took us close to Wichita, Kansas. Wichita was much farther than we had anticipated. It was late at night, so we decided to stay when they stopped at the rest area to use the restrooms. We often found that rest areas were a great place to sleep, as they had bathrooms and, sometimes, showers. There were usually snack machines available as well. And, of course, we could always panhandle. We would be in Kansas City the following day if all went well.

The Story of Freak Getting Hit by a Car

We woke up the following morning, cleaned ourselves up, and were off to an early start toward Kansas City. Sometimes, people in rest areas would invite us into their motorhomes for coffee or something to eat, but that didn't happen on this day. When I was traveling through the Midwest on my East Coast Hitchhiking trip the year before with my dog, Freak, and my hitchhiking partner, Norm, we were at a rest area similar to this one. In many places, there are rest areas on both sides of the freeway. In the situation with Norm, we met some people on the other side who had invited us for a cup of coffee. I don't remember how we met them, but they were on the other side of the freeway. We had left Freak behind to guard our packs, which he was very good at doing. Being half German shepherd, he was no one to tangle with when it came to protecting our equipment. If I told him to stay, he would. The problem was when we returned after having coffee, he got overly excited about seeing us and darted across the freeway without looking. He was hit by a car going about 60 mph and drug about 50 yards down the highway before the car finally came to a halt. He was still alive but seemed to be unconscious.

We were all standing around wondering what to do about him when someone said, "I've got a gun. We should shoot him. It doesn't look like he's going to make it."

As soon as the word "gun" was mentioned, Freak jumped straight up and ran in circles. The only thing I could figure out was, just before quitting my job on the railroad, a bunch of us had gone out to a deserted place one evening and were target shooting with guns. Freak was with me and took off running to the extent that we couldn't find him. Finally, we had to leave without him. I returned to the same area the next day after work, and he was there waiting for me. When Freak heard the word "gun," I think it scared him, and he jumped up quickly. Freak seemed alright after being hit, but a little out of it. I wondered if he had some internal injuries. A week or so later, someone stole him from me in Connecticut. Being at rest areas always reminded me of this story. As Hobo and I were sitting at the rest stop on-ramp, I told him about Freak's experience of getting hit by a car. I had no sooner finished telling the story than we got a ride from someone exiting the rest area.

Kansas City and the Aggressive Jesus Freaks

We were on our way to Kansas City, which was only another 200 miles. If all went well, we would be there by mid-afternoon. Our first ride took us as far as Emporia, which was about halfway. Our second ride took us right into the heart of Kansas City on the Missouri side.

We arrived in Kansas City around mid-afternoon and began walking around, just checking things out to see what was happening while looking for an excellent spot to panhandle. We hadn't had anything substantial to eat in quite a while, which meant we were hungry. We were able to find a good spot, and it wasn't long before we had enough money for a couple of hamburgers and fries. We discovered at the beginning of our journeys that it was necessary to ensure we took care of our basic needs before concentrating on what to do in any given place. Usually, when we arrived at a new destination, we didn't have much of a plan. We had pretty much learned, by now, to make the most of each situation by hustling our way into whatever it might provide for us.

It wasn't long before a couple of Jesus freaks came over to where we were hanging out and started a conversation, wanting to know where we were from and what we were doing. During our conversation, they realized we didn't have a place to stay, so they invited us to their commune. They were a part of a Jesus freak[12] community with different houses in which they all stayed but were near each other. Even though they had more than one house, they all ate communally. We took them up on their offer, thinking that one night with them couldn't be all that bad. Tomorrow will be another day to explore Kansas City.

Everyone at the community house greeted us warmly and seemed excited that someone new had entered their presence. We would soon discover that they relished persuading others to convert to Christianity and Jesus. In this case, we were their unlikely victims. We had dinner with them. It was spaghetti or something—nothing special, but towards the end, they began to hit us hard with the gospel. They were nothing like the Jesus freaks we had met in Florida; these people were much more aggressive in their tactics. I didn't bother to tell them that I was already quite familiar with Christianity. It was interesting to let them go on and see what approach they would use. They didn't seem too interested in probing where we might be in our spiritual experiences but were more set on simply preaching to us. As the evening wore on, they began to see they were getting nowhere with us, especially Hobo. He often tried to counter what they were saying with what he'd been reading in the Aquarian gospel, which made little sense to them. I just sat there for the most part and took it all in as I chewed on a toothpick that I had worn to uselessness. I later discovered they took that as a sign that they were getting through to me. It was something I always did with toothpicks.

Eventually, they escorted us to another home, giving us the front room to crash. I got the sofa, and Hobo had to sleep on the floor. Around 5:00 the following morning, Hobo and I were awakened by a discussion that was going on in the hallway. One of their fellow Jesus freaks had gone astray during the night and had reverted to shooting up heroin and was being given the third degree by one of the leaders of the group. It was quite a conversation. He was being assigned to me for his penance because they suspected I was close to breaking, based on what they had observed about the toothpick.

We heard them say, "Don't bother with Hobo; he's too far gone."

It was all quite amusing. After it was all over, Hobo quietly commented to me. "Hey, Space, did you hear all that? You better be ready because they're coming after you in the morning."

---

[12] In the early 70s, the term Jesus freak was a common term used to describe hippies who had turned to Jesus.

We chuckled and went back to sleep. The following day, when we were all up and having breakfast, they asked if we had had a good night's sleep.

Hobo, never the diplomat, said, "Yeah, but I was awakened early in the morning with people talking about me."

We all got blank stares from them, like we were out of our minds. Then, after breakfast, the person who came in during the middle of the night (who had been assigned to me) approached us and said, "Which one of you is Space?"

"That would be me," I said as I wondered what he would say next.

He then proceeded to tear into me with the gospel. Looking back on it now, I feel bad because I gave him a hard time. It was now mid-morning. Hobo and I had decided enough was enough! We got our packs, took off, and wandered back into the city to see who would come our way as we were fed and ready for a new day. We had nothing better to do, so we started panhandling as we walked along. We spent the rest of the morning and the early part of the afternoon just hanging here and there with hopes of scoring some pot and a place to party. After a couple of hours, we found a bar serving food. We were able to hang out there for a few hours. Sitting at the bar after making a few bucks panhandling, we were enjoying ourselves, talking with a middle-aged man who was there on business.

Noticing our packs and wondering about us, and said, "Hey! Where you guys off to?"

Hobo said something to the effect, "No place in particular, only that we're headed north and then eventually to Washington State and Canada."

"How would you guys like to go to Madison, Wisconsin, with me? I would gladly give you a ride, provided you could drive for me."

Hobo said, "Sure, we could do that."

I thought, "Yeah, right! You'll expect me to do all the driving."

I had already realized from experience that Hobo didn't drive. He said it was because of his eyes. Hobo was constantly squinting because he didn't see very well. I suspected he didn't even know how to drive.

Our new friend's name was Daniel. He informed us he still had another meeting to attend but wanted us to meet him back at the bar later that evening if we wanted to take him up on his offer. Unfortunately, it was around the middle of March, and we were still unsure about going too far north and dealing with cold weather.

I thought this wasn't a great idea because of the weather, so I told Daniel, "We need to think it over some more."

"Well, if you want to go, just be here tonight at 8:30."

After we left the bar, I expressed my reservations to Hobo because it would still be cold up North even though it was March. I could tell Hobo wanted to go. He seemed anxious to be heading toward Canada. He was always telling me what a great time we would have there. After talking it over, we decided to go for it. I finally caved in, thinking that fate seemed to be moving us in this direction. It would be about an eight-hour drive, so I would most likely be driving all night.

We spent the rest of the afternoon just hanging around the inner city, watching people, and chatting with whoever came by. We met back up with Daniel later in the evening. He was happy to see us and offered to buy us dinner. So, we all went into the bar once again. It was close to 10:00 before we finally made our way out of the city and onto the freeway. We would take I-35 North through Missouri and Iowa to U.S. Highway 20. Daniel said he would drive for the first hour or so, and then I would take over and drive through the night.

Hobo sat in the front seat and kept a running conversation going with Daniel while I tried to sleep in the back seat. I was in for a long night, so I wanted to try to sleep for an hour or so. I had dozed off a couple of times and would wake up to their voices as they continued in their conversations. The car had stopped at a rest area, and Daniel told Hobo to wake me up because it was my turn to drive. I have always enjoyed driving, especially long trips, so I didn't consider this drudgery. I liked the driving time to let my mind wander and think about things.

I began thinking about our evening with the Jesus people in Kansas City as I drove along. I realized my heart was getting hardened, and I was becoming somewhat disengaged from what Jesus had begun to do in my life. Would I ever find my way through this spiritual maze I found myself in, and would I ultimately turn my life over to Christ at some point? What was I trying to prove by wandering all over the country? What about Hobo? We were bound to split up at some point and go our separate ways. How would that all work out? The biggest question was the Jesus thing. Despite my somewhat disengaged heart, I knew the seed was still there, and I didn't want to lose it. In some unique and mysterious way, I sensed God was leading me despite my stubbornness and refusal to submit to Him. Knowing God hadn't given up on me gave me a sense of peace. But the question was, how long would He continue to allow me to have my way?

The weather was getting worse as we drove through Iowa. It had started snowing. I was no stranger to driving in snow as I grew up in North Central Washington, where we would sometimes have up to a foot and a half of snow. Hobo was sleeping but was now awake in the seat next to me, while Daniel slept in the back seat.

"Hey, it looks like it's beginning to snow."

"It's been snowing for a while, but I think we're doing ok. It's not snowing that hard, and I don't think it's sticking. Besides, I grew up driving in snow; I'm used to it."

As the snow continued to fall, I said, "Do you think we did the right thing coming north this early? We could end up spending some cold nights outside. I am sure we're going to have some chilly nights. What do you think?

Never one to give in, he said, "It can't be any worse than sleeping in the rain. I don't think it's a big deal. We will deal with it when the time comes. I am sure we'll be all right. It's the middle of March. It can't stay cold forever."

I said, "Maybe not, but I'm sure we will have some cold nights, and we'll wish we were still back in Texas."

"Well, it's too late now. We're already on our way, so we might as well make the best of it."

Noticing the gas was getting low, I said, "Hey, it looks like we're starting to get low on gas. We should wake Daniel up and tell him we should stop for gas. Besides, I could use a cup of coffee."

We stopped at the next gas station we saw and went in and bought some snacks and coffee. Of course, Daniel paid.

As we got back in the car, he said, "We're only a couple of hours away from Madison. When we get close, stop, and let me drive."

It was early morning when we finally rolled into Madison. Daniel dropped us off in the city center and thanked us for taking the trip with him. That was the last we saw of him. Though it had stopped snowing, it was still a brisk morning. We decided to find a coffee shop to hang out in for a while. Daniel had given each of us 20 bucks, so we had money to burn.

We were about as far north as we cared to be. So, what would the next few days hold for us? We were ready to find out.

Madison, Wisconsin
Chapter Nineteen

We slept through most of the day at a cheap hotel. It was late afternoon, so we decided to look around and see what Madison had to offer a couple of freaks like us. From what we had seen earlier in the morning, it looked like just the sort of town in which Hobo and I would do well. It was a larger city with a college, which we realized usually afforded us the opportunities we liked. We made our way up the street from our hotel, where we located a bar, thinking we would check it out later that evening. Since we had some money, we figured we would probably be drinking and didn't want to be too far away from our hotel room, not knowing what kind of condition we might be in when we returned. Our hotel room only cost us ten bucks, which left us with plenty of money to have a good time.

We hadn't eaten all day except for the snacks we'd purchased at the gas station and the donuts we had with our coffee that morning. We were ready for a meal, so we found a cheap diner and ordered hamburgers. After taking care of our hunger pangs, we decided to stroll around the city, taking in everything as we acclimated to our surroundings. It was always good to know where the best panhandling spots were: coffee shops, where cool people hung out; different types of bars, grocery stores, laundromats, and other places of interest. We also liked to have a place where we could meet up in case we got separated for whatever reason. We found a long brick wall where you could sit and watch what was happening. We sat there for about an hour, smoking cigarettes and watching people as they strolled by. It was starting to get dark and chilly, so we took off for the bar we'd spotted earlier. Fortunately, I had a warm jacket. When we were in Arizona with Bill, he gave me a nice suede jacket to keep the chill off me. Finding the bar, we found an excellent place to sit and ordered a pitcher of beer.

Drunk and Beat up in Madison

By the time we had downed the first pitcher, I was feeling good. I had spotted a couple of guys over at the bar and decided to hit them up for some spare change. I asked them for a couple of bucks. Unfortunately, they got very belligerent towards me and told me to get lost. I said some choice words back to them and almost got into a fistfight. Hobo and I then ordered another pitcher of beer; I told him we might be having some trouble before the night was over.

"Did you see what went down with those two guys at the bar and what they said to me?"

Hobo looked at me funny, "Yeah, I saw it, and I think you're lucky they didn't punch your lights out."

I am usually a peaceful person, not aggressive or violent at all. One of the reasons I was never a big drinker is that drinking seemed to bring out a lot of aggression in me. We were reasonably drunk by the time we'd finished our second pitcher, and I felt insanely aggressive.

The two guys were still at the bar drinking, so I walked over to them and began to harass them. Hobo was now with me, and the next thing we knew, we were all headed outside for a brawl. We both got the living daylights knocked out of us. They landed several blows to my ribs and my head. I felt like my ribs were going to explode. For some reason, I thought Hobo, being an ex-marine, would be able to handle them. I was wrong! We were both too drunk. They left us lying in the street licking our wounds. We somehow made it back to our hotel room. Thankfully, our hotel was only a block away. We were able to stumble into our room without further mishap.

We woke up the following morning in a lot of pain and hangovers. For me, it was my ribs that had taken the worst beating. I had a little knot on my head but no black eyes. The side of Hobo's face was a little bruised, but other than that, he wasn't in bad shape. Our first night in Madison didn't end well, but we hoped the second day would be much better.

The first thing we did after getting a shower was to head up towards the coffee shop to get something to eat and put some coffee into our systems. Before hitting the road, I had never been a coffee drinker. However, we often discovered that coffee shops were cheap places to hang out when we needed to seek refuge from the street. It had been a few days since either of us had any pot to smoke, so we set out to find some people we could get high with. With this in mind, we headed to the college to see what might come our way.

Even though it was Saturday, small clusters of people were hanging out here and there. We immediately found a comfortable spot to hang out and check out the place. It wasn't long before a group spotted us with our packs and wondered why we were hanging out at a college campus. As we sat there getting acquainted, they pulled out their refers and asked us if we wanted to join them. We hung out there for a good while, smoking pot and shooting the breeze, enjoying each other's company. Then, as we were getting ready to leave, they said, "Hey! Why don't you guys drop by our frat house later in the day, and we'll smoke some more weed? We're only a couple of blocks away. Our place is easy to find."

Hobo replied in his usual comfortable voice, "That sounds like a great idea. We'll catch up with you a little later."

Our new friends seemed genuinely interested in knowing more about our experiences on the road and how we were making out. So, our day was off to a great start despite starting with hangovers. We continued to hang out around the college area for another hour, enjoying the high from the pot we'd just smoked. And we were then headed to our new friends' house. We had no problem finding their place as they'd given us good directions. When we arrived, they were there and seemed excited to see us.

The Frat House and More LSD Trips

We spent the next couple of hours sitting around smoking pot, telling one story after another. They were all interested in us. We talked about some of the LSD trips we had taken during our travels. Talking about LSD seemed to interest them, as we soon discovered they were into it. They just happened to have some on hand, brought it out, and invited us to partake. When I had taken LSD in the past, it was only one hit at a time. This time, we all took two hits each. After taking the LSD, Hobo and I wanted to go out on the town rather than sit around; they wanted to observe us as we started to get off, so we stuck around for a while. I ended up in an upstairs room with someone who was into the whole meditation thing. We were sitting there starting to get off on the acid when he realized I was meditating right along with him.

He was surprised that meditation had become so natural to me and said, "How and when did you learn to meditate?"

I said, "If you spent as much time sitting on the side of a road waiting for rides and riding freight trains, you would understand."

I have always been more of a contemplative thinker, so meditation came naturally.

Hobo was getting antsy to go, so he found me and said, "Come on Space! Let's get out of here. This is really good acid, and we need to be doing something besides sitting around here."

We told them we wanted to go out on the town and check out some of the bars. They said we could come back and crash there if we wanted to. With that said, we left for the evening, leaving our packs at the house. Since checking out of the hotel earlier that morning, we had our backpacks with us. So, we were happy to take them up on their offer since we had nowhere to stay. However, as we walked toward one of the bars we had checked out the day before, I started to panic a little. I was beginning to get off on the acid in a big way.

I thought, "What have I done?"

I was getting these big rushes, one after another, with wild hallucinations, and wondered whether I had overdone it by taking two hits. We eventually made it to the bar and had just settled in; when I looked down at the beer I was drinking, I realized it was green. At first, I thought I was hallucinating until someone told me it was green because it was St. Patrick's Day. After a couple of beers, I began to relax and enjoy the trip rather than worry about the amount of acid I had just taken. I started to think about how we were in Denton, Texas, partying at a nightclub just a week ago, and now here we were in Madison, Wisconsin, drinking in another city. What a life we were leading! As I thought about this, I began to chuckle a little bit at myself and my journey. It was all quite amusing. It all seemed like one long acid trip that kept going on and on.

The bar was located near the college, meaning many students frequented it. It was just a few blocks away from where we were staying. I was now enjoying the trip and letting my mind wander around the room, taking it all in. I noticed many people—hippies, straights, and even a gay couple. I had never seen a gay couple interacting the way this couple was doing. Out of curiosity, I let my attention pause on them for a moment too long. Unfortunately, they caught my gaze and must have thought I was gay. The downside was that they constantly stared in my direction, making me feel weird. As the evening wore on, they made their way over to where I was sitting. They even tried to engage me in a conversation. By this time, I was stoned out of my mind, and the only thing I could think to do to get rid of them was to take my glass of beer and throw it in their faces. Hobo was sitting next to me, deeply engrossed in a conversation with a gal sitting close to him.

Hobo turned to me and said, "Space! What do you think you're doing? You can't just throw beer in people's faces."

"Well, they deserved it and knew exactly why I did it."

Fortunately, that was all there was to it. When the two guys saw that Hobo was with me, they were afraid to start anything. By this time, Hobo was ready to go. He was hitting it off with the gal and wanted to split up for the night. Usually, we didn't split up under these kinds of circumstances. However, we split up since we already had a place to return to for the night. We both left the bar, with Hobo taking off with the girl while I spotted some people smoking pot outside around the corner and joined in with them.

Totally Wasted and Freaked Out on LSD

The next thing I knew, I was somehow in another frat house, and everyone was either drunk or high. I was hallucinating like crazy. I don't even remember how I got there. In my hallucinations, I began to see I was in a house full of demons and was a representative of the light. Suddenly, the demons started to come after me, trying to harm me. I thought they intended to kill me. I was really freaked out, but I somehow escaped and found myself back on the street. I realized the following day that I must have left my jacket behind because I didn't have it on when I finally returned to the frat house.

I had to figure out how to get back to the house where Hobo and I had been earlier in the evening. I knew I would be safe if I could get back there. It would always amaze me, even while on LSD, how I could sort things out and find my way. I had quite a few beers during the evening, so the alcohol effect was also upon me as well. I knew if I could find my way back to the center of town, I could probably figure out how to get to where I was going. As I found my way, after walking a block or so, I would lean against a building until I found my bearings. Then, I would take off again. I somehow made it back to the frat house and knocked on the door until someone finally came and let me in. Once back in the house, I found a quiet corner to kick back while coming down off the acid. It wasn't one of the better trips I had ever been on, but I survived. It had been a weird night, and now, over 40 years later, I remember almost every detail of that night.

Looking back, I'm, once again, reminded how thankful I am that I made it out of the lifestyle of drugs and everything else unscathed. Today, I am amazed at how much I enjoy life without mind-altering drugs. The thought of taking drugs or alcohol is so foreign and repulsive to my thinking.

The next day, I woke up around noon and figured I had better head down to the meeting place Hobo and I had spotted earlier. I found Hobo sitting on the brick wall smoking a cigarette in the same spot we were at a couple of days earlier.

When Hobo saw me, the first thing out of his mouth was, "Man, you were wasted last night. I was watching you as you tried to find your way back. You looked like that guy on the Jethro Tull Aqualung album."

"Yeah, it was quite a trip. I don't remember ever being that stoned and out of my mind. I was quite freaked out."

I never thought of asking him if he felt I was so wasted; why didn't he try to help me? He seemed more content to enjoy the amusement of me trying to find my way.

We then returned to the coffee shop we had been frequenting. Though we were not ready to leave, we talked about where to go next. Hobo still wanted to go to Canada. He was from there and had dual citizenships because of his tour with the Marines. He was from a town in British Columbia called Kelowna, which happened to be only a few hours from my hometown, Wenatchee.

I said, "We should stop by my home in Wenatchee first. It would be good for me to check in with my family."

I hadn't checked in with them much while traveling with Hobo. I suspected he wanted to check in with his family as well. I had only called my parents twice since leaving in October. I am sure they were worried about me and wondered what I was doing. It was also a reasonable probability that my dad would have done my taxes from the time I had worked on the railroad and the fruit sheds, so I probably had some money waiting for me.

We were not in any hurry to leave Madison, especially since we had a place to crash and leave our backpacks while exploring the city. It was as if we had hit the jackpot with the place where we were staying. There wasn't much going on, so we wandered around awhile and then headed back  to the frat house. Once back at the frat house, our new friends wanted to know what had happened to us after leaving the house the previous night. So, we spent an hour or so just sitting around sharing our stories and listening to them tell their stories of college life and tripping out. After a while, we told them we would like to crash for a couple of hours before going out again. Hanging out in the frat house with a bunch of guys reminded me of my days in Nam when all of us would sit around in the evenings in our hootch, smoking pot and listening to music while shooting the bull with one another.

They were all smoking pot when we woke up, so we joined them. They seemed to have an endless supply of LSD and pot and wanted to know if we wanted to take some more acid.

Our answer was obviously, "Let us do it! We're game."

Hobo and I never turned down opportunities for free drugs, especially LSD. For both of us, LSD was our drug of choice. Moreover, we both loved tripping out.

We took off for a bar our new friends had told us about after taking the acid. It had an upstairs mezzanine from which you could see everything that was going on below, including the dance floor. We found a quiet spot upstairs as we started to get off the acid. I was in a much more relaxed mood that evening compared to what had happened the previous evening. I just took too much acid the night before and had too much to drink along with it. So, it wasn't one of my better trips. I was also still a bit agitated from getting beat up the night before. Hobo noticed I was in a much more peaceful state of mind and said something to the effect. As we were sitting there, he saw a couple of pretty gals sitting by themselves.

He asked me, "Do you think we should try and make a move on them?"

"No, I'm perfectly content just to sit here and enjoy the music and watch what's happening."

The truth was I didn't have the emotional energy to do anything—the last couple of days had taken a toll on me. I just wanted to relax and enjoy the trip. They were playing the Beatles, the Stones, and other groups like them, which were my favorite types of music. We spent the next two hours nursing our beers, not drinking too much. We reminisced about the many adventures we had been through since we started together in Tempe many months earlier. We had some good laughs over the things we had done and experienced. We were getting off on the LSD and enjoying the trip. After a while, we returned to the frat house and spent the rest of the evening smoking pot with our new friends. As the evening wore on, they let us know that the following morning was Monday, which meant they had to get back into their school and study mode. They made it clear it would be time for us to move on.

The following day, Hobo and I packed our stuff and headed for the coffee shop to discuss our immediate plans. Our new friends were kind enough to send us on our way with a bag of weed from what seemed like their endless supply of it. Looking back on it, I am sure they were dealers. At the coffee shop, we solidified our plans to head west to my home in Wenatchee and then to his home in Kelowna, British Columbia. We would travel on Interstate 90, taking us through the Black Hills, which meant we would be going to Mount Rushmore. Hobo had never seen it, but I had when I was on vacation with my parents as a kid and then again with Norm on my hitchhiking trip to the East Coast the year before.

We hoped to try to make it as far as Sioux Falls, South Dakota, which would be possible if we were to leave right away and get some good rides. So, with this in mind, we took off, with our thumbs out, waiting for our next free ride to adventures unknown. Madison had been quite an adventure, and now we were ready for whatever new escapades would be awaiting us as we traveled toward Washington and Canada.

Homeward Bound
Chapter Twenty

It was mid-morning by the time we got out of the city and on our way to Sioux Falls. I had awakened that morning with a toothache. I had sensed it coming on for quite a few days, but it was getting progressively worse. Being sick or having problems like this was something neither of us had experienced yet. Neither of us had been ill throughout the winter in Florida, New Orleans, Los Angeles, and Arizona. The evening was upon us as we rolled into Sioux Falls. It had been a long day, and we had nowhere to sleep, which meant finding a place outside in the cold. My toothache had become very painful, and I wasn't sure what to do about it. We had purchased some aspirin, but it wasn't helping much.

A Bad Toothache and a Visit to the Dentist

We were hanging out in a grassy area in downtown Sioux Falls after a sleepless night of pain.

Hobo noticed I was chain smoking and made a snide remark, saying, "Chain smoking isn't going to help your pain."

He was right; it wasn't, but it helped to take my mind off the pain a little. By this time, it was hurting badly, and I didn't know what to do about it. I was genuinely concerned, knowing we didn't have the money to see a dentist.

He finally got fed up and said, "I'm tired of sitting here watching you chain smoke while you suffer in pain! "Let's go find a dentist and see if they'll work on your teeth for free."

Believe it or not, we found a dentist who went to work and filled the cavity for me. What a relief it was to be pain-free. By early afternoon, I was as good as new and ready for whatever the day had in store for us.

Mt. Rushmore

We didn't waste any time as we were anxious to get back on the road. So, we stuck out our thumbs again and headed towards the Black Hills and Mt. Rushmore. We ended up camping at a rest area on the I-90 freeway. Unfortunately, we only made it a couple of hundred miles and were still considerably short of our destination by the time it got too dark to travel. Facing another night of sleeping in the cold, the thing I had feared about the cold weather was now upon us. Oh well, another cold night under the stars. Thank God for our warm-down sleeping bags.

After another cold night under the stars, we arrived in Rapid City, South Dakota, around noon. After panhandling, getting enough money to eat, and filling our packs with food for the road, we were ready to visit Mt. Rushmore. We got a ride right away and arrived within the hour. Hobo was surprised at how small it seemed compared to what the pictures made it out to be. I had been there before, so I wasn't surprised.

In my hometown of Wenatchee, there is a natural rock formation called *"Lincoln Rock"* on the road to Chelan, just past Rocky Reach Dam. In my opinion, it is much more impressive simply because it is a natural rock formation.

All in all, it was a great day that ended well. We spent the evening at a nearby campground, eating some of the food we had purchased earlier that day. The next day, Hobo told me he was getting antsy about getting to Canada. It seemed like the closer we got, the more in a hurry he was to get there. I agreed, and from now on, we will try to get to my home in Washington as fast as we can without any more sightseeing.

The next few days were relatively uneventful, traveling toward Washington until we got to Spokane. We had gotten a ride through Spokane, and the person who had given us the ride dropped us off at a freeway exit ramp. Unfortunately, he was headed in a different direction than us. So, we had to walk on the side of the freeway to get to the onramp we needed. Consequently, it was a short distance before getting to the one going in our direction. We tried to scramble as fast as we could, but a cop stopped us before getting there. We tried to explain our predicament to him, but it was to no avail.

Jail Again

In Washington, hitchhiking was legal if you stayed on the on-ramps or were on a road that wasn't a major freeway. The policeman was a real hard-nosed guy who immediately took a dislike to us and hauled us off to jail in Spokane. So, there we were, less than 150 miles from my hometown, in jail again. I used my phone call to call my parents but knew it would be useless. Hobo insisted I call them and give it a try.

He said, "You have to call your parents and see if they'll get us out of this mess."

My parents made it clear to my three brothers and me never to expect to get bailed out of jail by them. I was right; even though they hadn't seen me in several months, they said, "We love you, but it's your problem."

So that was it; they weren't going to help. Jail in Spokane was the same as in Key West—just a bunch of guys hanging out together with nothing better to do than play cards, watch television, and shoot the bull with each other. I was always more of a listener than a storyteller, but Hobo would egg me on and get me to tell stories about Vietnam.

Reflections: Almost Busted for Dope in Vietnam

This time, I told the story of another incident when I almost got busted for smoking pot. It was a setup—a plan had been put in motion to catch one of my buddies and me in the act. In our company, we had a bunker in the middle of our company area for protection whenever we were rocketed or mortared. The sirens would go off, and we would congregate there and be safe. On top of the bunker was a sundeck where we would hang out and smoke dope. We always felt safe there because nobody could get to us fast enough to catch us red-handed. Another buddy and I were on a particular detail digging a ditch at the base of the bunker. We didn't realize it, but our NCOs and Officers were gathered in our movie building, about 25 yards from where we were.[13] They were waiting for the moment we would take a break and go up to the sundeck to light up a joint so they could be ready to pounce on us.

It wasn't long before their plan materialized, just as they anticipated. We eventually both got tired and bored with digging the ditch, so we went up to take a break and smoke a joint. I was carrying a film canister of pot in my pocket. We had the joint about half-smoked when suddenly, we saw them coming after us. It happened so fast that I barely had time to drop the joint and smash it into a crack, but I still had the canister in my pocket. Our habit was to carry a small film canister of pot in our pockets or have a few rolled joints tucked away in a cigarette pack. We

---

[13] N.C.O. is the acronym for non-commissioned officers. Non-commissioned officers are those who have stripes to determine their ranks such as corporal, sergeant, staff sergeant, etc.

would keep our big stash hidden in our hootch.[14] We had a secret compartment built into our wall where we kept the pot hidden. We would also hide the stems and seeds, once the pot was cleaned, in a more obvious place. When our hootches were searched, that's what they found. They would think they had found something and give up the search for more.

A month before this incident, we had all been smoking pot at another of our favorite spots. It was in the back of our barracks on a large log along the perimeter line. We were talking about what we would do if we ever came close to getting busted.

I said, "I know exactly what I would do. I will take off running and throw the stuff away."

As we were all standing there with the Officers and NCOs feeling good about themselves for having caught us in the act, they decided to march us into the orderly room. When I reached the bottom of the steps, I ran as fast as I could around the back side of the mess hall and threw my canister away into the grease pit that was back there.

The way I looked at it, I had nothing to lose. If they caught me with marijuana in my pocket, I would be on my way to LBJ (Long Binh Jail) for the remainder of my tour or who knows how long. So, after throwing the canister away, I ran to the orderly room and waited for them to catch up with me. They gave me a hard time for running, but I didn't care. To say they were mad was an understatement. They were thoroughly upset! They had blown their opportunity, and they knew it.

I said, "I was running to speed the process up. What's the problem?"

Once in the orderly room, we were both thoroughly searched, but to no avail. They were upset at blowing an opportunity to make an example out of us. The company commander ordered that anyone in the future be searched on the spot. Once again, I had evaded getting busted.

---

[14] While in Vietnam we simply came to refer to our sleeping quarters as hootches. I believe it was a term that was derived from the typical Vietnamese homes in which rural farmers or peasants lived.

These were the sort of things that eventually led me to receive a general discharge from the army rather than an honorable discharge. My general discharge was under honorable conditions, meaning I couldn't adapt to the military lifestyle.

The guys got a big kick out of the story, making my stay bearable. I was thoroughly accepted. We still didn't know how long we would be in jail. It would be a couple of days before we got an opportunity to go to court and find our verdict. Our day in court finally came. The judge sentenced us to time served, which was a great relief. Thankfully, Hobo didn't mouth off to the judge this time and was released as well. It was still mid-morning, which meant—if all went well—I would be sleeping in my bed that night. Once on our way, we were careful to stay on the on-ramps. The last thing we wanted to do was to end up in jail again.

Meeting up with a Friend from the Past

Leaving Spokane, we got a couple of great rides and were in Moses Lake, Washington, within a few hours, which meant we were only about an hour away from my home. While waiting for a ride in Moses Lake, a car stopped, and the gal in the car immediately yelled out my name. As it turned out, she was one of the gals from a group of friends I had hung out with for a while back in Wenatchee before hitting the road. We called her "Better." I was never quite sure if that was her real name or not. I was surprised she had recognized me as my hair was much longer, and I also had a beard. After introducing Hobo to her and her friend, we all decided to go to her home in Moses Lake and catch up on old times. They had some mescaline, so we all partook. I always liked mescaline. It was much more of a mellow high than LSD.

The Mescalito Spirit

After the visit with my friend, our first ride appeared after the mescaline began to take effect. The driver was a hippie-looking guy. As soon as we entered the car, we sensed the Mescalito spirit.

All three of us responded simultaneously by saying, "Mescalito."

I had never experienced anything like this before where the presence of another spirit was so strong and unmistakable. Hobo and I had been reading a book by Carlos Castaneda, *"The Teachings of Don Juan."* We were familiar with his understanding of the Mescalito spirit, but this was the first time either of us had encountered it. The mescaline we had taken was quite strong. Both Hobo and I were getting off on it in a good way. It brought back to me the vision I had while in Vietnam when I saw my whole life flash before my eyes. I began to share the details of the vision with Hobo, who was quite intrigued by it. I am sure I had shared it with him before, but not with the intensity and detail I was now sharing.

The mescaline trip was beginning to have a very sobering effect on me, even though I was enjoying it. As I reflected on my vision while in Vietnam, I realized I was still very much lost and hadn't gotten any closer to connecting with the reality of what I had experienced. I seemed to be drifting further and further away from it rather than closer. In the past, I would have fleeting visions of having it almost within my grasp; now, it was becoming more distant. At the same time, I realized I was drifting further away from what I had begun to discover about Jesus and the Bible while in Vietnam. I was now beginning to have spiritual experiences such as meditation—and now the Mescalito spirit—both were different than what Christianity espoused.

The experience with the Mescalito spirit added to the confusion I was trying to navigate in this spiritual maze of other beliefs. Finding my way through this spiritual mystification was becoming more and more difficult as I became increasingly uncertain about what I believed. It seemed like the waters were being muddied rather than becoming more evident. The only thing that seemed to make sense was to accept the journey that was now taking me down a few different paths to spirituality. In the end, this was all good because I eventually saw these paths as dead ends. None of them led to lasting peace and a sense of purpose, which I desperately wanted.

After the Mescalito guy dropped us off in the middle of nowhere, another car stopped after a long wait. This ride took us to Wenatchee, which meant that this would be our last ride before reaching my home. It was late afternoon when our ride dropped us off at my parent's home in East Wenatchee. It was good to be home but weird at the same time.

It had been six long months since I had left town on a freight train with Jack and the other friends from Minnesota. So much had happened to me in the last six months. I was pretty much a different person in many ways. How would everyone react to me? My brother had gotten married during this time. I was in Arizona at Bill's home when the wedding took place. I remember calling home from Bill's house and my mom not having the time to talk to me because it was Bob's big wedding day.

My mom was sitting in the kitchen when we arrived and was happy to see me. My father wasn't home but was working the plant's swing shift. Hobo and I were still extremely high on the mescaline, and my mom realized we were high right away as my eyes were dilated.

She said, "You're high on something, aren't you?"

I didn't lie but said, "Yes, we ran into someone I knew back in Moses Lake, and she gave us some drugs."

She said something to the effect, "Well, you didn't have to take them."

"I know, but we did."

She wasn't happy with that, but it was something I think she had come to expect from me. I had never made it a habit of trying to hide the fact that I did drugs from my family. They all knew. When I was in Vietnam, I once sent a picture of me with a joint hanging out of my mouth and had written on the back of it, *"G.I. smoking pot in Vietnam."* I had shared this with Larry, one of my buddies at the time, and he told me what a stupid thing it was to do.

He said, "Man, our parents have enough to worry about with us being over here in danger day in and day out, and then to send a picture like that—what were you thinking?"

On another occasion, when I had returned from the Satsop Rock Festival I referred to in an earlier chapter, my mom and one of her friends were in the kitchen when I arrived home.

My mom asked me, "Well, did you do drugs while you were at the festival?"

I said, "Of course!"

It was a strange reunion. My mother didn't know what to think of me, especially Hobo. As I look back on it, I am deeply ashamed of the way I treated my parents during this season of my life. I seldom called them and let them know what I was doing or where I was. I can only recall calling them two or three times during the six months I was gone.

Their friends would ask them from time to time how I was doing or where I was, and their only response would be, "We don't know, but we're praying for him."

I was so self-centered that I hadn't even taken the time to think about how my lifestyle and non-communication affected them.

Reflections: My Father and Mother

My mother and father were both products of a religious system that gravitated more to the "do's and don'ts" rather than grace and love. As a result, we were disciplined and made to toe the line without much affection. What this produced in me was a callous heart. Sometimes, I didn't even know how or what to feel. I had come to identify with the John Lennon song *"How,"* in which he expressed how his feelings had always been denied and didn't know how he could go forward when he didn't know which way to turn or was unsure. The song summed up my life and what I was doing with it. I was following whatever instincts and intuition that filled my heart and mind. It was my way of trying to find my way forward into something I was unsure of where I was headed.

My parents have gone to be with the Lord in the last few years, and I miss them dearly. Despite their shortcomings in some of the ways they raised us, I've never held it against them, nor had a lack of forgiveness towards them. I understood that was how they were brought up as well. They did the best they could with the tools that they had. It must have been difficult raising four ornery boys and two girls. Yet, they loved us unconditionally. They lived the Christian life and loved God with sincerity and wholehearted devotion.

It was the prayers of my mother and father, who prayed me into the kingdom of God, and their steadfast and faithful testimonies and service to Jesus Christ influenced me. They may not have done everything right because of their rigid upbringing, but their hearts were always for their children to know the Lord. For that, I will be eternally grateful.

Later in life, when I was the Senior Pastor of a church in the Sacramento area, my parents moved to California to be near my wife and me. It was a great time when we could spend lots of time with them, playing games, camping, and enjoying each other's company. They were members of our church and were so proud to hear me preach each Sunday. I felt like I was giving back to them the years I had made them miserable with my selfishness.

As of the writing of this book, my father recently passed away at the age of 95. However, on one of my last visits with him, he said something that touched me very deeply.

He said, "You know, Kenny, of all the preachers I've heard over the years, you're the best."

He said it in a way that I knew he believed it.

There was an occasion several years ago in which I was at a men's gathering from the church I am presently involved with, and the speaker was speaking on the fruit of the Spirit. He shared how difficult it was for the fruit of the Spirit to get worked out in our lives. I sat there thinking, "This wasn't true in my life." Yet, the fruits of the Spirit seemed so natural to me. It was then that I had an epiphany. I realized the fruit of  the Spirit came easily because of the impartation through the life of my wonderful and gentle father. He had passed on to me a generational blessing in that area rather than a curse. I see these same fruits in the other members of my family.

 So, there I was, sitting at the kitchen table talking to my mother, with Hobo listening in, trying to convince her that I was doing well and was healthy. Finally, I asked her, "What's the problem? I'm healthy."

After the conversation with Mom, I showed Hobo around the house and our basement, where we would be sleeping, while my mom busied herself to fix us something for dinner. Our home had a full basement beside the two bedrooms and a living room upstairs. I also took the time to show Hobo all my pictures in Vietnam. He was quite intrigued by them.

Back in My Hometown, Wenatchee
Chapter Twenty-One

Following a wonderful, home-cooked dinner, Hobo and I decided to go out and see what was going on. I suggested we go to The Huttle, one of my favorite bars in town, where some friends hung out. We still had the effects of the mescaline working in our system, and we were starting to come down, so it would also be good to get a couple of beers into our system. Neither one of us was in the mood to do any serious drinking. We just wanted to get out and have a couple of beers.

Meeting up with Old Friends

At the Huttle, I ran into a high school friend. We talked and discovered that we had been to the Gatlin Creek Rock Festival in Texas. We were both equally surprised.

We compared notes and realized, "Yeah, we were both there."

The following day, when we awoke, my dad showed me my income tax check, which had just come. It was about $250.00, the most money I had gotten since hitting the road many months earlier. Hobo and I decided to do a little shopping with the money. Hobo desperately needed new boots, and we both needed new jeans, so off we went. My brother, Dick (Junior as he is now called), who had recently been married, had left a nice pair of boots at home. Since we both wore the same size, I decided to avail myself of them. Hobo wanted boots like the ones I now had.

Hobo and the 22 Rifle

After purchasing what we needed, Hobo tried to convince me we needed a 22 rifle. Of course, I thought this was ridiculous.

So, I asked him, "What are we going to do with a 22 rifle?"

He didn't have much of an explanation. He just wanted one. I eventually gave in to him, even though it was a stupid thing to do. I had realized a while back arguing with him when his mind was made up wouldn't do any good, so I gave in. It could easily be broken down into more than one part to fit into his backpack. I sure wasn't going to be the one to carry it.

Once we had purchased everything, we returned to my house, where Mom had already prepared dinner. My younger brother, Jerry, and my younger sister, Janice, were there. They were the only ones out of the six of us living at home, as they were both still in high school. My brother, Bob, who had recently married, had popped in the day before for a short visit. Junior had moved to Montana and was still working for the railroad after being promoted to crew foreman. My older sister, Bonnie, lived in Alaska with her new husband. She had gotten married just a couple of weeks before I had returned home from Vietnam.

After dinner, Hobo and I decided to head out to The Huttle again. We had an excellent time the night before, so we were game for another night in town. Once again, I ran into another high school friend. She was with a very pretty blonde. Hobo began to hit it off with my high school friend while I was getting to know her friend. As the evening wore on, we would all go outside periodically to smoke pot and then come back in to drink more beer. We were all having a great time and getting along well to the extent that we ended up at their home that night. As it turned out, the two gals were roommates.

The next afternoon, the gals decided it would be a good idea for us to move in with them while staying in Wenatchee. We, of course, were very agreeable to the idea, which meant going back to my home and picking up all our stuff. It was awkward when I told my mom I was leaving again, but that's how it was. I didn't care about anyone but myself.

As we were leaving, Hobo joked with the girls and said, "Space is running away from home."

We ended up spending three or four days with them, smoking a lot of pot and drinking Tequila and whatever else they had around.

One night, Hobo and I stopped at a pizza parlor to get some pizza, and I ran into my high school girlfriend. It was a very awkward moment as she was now with another guy. The guy she was dating was someone I knew from basic training. He was my platoon guide in basic training at Ft. Lewis, Washington.

She looked at me and said, "You look burned out."

Interestingly, we recently connected on Facebook and had a pleasant visit while my wife and I were visiting family in Wenatchee.

Hobo was getting antsy about entering British Columbia, Canada, so we planned to leave. We had done about as much in Wenatchee as we cared to do. So, once more, we were off on another adventure.

Hobo and I stopped by my parent's home before leaving, and I said goodbye, not knowing when I would see them again. I'm sure my mother and father were unhappy about it, but that's how it was. My thinking was I had been to Vietnam and away from home for two years, so it wasn't like I was living at home. Before starting my hitchhiking adventures, I had been living in the railroad, sleeping cars, and at the Columbia Hotel. I was very independent and didn't feel I had to answer to them or anyone for that matter. I needed this time to be on my own without their values dictating who I should be or what I should be doing. I needed to discover who I was to be in my relationship with God and whatever might come my way.

Off to Canada

We had visited my hometown, and now it was time to visit Hobo's hometown, where his parents still lived in Kelowna, British Columbia. It was only three hours away from Wenatchee. We had one major problem, though. Getting into Canada with a 22 rifle wasn't going to be easy. Hobo still had the rifle and didn't want to get rid of it. I wasn't sure how I would get in without much money to support myself while there. He was a Canadian citizen and a U.S. citizen, which meant he could come and go across the border without question, except for the fact he had that stupid rifle with him. We figured our only possibility of getting in was to sneak across the border as we set our new boot heels to wandering. It is incredible what you can do once you set your mind to something.

On our first day out of Wenatchee, we got no further than the Omak area on Highway 97. We spotted a river nearby and decided to wander down to it and enjoy some shooting practice. It was off the road a way through a large field, which caused us to feel safe—as we were well out of the way of anyone discovering what we might be doing. We spent the afternoon having fun with the rifle, shooting at various targets. We ended up making camp by the river. We would continue our journey to Canada the following day and figure out how to cross the border. Later that night, lying in our sleeping bags, we heard people coming our way with flashlights. We could hear them talking and wondering where we were. Evidently, someone had reported us, and they were now looking for us. Fortunately, we were just beyond an embankment, and they didn't find us.

Nevertheless, it was a close call. We could very well have ended up in jail again. I felt this stupid rifle would get us in trouble again, but we somehow escaped the consequences this time. We still had to get across the border with it.

Plans to Sneak Across the Canadian Border

The following day, we hurriedly packed our stuff and got out of there as fast as we could, fearing that whoever was looking for us the night before would be back again. Luckily, we got a ride immediately and were miles away in less than an hour, which took us to a park within a mile or so from the Canadian border. At the park, we met some other freaks just hanging out. They knew exactly how to cross the border without going through the checkpoint. They took us to where we could cross and showed us how to do it. We then went back to the park and hung out with them for the remainder of the day. We wanted to wait until around midnight to sneak across the border. We would have to run about a quarter mile through a field. By doing so, it would put us about that far ahead of the checkpoint. As the time got closer, we were confident we could do it but a little scared simultaneously. What if we got caught? We had no idea what would happen to us, but we were up for the risk.

The time finally came. We jumped in the car with our new friends, and off we went, trying to slip across the border like a couple of criminals. We were freaks doing a stupid thing, but it worked. We were across the field and onto the highway in no time. As soon as we got to the highway, we stuck out our thumbs and waited for a ride. In a short while, we were on our way to Kelowna.

Canada, here we come!

Discovering Canada
Chapter Twenty-Two

Once we made it across the border, without being detected, we traveled through British Columbia towards Kelowna on our first ride since arriving in Canada. It was after midnight, but we wanted to travel to get as far away from the border as possible. We didn't want to take any chances of getting caught and hauled into jail.

Visiting Hobo's Hometown, Kelowna, BC

We arrived in Kelowna in the early morning and thought it would be better to find a place to sleep outside. Later in the day, we would go and see Hobo's parents. We hoped to be able to stay with them for a few days until we met some people we could hang with for a while. It was late morning before we woke up and got our day started. We had been fortunate enough to find a secluded spot to sleep without being detected. It had been a long time since Hobo had seen his parents, so he was very anxious to get going.

We arrived at their home shortly after noon. They seemed glad to see him, but I sensed they were not very accepting of his lifestyle or appearance. After an hour or so, his dad suggested we all go to a local pub. His dad, his younger brother, Hobo, and I all left. His mother chose not to come. It seemed strange to me that we would go to a pub in the middle of the day, but I soon discovered that pubs in Canada were somewhat different than what we call bars or saloons in the States. I was surprised to see so many people hanging out at the pub in the middle of the day. I had always considered bars to be where people go in the evening to party with their friends. Instead, I discovered that the pub was a natural place for people to gather and enjoy each other's company. We found a table where his father ordered drinks for everyone and wanted to know what we had been doing. I may have been a little too forthcoming in things I said because, later in the day, Hobo got on my case for talking too much. We sat there for about an hour or so, enjoying each other's company, and then his dad said it was time for him and Hobo's brother to leave. We told them we would meet them back at the house later.

Not Welcome at Hobo's Parent's Home

Hobo had picked up on some vibes I had missed. He told me he didn't think his parents were going to let us stay there. When we reached his home, we found our packs on the front step with a note saying we weren't welcome. I thought that was rather cold, but I didn't know his family history. Hobo had never talked about them much except to say that in his childhood, he lived with his grandparents quite a bit. It was still early enough in the afternoon, so we took off looking for a place to hang out around town in hopes of finding a place to party.

We found a place to park ourselves in what seemed like a likely place to meet people. It wasn't long before a hippie-looking couple approached us, wanting to know what we were up to and where we were going. Their names were Craig and Susan. They seemed like a hip couple. Even though we were longhairs and hippie-looking, there was a look about us that set us apart from the locals. I'm sure our backpacks had something to do with it, but it was more than that. We were grungier looking. Regardless of what it was, we knew it was working and took full advantage of it. It wasn't long before Craig and Susan invited us back to their home. They informed us they were living in a community house with several others. As it turned out, it was a party house—just the type of place we hoped to find.

Party House in Kelowna

The place where Craig and Susan were staying was incredible, with lots of people coming and going and beautiful girls. It was pretty much a hippie community home. They had a room for a band to come and practice with everyone jamming. There were also plenty of drugs floating around as well. We felt like we had hit the jackpot in places to stay. As usual, Hobo's engaging personality got us into places like this. The first evening was a taste of what our stay would be like. People were coming and going; weed was flowing, music was constantly playing in the background, and there were girls, too. What more could a couple of road freaks want?

I discovered very quickly that Craig and Susan were not a committed couple. Instead, they just hung out together. The reason I knew this was that Susan began to hit on me, and I ended up in bed with her.

The following day, Hobo gave me a hard time, saying, "What do you think you're doing? These cool people invite us to their home, and you sleep with the guy's girlfriend."

I tried to explain to him by saying, "They weren't boyfriend and girlfriend, and it was cool between them."

"Nevertheless, it was still a stupid thing to do."

"What was I supposed to do? She's the one who came on to me." I'm sure everything's going to be okay." You'll see!

He let it go at that.

One night, while we were there, a band came over to play and let Hobo play with them. I didn't even know he knew how to play the guitar. I don't think he knew how to play that well because one of the guys in the band kept trying to show him how to play the chords more perfectly. Eventually, they just let him play the best he could. Somehow, Hobo ended up owning a guitar after that night. Someone took a liking to him and gave him a beat-up guitar with a case and everything.

After about a week of partying with them, we were ready to move on. We planned to hitchhike across Canada and end up in Toronto. Our next destination was Calgary.

Starting to Get Weary

Before leaving Kelowna, someone gave us some acid. We both took it immediately and then hit the road after saying goodbye to all our new friends. However, we were in for a surprise when we got to the on-ramp. A lot of people were lined up waiting for rides as well.

Wondering what was going on, I asked Hobo, "What's going on with so many people waiting in line?"

"It's because of all the youth hostels. It makes it easy for them to go from one place to another, so they're really into hitchhiking."

We were about to discover traveling through Canada would be relatively slow compared to the States. However, we were now getting off on the LSD while watching others get rides, so we didn't mind that much. We waited a couple of hours before it was finally our turn to get a ride.

I had a problem! Something had happened to my right elbow, and it was beginning to swell up and hurt. In the days ahead, what was happening to my elbow would cause me extreme pain and anxiety as we traveled through Canada toward Saskatoon. As the LSD began to have its effect, I wondered how long my partnership with Hobo would last. I was starting to get weary of all the traveling. I was beginning to sense I had experienced enough of this lifestyle. As I sat there getting lost in my thoughts with the acid's full effect, I realized I wasn't getting any closer to what God wanted to do in my life. I sensed some disillusionment coming upon me. Despite all the new experiences, I was still very empty and unfulfilled. Whatever I was doing didn't seem to be working. I didn't bother sharing any of this with Hobo because I wasn't sure how he would take it, although I knew he would get along fine without me. We had been good partners, so I was committed to at least traveling through Canada with him as far as Toronto. Besides, I had never been to Canada and wanted to see as much of it as possible. Who knows what the future holds? I was along for the ride but was sensing that it might be coming to an end soon.

Onto Calgary and Edmonton

Our trip to Calgary would take us through two National Parks—Glacier and Banff. It was well over 300 miles to Calgary, so we didn't have much hope of making it there in one day. On our first day out of Kelowna, we ended up stranded on Canada Highway 1 northeast of Kamloops. It looked like we were in the middle of nowhere as car after car passed as if we were invisible.

I thought to myself. "I hope this isn't an indication of what the next several days will be like."

As dusk settled in, Hobo says, "We might as well go over to the lake and make camp. It doesn't look like we're going to get a ride."

We had noticed the small lake when we first arrived and had already considered that we might have to spend the night there.

Fed up with being cold, I said, "That sounds like a good idea. I am ready to settle in for the evening. Maybe we'll have better luck tomorrow."

With that decided, off we went, hoping to find a good spot to camp where we could make a fire to keep warm and make something to eat. We had more cooking utensils with us now as well. When we were in Wenatchee, we picked up some of the camping gear my parents had lying around, and nobody was using it.

Killing and Eating Muskrat

As we were checking the lake out, we noticed muskrats everywhere. So, we got our .22 rifle out to see if we could kill a couple of them to put in the stew we were going to make. I figured I could shoot well enough to kill a muskrat. In the army, I qualified with the M-14 and M-16 as an expert marksman in basic training. I doubted whether Hobo could see well enough to shoot anything, but he gave it a try anyway.

It didn't take us long before we shot a couple of them. Hobo wanted me to wade into the water, even though I wasn't feeling that great because of my elbow. I took off my boots, rolled my jeans up, and waded to the dead muskrats. Thankfully, the water wasn't too deep, but it was freezing cold. I volunteered to skin them. I knew from skinning rabbits as a teenager that it wasn't difficult. When I was in Jr. High and High School, my brothers and I raised rabbits. We learned to skin and dress them out. We always had rabbits in our freezer. In my High School Vocational Agriculture class, raising rabbits was my project.

As I was skinning and preparing them for the stew, Hobo built a fire. I was unsure whether muskrats were even edible, but we were hungry and willing to try them. As I was writing this part of the story, I looked it up and discovered they are, in fact, edible as they feed on fleshy roots, stalks, and other parts of the vegetation that grows in the water or on land near their homes. They also eat mussels, frogs, crayfish, and some insects. Most people will not think of eating them because of their rat-like tail and the "rat" part of the name. However, restaurants have been known to serve them; only they are called "marsh rabbits." So, if you have ever eaten marsh rabbit, you have eaten muskrat. The stew wasn't that great, but it was edible, and we also had a warm fire going to keep us warm as it was getting cold. Unfortunately, it was now late, so we called it a night after stoking the fire again.

Concerned About My Health

We woke up the following day covered with more than an inch of snow. Once again, my fears about going North too early came true. But unfortunately, it was a decision we'd made, and now we were stuck. Oh well! At least with the snow, our sleeping bags didn't get soaked like the times we got stuck in the rain, but it was cold as we got up and got our fire going.

We finished our stew for breakfast and then headed to the highway to wait for a ride. We hoped it wouldn't be a long wait. My elbow had swollen up quite a bit, and I was also beginning to run a fever. I was getting more concerned about my health and wondering what I would have to do to get it fixed. After all, I was in Canada and not the States. Would I be able to see a doctor as quickly as I had seen the dentist when we were in South Dakota? I wondered.

The issue with my arm was causing me to think that maybe this was a sign that my time on the road would end in the not-too-distant future. I was beginning to think seriously that this season in my life might be ending soon. It was a good two hours before we finally got a ride, but they were going to Calgary, which meant we would see Banff National Park through the comforts of a nice, warm car. Banff National Park was beautiful, but we were content to stay with our ride rather than stop and explore. We probably would have stopped if it had been a warm, sunny Spring Day. We both wanted to get to Calgary and sleep in a warm bed after waking up in the snow.

Calgary and Edmonton

Once in Calgary, we set out to find a place to spend the night. The great thing about Canada was there were many free places to stay. We were able to find a hostel that was somewhat like a YMCA. We ended up having a room to ourselves. Being a Canadian citizen, Hobo seemed to know all about these places. However, he should have clued me on how to read off my Social Security number. When we checked in, I had to tell them I was a Canadian citizen or wouldn't be allowed to stay. When they asked me for my Social Security number, they kept asking me to repeat it. I couldn't understand why. The guy at the desk finally said that I kept reading it off like an American number. In Canada, their number reads 123-456-789 instead of 123-45-6789.

I finally convinced them to let me stay. I told them I was extremely sick and confused because of the swelling on my elbow. I showed them my elbow and how swollen it was. By showing them my elbow, I was hoping they would have mercy on me. It worked, even though they probably knew I wasn't Canadian. Hobo gave me a bad time for reading my number wrong, but it was his fault for not warning me. My elbow was getting worse and worse. I was in a lot of pain and running a fever, but there was nothing I could do about it. I just needed a good night's sleep. When I woke up the following morning, my bed was drenched from sweating all night from the fever. I was horribly sick and was becoming very worried about what was happening with my elbow. I was scared!

After getting up and having breakfast, we left to explore Calgary to see if we wanted to spend any time there. As we walked around, we didn't like the feel of it for one reason or another and decided to continue to Edmonton. Our goal was to head toward Toronto eventually. We had heard from someone we had met that Saskatoon would be a great place to visit; otherwise, we would have just continued Highway 1 toward Winnipeg. The real issue for not wanting to spend time in Calgary was probably that we were headed toward Toronto and didn't want to waste our time unless something resonated with us. In the back of my mind, I was thinking, "I'm getting very weary of this whole thing." Toronto was beginning to take shape in my mind; the road's end was near. Because I was sick and hurting served to reinforce these thoughts to the forefront of my mind. Yet, for some reason, I was at peace as these thoughts flowed through my mind.

It was only about 170 miles to Edmonton, which meant we could make it there in about four hours if all went well. It was mid-morning, and we planned to be there by late afternoon. Just as we suspected, we arrived in Edmonton around mid-afternoon and set out to find a place to stay for the night. It was too cold to sleep outside even though we had down sleeping bags. My fears, back in Kansas City, about going North too early were now fully realized. We eventually found a place, but it wasn't to my liking. It was more of a house for people with drug and alcohol problems and was filled with older people. We both felt like a fish out of water. I don't remember how we found this place, but we did. While there, one of the men was going through DTs.[15] He was having seizures, which freaked me out. Having been through convulsions, I knew what it was like and didn't particularly want to remind myself of how terrible they were.

Getting Sicker and Sicker

We woke up late the following morning. The swelling in my elbow was terrible. I was getting increasingly frightened that something serious was happening with my arm. It was beginning to look like a balloon. On top of that, the guys at the hostel gave us a hard time for sleeping so late. They thought we should have been up early and on our way. They didn't make us feel welcome at all. It was a strange place, and I was ready to leave despite the pain and the fever.

It was about 340 miles to Saskatoon. We would need to have a good day hitchhiking if we were going to make it in one day. It was already late morning, so it didn't seem like it would happen, especially if things went as slow as they had been since starting our trek across Canada. We were right. We only made it about half the distance, and it took us three or four rides to get that far. I was getting sicker and sicker, and the swelling in my elbow was getting worse and worse. What was I going to do? I knew I would somehow have to find a way to see a doctor once we

---

[15] DT's is slang term for delirium tremens, a "shaking frenzy" with convulsions usually caused by withdrawal from alcohol.

got to Saskatoon. To make things worse, we had to spend the night on the side of the road, sleeping outside in the cold.

We found our way to a coffee shop the following day and ordered a hearty breakfast. We still had a little money I had gotten back from my taxes, which we were using sparingly. Our first ride of the day took us about half the distance to Saskatoon and dropped us off at a gas station. I was in the restroom when the swelling in my elbow broke loose. It was one of the strangest things I'd ever seen. Pus and blood started streaming out of my swollen arm through my elbow. I then squeezed it until it was all out. I was relieved as I pressed my arm and saw the blood and puss pour out. I was getting worried sick that something terrible was happening to me.

Our next ride was with two guys and a gal. They were traveling to Saskatoon. We had a great time chatting with them about our adventures and travels, although Hobo did most of the talking. Still worn out from the infection in my elbow, I tried to nod off. I hoped it was getting better now that the pus and blood had drained. Fortunately, I nodded off several times during the ride.

Saskatoon

Upon reaching Saskatoon, they dropped us off in the heart of the downtown area. Both Hobo and I sensed a liking for Saskatoon right away. We sensed it was going to be a good experience. We set up shop on a busy street corner, where we felt at home. Hobo now had his guitar, which he would bring out and pretend to be playing something. He didn't know how to play that well but seemed eager to learn. It wasn't long before people came by, checking us out and wondering what we were doing in Saskatoon. We got into several conversations, including one with a small group of people telling us about a party happening later that evening. Quite intrigued with us, they invited us and gave directions. We spent the next couple of hours hanging out on the street corner while people strolled along. Some stopped by to satisfy their curiosity, and others just moved on. We were killing time since we had a place to go for the evening. We eventually got enough money panhandling to get something to eat before heading over to the party. It was getting into the early evening, so we found a place to eat. By the time we finished, it was time to head out to the party.

We arrived at the party around 8:00, and it took us about half an hour to walk there. When we arrived, the house was full of people sitting around smoking pot and drinking beer and wine. The music was blaring, with a few people dancing. It looked like it was going to be a great evening. The people who had invited us were also there and introduced us to the others. To our surprise, the people who gave us a ride into Saskatoon were also there.

Meeting Stacey

I started a conversation with Stacey, the gal who had given us the ride, and we began to hit it off very well. She was just as surprised to see us. It seemed like fate had its way. As we talked, she began questioning me about what kind of drugs I had been taking.

She asked. "Were you on heroin earlier in the day when we picked you up? You kept nodding off like you were on heroin."

"No," I told her.

"I had just been sick from an infection in my arm."

I showed her my elbow and said, "I'm feeling much better now that all the puss and blood drained out."

We spent the rest of the time at the party getting to know each other and were incredibly comfortable together. Sitting there drinking wine and smoking pot, we began to get cozy with one other. The next thing I knew, I was invited back to the house where she was staying. It seemed like she was kind of a nomad herself. I wasn't too worried about Hobo. He seemed to be having a great time. Every time I glanced at him, he was thoroughly engaged in a conversation with someone. There were plenty of other girls, so I was sure he would be fine. We had our spot on the street corner where we could meet up the next day, as it looked like we were going our separate ways for the evening. It was starting to get late, and both Stacey and I were anxious to get going. I found Hobo and explained to him what was going on.

I said, "Stacy and I are hitting it off, and it appears that I will be spending the night with her. Is that cool with you?"

He told me, "Sure, no problem! I've got a place to stay as well."

I didn't know it then, but this was the beginning of the break between us.

Getting Settled in Saskatoon

Over the next several days, Stacey and I continually hung out together and would run into Hobo and others around town. We would even hang out together in coffee shops, but for the most part, we were starting to go our separate ways. Because we were hanging out with the same people and frequenting the same homes, we continued to run into each other, not giving much thought to it. We had landed in a community of freaks, and we were all getting along great. Everything was going great, especially now that I wasn't worried about my arm. It was healing up rather well. Hobo had found a place to stay with a gal in the downtown area where we would hang out from time to time. I would drop by and hang out with Hobo and his new girlfriend when I wasn't with Stacey.

Hobo and I were both starting to settle in Saskatoon. I had even gone to the dentist to get another cavity fixed and was able to receive food stamps. It was beginning to look like we might be there for quite a while. Then, one day, Stacey said something to me that would change my life again.

She said, "Some of my friends and I are going to Toronto in a day or two, and I'd like you to come with us. What do you think?"

It took me totally by surprise, so I said, "Let me think about it."

Leaving Saskatoon had just come up out of the blue and caught me off guard, so I wasn't ready to give her an answer. It got me thinking, though. I still wanted to go to Toronto, even though I was enjoying the time of my life here in Saskatoon. I seemed to be settling in, but what would it be like in Saskatoon without Stacy? I knew once I got to Toronto, I would most likely finish with this phase of my life. It was a lot to consider. Was I ready to return home and get on with my life, whatever that would be? There was quite a tug-of-war going on with my emotions and thinking. I was now completely over the infection in my elbow and was enjoying myself with all the new friends I was meeting. But, on the other hand, I wanted to be with Stacey, and she was ready to leave.

Was it fate or God's plan that brought Stacey and me together at the party? Was Stacey part of God's plan to separate me from my partnership with Hobo? When God calls us, does He work with us and guide us despite our resistance? Was this His plan to get me moving in the direction that would eventually lead me back home? In the back of my mind, I knew I had to finally find my way back home to Wenatchee if I was ever to settle down long enough to allow God to work in my life. Even though I was presently immersed in myself and trying to experience what the world had to offer, God was never far from my thoughts. God's grace, mercy, and long-suffering with us are beyond our understanding. He loves us despite ourselves and never gives up on us.

Romans 5:8 says, "But God demonstrates His own love toward us, in that while we were still sinners, Christ died for us."

In addition, *1 John 4:19 says, "We love Him because He first loved us."*

He continues to woo us into His presence, even when we oppose Him. Eventually, we either see the light and repent or reject Him by further hardening our hearts to Him. I knew I had hardened my heart, but was I willing to continue to do so?

So Long, Hobo

I ran into Hobo later in the day and told him what Stacy had said: "I'm seriously thinking of going to Toronto with her."

He was quite taken aback and said, "I'm not ready to leave Saskatoon and won't be for quite a while. This place is happening for me in a good way. So, I'm not leaving."

I said, "Well, I'm seriously thinking I'm going to go."

He then got a little angry with me and said in a very sarcastic way, "What are you going to do? Go back to Wenatchee?"

"Who knows what will happen! You know how it is; go with the flow and figure it out."

That was it. I made up my mind right then and there. I was going. I was leaving, and Hobo was staying. We had been together for about eight months. We had met each other the previous October, which was now the middle of May. It was sad, but I sensed that this day was coming. My emotions were conflicted, but in my spirit, I felt God was preparing my heart for this from the time we left Kelowna, even though I was still at odds with Him. As it is often said, "God works in mysterious ways." His ways are usually a mystery to us as we try to discern what He's doing.

Leaving for Toronto with Stacey

Hobo and I had a couple more conversations, and he finally came to terms with the fact that I was leaving. I left on good terms with him and two days later found myself in a Volkswagen van on my way to Toronto, about 1,800 miles away. The only catch was that none of us had very much money. Mine was now gone, as we had been eating out a lot and weren't spending much time panhandling. We would all have to panhandle on the way whenever we needed gas or food. Well, that is what hippies do!

We stopped a couple of times between Saskatoon and Winnipeg to panhandle, and then we would all climb back in the van, and off we would go again. At one point, we pulled over during the middle of the night and slept for about six hours. So, it took us a couple of days to get to Winnipeg.

Once we arrived in Winnipeg, we decided to stay there for a day before continuing our trip. We were all panhandling, and each time we came back, Stacey would want to know how much I was doing compared to her. She would usually take off on her own because she could do much better when alone rather than being with one of the guys. Stacey would always have two or three times more than any of us. She was very streetwise. I was beginning to pick up the vibe; Stacey thought she was better off without me and the others. I had been sensing she was starting to be somewhat cool toward me. I figured I probably wouldn't see much of her once we got to Toronto.

Toronto, the End of the Road for Me

It was another couple of days before we finally rolled into Toronto. It had been a long trip, and I was getting weary of everyone's company, including Stacey's. I was relieved when she told me she had things to do in Toronto and would rather be alone. I was stressed from being cooped up with everyone for the last few days, so I just took off alone to discover Toronto. As an introvert, I needed my own space from time to time. I needed it now, so I was happy to part with everyone. My first order of business was to find a place to stay, which I found rather quickly. I found a YMCA after talking with a couple of hippie characters I had met on the street. It had a huge room full of bunk beds with a smaller room off to the side. I ended up in the smaller room. I wasn't too fond of being in a massive room with a bunch of guys.

By now, I had realized Stacey had given me the clap.[16] Therefore, I needed to find a clinic to get the antibiotics I would need to get over it. Having had in Nam, I knew the drill. I now suspected Stacey knew she had it and had given it to me. It was probably one of the reasons she was in such a hurry to leave me. So, I found a clinic right away and got the antibiotics needed. The only problem was I wouldn't be able to drink any alcohol for a few days. Whenever I went to bars, I had to drink Coke or some other soft drink. There wasn't much fun in doing that.

Amazingly, I had settled into street life without relying on Hobo and his antics. I felt unusually confident as I hung out daily with some of the guys I'd met at the YMCA. With Sunday just around the corner, we heard about an outdoor concert happening, so we all made plans to go.

---

[16] Clap is a slang term for gonorrhea—a common STD.

My new friends and I would go to the bars together, play stick hockey, ride the subways around the city, and even drop acid together on one occasion. I also had plenty of time to explore things independently, which was fine. I was enjoying myself quite a bit. Even though I had discovered new-found freedom in not depending on Hobo's extroverted personality to help me get by, I sensed the time was coming when I would be hitting the road again. After spending so many days cooped up in a VW bus, Toronto was a nice reprieve, but I knew it couldn't go on forever. Staying at the YMCA was sure to get old eventually.

The day of the concert came, and we all went together. To my surprise, Stacey was there too. She spotted me and came over to see what I had been doing since we departed. We talked for a bit to see how we were both getting along. I didn't mention the clap to her. One of my friends whom I had met gave me a hard time about not telling her.

He said, "Who knows how many others got it because of her irresponsibility? You should have told her."

I said, "Well, I didn't, and that's that. I can't do anything about it now. Besides, I am sure Stacey knows she has it. That's most likely why she split from me."

At the concert, I realized I was ready to hit the road and return home. I had experienced enough in the past year to satisfy my yearning for an adventurous lifestyle, which seemed to be leading nowhere. I was nowhere close to what I had been searching for and still empty inside. I was the nowhere man John Lennon sang about. It seemed as though I was wandering in circles without any purpose in what I was doing. It appeared the end of the road for this phase of my life had finally come. I was ready to head home and try to figure out what to do next. So, the next day, I packed my stuff and hit the road.

"So long, Hobo! It was fun while it lasted. You were a great friend and partner."

Going Home – So Long, Hobo
Chapter Twenty-Three

Once I left Toronto and headed home, I wanted to get back to the States as quickly as possible. Hitchhiking was much slower in Canada, and I didn't want to waste time. I had seen and experienced enough. Canada was a great place, especially Kelowna, Saskatoon, and Toronto, but it was time for me to end this phase of my life. It was sad to leave Hobo, but I knew it was time for us to go our separate ways. I had become very intuitive and had known for a while that this part of my journey was ending. I had more to learn about the person I was to become and what God had in store for me in the next phase of my life.

I will always be grateful for the partner Hobo was to me and for inviting me to travel with him to New Orleans from Tempe, Arizona. It was the beginning of a great friendship and a time of discovery for me. We had many great adventures together. I wish I could remember them all, but too many years have passed. Nevertheless, I am fortunate to have retained the ones of which I have written.

God saw me in this un-surrendered state of mind and had a lot of patience toward me. He knew I needed someone like Hobo to travel with to help keep me safe from whatever unknown dangers may have been lurking. God knows us from beginning to end, and He knew I would eventually surrender my life to Him. So, he sent Hobo my way as sort of a guardian angel. If it had not been for the fact that I had met Hobo or someone like him, I probably would have given up on the road life and gone home much sooner. I don't think I would have lasted long on my own. It just wasn't in me. It would have been too much of a struggle. Instead, with someone like Hobo, I could step out of my introverted personality and experience things I would never have experienced—both good and bad. I needed to cut loose and get my Ya Ya's out after Vietnam and all I experienced there. Even though I have regrets for things I did and for people I may have hurt, I needed to come to the end of myself. God needed to bring me to the point where I would eventually surrender my life to the Lord Jesus Christ.

Had I not hit the road and kept moving, I think I would have gotten bogged down and addicted to heroin. Staying on the road during this adjustment time kept me from destroying myself. Even though my life seemed to have taken a crooked path at this juncture, I was still somewhat focused on finding my way and seeing how God would fit into it. I hadn't given up on God, nor had He given up on me. I was taking it slow, as I had said to Him, when I received the vision of my life flashing before my eyes way back in my Vietnam days. I was now on my way out of Canada. Kelowna, Saskatoon, and Toronto were cool places, but there was nothing more there for me, so I left Canada and Hobo behind with no regrets.

Meeting up with a Carload of Hippies

Once the decision was made to return home, I crossed the border and decided to head towards Interstate 90 near Toledo, Ohio, which would take me home. As I was nearing Toledo, a carload of pot-smoking hippies picked me up. It was early evening, and they were more than willing to let me spend the night with them.

I was a little surprised they had invited me to spend the night because I was hitting it off with one of the girls who was sitting in the back seat. I could tell one of the guys in the front seat wasn't too happy about it. As a result, I played it cool and didn't get too involved with her. At their home, I took a shower and cleaned up before joining them for the evening. As I was taking a shower, I noticed a razor and decided to cut my beard off, leaving the mustache. I was getting tired of it and wanted a cleaner look for my return home. I ended up spending the evening partying with them and their friends. After a good night's sleep and hearty breakfast, I was given a ride to the Interstate 90 on-ramp to begin my second day since leaving Canada. The next few days were relatively uneventful as I kept going with one ride after another, sleeping at rest stops when it got too late to travel.

Arriving Home Unscathed

On the fourth day after leaving Toronto, I arrived at my home in East Wenatchee. My parents were surprised to see me as they had no warning I was coming. Though surprised, they were happy to see me, especially after telling them I was home and done with traveling around the country. I could tell they were relieved I had ended this phase of my life relatively unscathed. The prayers of my mother and father were answered.

It was the beginning of June 1973. I was finally home, but not sure what to do with myself. I needed time to gather my thoughts and think about what I had just been through and what I should be doing in the future. I had no sooner started to get settled into my parent's home when our family friends who owned the apple orchard on Lake Chelan stopped by for a visit. My parents must have alerted them that I was home.

Paul Peters and His Apple Orchard

Paul Peters had been a part of our family's life for as long as I can remember. When my parents moved our family out West to Washington State in 1953 from Detroit Lakes, Minnesota, I was three years old. Our first home in Washington was a small house in Paul's father's apple orchard. Some of my earliest memories are of eating cherries from the cherry tree on the side of the house.

My father and his brothers first came out west to Oregon and California in 1936 by hitchhiking and riding freight trains to work in the wheat fields, the pea harvest, and the apple orchards. *(Maybe that's how hitchhiking and riding freight trains got into my DNA.)* They were sitting at the unemployment line in Chelan, Washington, when Paul Peters, Sr. picked them up to work in his orchard.

The Peters family took a real liking to my father and his brothers.

Over the years, they continued to work for him and then his son, Paul, until 1984. My father would take his vacations and pick apples every year for Paul. My uncles would do the same. Every year, my father and his brothers would have an apple-picking reunion in the Peters' orchard. Paul was always very generous to them, paying them better wages than the other growers around him would.

During every summer of my high school years, my brothers and I worked in his orchard during the summer months. We thinned apples and put the props under the trees. I developed much of the work ethic I have today during those summers working in Paul's orchard. Even though he was very generous and kind to our family, he was also a person who expected you to work hard—no goofing off.

Paul and his wife, Carol, arrived at my parent's home to visit a week after I had been home from my hitchhiking experiences. During the visit, we discussed what I planned on doing with my life in the immediate future. I didn't have much of an answer. Paul then offered me a job working in the orchard during the summer, thinning apples. It seemed like a good opportunity for me. I needed something like this to gather my thoughts and figure out what was going on with my life. Oddly enough, I felt more lost and without purpose than when I first started on my hitchhiking adventures. But, at least this offered me something I was familiar with, which would give me peace.

The next thing I knew, I was sitting in a barber shop in Manson, Washington, getting my hair cut. Paul Peters made one thing clear. He wouldn't have a long-haired hippie working for him, so I submitted to having my hair cut.

Home, But Still Lost
Chapter Twenty-Four

It was the middle of June 1973. I was settling into my new home for the summer, which was in our family friend's orchard in Manson, Washington. It is the same house my parents first lived in when they moved to Washington from Minnesota in 1953. It is a two-bedroom house with a living room and a kitchen. I would be sharing the house with my Uncle Paul, who was somewhat of a migrant farm worker.

Uncle Paul

Uncle Paul had always been the black sheep of the family. He had an alcohol problem that would cause him to go on binges periodically. Paul and I became good friends since we connected philosophically and were drinking buddies occasionally.

During the summer between the eighth grade and my first year of high school, my brothers and I worked on Uncle Paul's strawberry farm in Silverton Heights, Oregon. He had just purchased this beautiful piece of property and was anxious to make a go of the strawberry farm. Unfortunately, it didn't work out since his mother-in-law insisted on being the row boss. She would drive a lot of the workers crazy, and they would quit on him. I am sure there were other reasons as well.

This is a picture of the Birks' Homestead in Independence, Oregon

At the beginning of that summer, our family went on vacation to Independence, Oregon, where most of our relatives on my dad's side lived. They had about 10 or 15 acres of land on which they had all built homes. In addition, there was also the old homestead that was already on the property, where my grandparents lived when they were alive. My uncle Lloyd, a Nazarene Pastor in Salem, Oregon, was also building a home for his retirement. It was in Uncle Lloyd's house where, once our vacation was over, my parents decided that two of my brothers and I would stay in Independence and work in the strawberry fields with our cousins. It was arranged when the strawberry harvest in Independence ended, along with my brothers, Dick and Bob, we would go to Silverton Heights and work for Uncle Paul. My mother would stay with us while we were in Independence, get up, and cook breakfast each morning at around 5:00. My father would go home and go back to work. Every morning with our cousins, we walked to the end of the street, where we would catch a bus to the strawberry fields. It was a great time. We had lots of strawberry fights but still managed to make money picking them.

Once the strawberry season ended in the Salem and Independence area, my mother went back home. As planned, my brothers and I went to be with my Uncle Paul and his wife at his strawberry farm. It was a great summer! Even though we were staying with my aunt and uncle, we were away from home and on our own. We got to drive tractors and even learned how to drive his car.

At the end of picking time every day, we went with Uncle Paul to the place where the crates of strawberries were unloaded and graded. Then, as my uncle drove the tractor, we would ride on the trailer with all the crates of strawberries. Instead of looking at every flat to see how many rotten strawberries were in them, they would only look at a few of the flats and determine from them how many the berries were good and how much they were worth. Sometimes, the man in charge would let us eat the rotten ones so they wouldn't count against my uncle. Even though they tasted terrible, we always got a kick out of the process. It was fun!

Now, instead of working for my Uncle Paul, we were both sharing a house and working for our family friend, Paul Peters, and his wife, Carol. Aside from my Uncle Paul, I had three cousins, Mary, Rachel, and Fatina, who also worked in the orchard that summer. They were my Uncle Lloyd's daughters from Oregon. They were staying at the house down the street at the other end of the orchard.

Both Paul and Carol Peters worked alongside us, even though they were the orchard owners. Paul Peters was a real fanatic at listening to all the news shows on the radio. He constantly had his radio blasting with Paul Harvey and others. It was June 1973, and our country was in the middle of the Watergate hearings, which meant that was what we heard day in and day out.

Uncle Paul and I hit it off very well. We were considered black sheep then, so we had that in common. He was the one who introduced me to Edgar Cayce and other books of spiritual enlightenment.

Uncle Paul had been saved many years ago while living in Independence, Oregon, near his brothers, Alan and Doug. Unfortunately, Alan and Doug gave him such a hard time with their expectations of how he should be acting as a Christian that he got disillusioned with the whole thing and gave up on it. There didn't seem to be much of an understanding of grace in their lives. I am sure there was another side to that story, but I never heard it. All three of them have since died.

As I got to know Paul during those summer months, I realized he had a spiritual side to his personality. Like me, Uncle Paul was into many weird ideas. He gave me a book about Edgar Cayce's life, which I found fascinating. Edgar Cayce was called the *"Sleeping Prophet"* because of his ability to go into induced sleep or trances, where he would give readings to people who came to him in need. Cayce claimed to be a Christian, raised as a Baptist in a Bible-believing church where he also taught Sunday school classes. He was also very much into reincarnation, which isn't something the Christian faith recognizes or adheres to as the Bible says, *"Just as people are destined to die once, and after that to face judgment"—Hebrews 9:27 (NIV).*

As the summer wore on, Uncle Paul and I continued to work together in the orchard while living in the house we were allowed to use. We continued to share our spiritual experiences and occasionally drank together at the bars. I can only remember one time when we got a little drunk. Most of the time, we just had a couple of beers, which was pretty much the extent. During this period, I wasn't smoking pot at all. I had been away too long and didn't have any connections.

Back in Wenatchee

Later in the summer, after we finished up with Paul Peters, we returned to Wenatchee and settled in at my parent's home in East Wenatchee while working in the orchard down the street. It is the same orchard my brothers and I often worked in after we finished working for Paul Peters during the summer months. This orchard also had pear trees, which meant there was work throughout the summer until apple harvest time.

Once back in Wenatchee, I began to find my way around town again. I was hanging out with friends I had met when I returned from Vietnam. I also met a few others, which meant that the pot was beginning to flow again.

I was still very much involved in reading new material, especially about Edgar Cayce and Carlos Castaneda, who now had a new book called *"The Journey to Ixtlan."* This book continued the lessons into a separate reality. Paul was reading a book about flying saucers and how people from other planets were trying to communicate with us. I also read the book but didn't find it as inspiring as he did. It seemed a little too far-fetched for me.

I had been looking to a few sources for spiritual direction this season. While in Vietnam, I read the book by Tom Wolf, *"The Electric Kool-Aid Acid Test,"* about Ken Kesey and His Merry Pranksters. Kesey was very instrumental in getting the whole LSD movement started in San Francisco and had become somewhat of a hero to me. Unfortunately, as I continued looking for new insight from him, nothing came forth. He was just another voice trapped in deception, which was feeding the deception I was in at the time. While in Vietnam, I began connecting with the music of John Lennon and George Harrison and their message of peace and love. They seemed to know what was happening and had something to say that would bring answers to the spiritual quest I was on. But, again, the more I looked at them and the others, it fed into the disillusionment I was sensing at the time. I was beginning to conclude they were voices of the enemy, to deceive and to keep me away from the actual reality that I had started to discover and experience in Jesus while in Nam.

Just Drifting and Existing

It seemed like I was doing nothing more than drifting and existing without purpose. I was becoming somewhat disillusioned and rather bored with everything. I continued to work in the orchards until I could figure out something better to do with my life.

September came around, and it was time for the apple harvest. I returned to Paul Peters' orchard with my dad, who took his vacation to pick apples to earn extra money. My three uncles—Paul, Doug, Alan, and his wife, Dorothy were also there. For my dad, it was sort of a vacation, getting to spend time with his brothers during this yearly outing.

Things were going rather well for the first week of the harvest. Then, unfortunately, one day, while working on an eight-foot ladder, I reached too far for an apple, and the ladder went out from under me, and I fell. I put my hands and arms out to break the fall and severely broke my wrists. I was in extreme pain!

Two Broken Wrists

I drove to the doctor in Chelan, about ten miles away. I had a 1956 Chevrolet pickup I had traded from my brother, Junior. He wanted the Chevrolet Impala I had purchased from my brother Bob. As it turned out, I had broken both of my wrists. My apple-picking days were over, but I would still get paid since I was injured on the job.

Kenny's Folly

Back home in Wenatchee, I was bored and had nothing to do with casts on both of my hands. For some time, I was pondering the idea of building a camper on the back of my pickup. If I decided to travel again, I would do it in style with a camper built onto my pickup. In addition, I had been pondering the thought of going somewhere in Mexico and parking where there were many peyote buttons to try and get in touch with the Mescalito spirit. At this point in my life, I was losing touch with reality and beginning to be more inclined to the separate reality that Carlos Castaneda mentioned.

Once I set my mind to building the camper, I began to do it. My first step was to go to a junkyard and find a flatbed from a truck like mine. I could buy one and bring it home to my backyard, where I started building. Building a camper didn't seem too difficult to me. As a child, I watched my dad and Uncle Alan build an extension to our home that enabled us to have a full-sized dining room and kitchen. Most of my uncles were also involved in building houses, so how hard could it be to build a camper?

I worked everything out on paper. Next, I figured out how much lumber I would need and the other fixtures that would go into it, such as a sink, bed, lights, windows, and electrical outlets. Once I had all this done, I purchased the necessary fixtures and lumber and began to build. Over the next few months, I worked diligently on the camper despite having two broken wrists. It was quite an enjoyable experience, working and building a project I had envisioned. It was a real escape from the disillusionment I was beginning to feel due to the loss of direction I was sensing. Once I had it built, I put it on jacks and attached it to my truck. Everything went well until I decided to take it for a test drive on our street. What I failed to consider was how heavy it was going to be. As I began to drive up our road, I discovered that the front end of my truck felt like it was being lifted off the ground as I drove. It was, in fact, much too heavy for the truck.

To my dismay, I had to dismantle it and put my regular truck bed back on the truck. All that work I had put into it would never work. It was just too heavy. The upside was it would serve as an extra room where friends would stay the night or family would come to visit. Other than it being too heavy, it was a great camper.

Just recently, when visiting my hometown of East Wenatchee, my brother Junior and I drove up to our old home to see what had become of the camper. Thirty-eight years later, it was still there. The people living on the property were using it as a storage shed. It wasn't in good shape, though. My mother always referred to it as *"Kenny's Folly."*

Isolation

During this period, I was hanging out with friends who were heavy drug users like me, smoking pot all the time and dropping acid as well. However, I found myself being very content at times to do LSD on my own while listening to the music of George Harrison, Ravi Shankar, John Coltrane, and others while meditating in the basement of my parent's home. I was beginning to isolate myself in many ways and didn't need people around me. This season of my life was peculiar. I had no inclination whatsoever as to where I was headed. I was still very lost in my mind, without any clear direction. I was still using drugs, but they no longer gave me the satisfaction they once did. I was pretty much just existing. The vision I had in Nam seemed like a distant picture in my mind that was quickly fading away. Yet it was still there nudging me along.

Failed Hiking Adventure

During the season of isolating, I read a book about a guy who had hiked the Pacific Crest Trail from Canada to Mexico. The book inspired me to think that going on a long hike on the trail would be cool. I was hoping to get some inspiration to move forward into whatever was next for me. So, I began preparing for the adventure with nothing better to do and plenty of time on my hands. The backpack I used for hitchhiking was worn out, so I bought myself a nice new one. I also purchased a new down sleeping bag, lots of dried food, and other equipment needed. The trailhead leading to the Pacific Crest Trail wasn't too far from my home. It was just past Leavenworth, Washington, in the Icicle River Campgrounds. During my childhood, our family camped there on several occasions, so I was familiar with the area. It had now been over six weeks since I had broken my wrists, so it was safe for me to take off. On the day of my departure, my brother, Bob, drove me to the last campground in the Icicle River Camp area, where the trailhead to the Pacific Crest Trail was.

Bear Trouble

I camped at the campground on the first night to begin my trek the following morning. In the middle of the night, I was awakened by a lot of commotion. To my surprise, a bear had grabbed my backpack and carried it up the trail. The commotion woke up another camper next to me. We both took off up the trail with our flashlights, looking for my pack even though I was pretty well shaken and frightened by the episode. Finally, about 300 yards up the trail, we found it with the bear nowhere to be seen.

After waking up the following morning, I decided the hiking adventure wasn't a good idea. The incident with the bear spooked me. What was I thinking, taking off on an adventure like this all alone? From all the drugs, I wasn't thinking straight. Hello! As I said before, I was beginning to lose touch with reality.

It would be a long walk out of the park since I was at the last campground, so I decided to just leisurely work my way out as I fished in the river periodically throughout the day. I got so caught up in fishing and enjoying myself that I didn't make it very far out of the park. Rather than locate a campsite at the campgrounds to sleep, I made a camp by the river. That was my isolation mentality taking over. I had already forgotten about the bear the night before. Had I been thinking about it, I'm sure I would have sought the safety of having others around me. I also would have had enough sense to put my pack in a tree like you were supposed to. But, as I said, I wasn't thinking straight and was burned out from all the drugs I had taken over the last several years.

As I settled down by the river at the camp I had made and was all snuggled up in my warm mummy bag with my pack lying next to me, my thoughts began to slow down. I started remembering the incident with the bear from the night before. No sooner had I begun to think about it than I sensed something dark brooding over me. As I looked up, I found myself staring another bear right in the eye. He looked right at me and then at my pack. He then laid down next to me, tearing open my pack to get to the food. He was so close; I literally could have reached out with my hand and touched him. However, I had read enough about bears to know not to make sudden moves. At the same time, while the bear munched away, I slowly unzipped my bag. I wanted to be able to make a run for it if needed, as if I could outrun a bear.

The strangest sensation came over me as I lay with the bear beside me, ripping my pack open and eating the contents. I was totally at peace, with no sense of fear. I just knew the bear wasn't going to hurt me. It was like God put his arms around me and said, "It's alright; I'm here watching over you."

After the bear had finished with the food, he got up, looked me squarely in the eyes, and walked away. I then got up, made a big fire, rattled my pots and pans to scare him away, and went back to sleep. However, I didn't waste time getting out of the park the following morning. I was home by early afternoon with a tale to tell. The bear had ripped all the pockets on my pack, which was evidence enough.

I knew I was lucky to be alive, which caused me to think soberly about where I was headed. I knew I was overdoing it with the drugs and getting increasingly out of touch with reality. I didn't know what to do. I could sense God jerking the line and trying to reel me in, but I was still fighting Him. So, instead of giving in, I continued using drugs to the extent that I was constantly either loaded or drinking.

The money I received for getting hurt on the job was running out, so I figured it was time to get a job. There was always plenty of work in the apple sheds around Wenatchee, so I went back to work at Washington Fruit Growers, where I had worked before taking off on my hitchhiking adventure. I was immediately hired and went to work packing apples. At least I was doing something familiar to me, which helped keep my sanity.

Back at Work in the Apple Shed

Working at the apple shed, I became increasingly disillusioned with life and drugs. I wasn't enjoying getting high as much and was even getting paranoid. I began withdrawing more and more from my friends and keeping to myself. I was hiding out in my parent's basement, feeling empty inside. I felt like I was losing connection with what had begun to happen to me in Vietnam with the vision and the relationship I had started to experience with Jesus. I was still one lost individual who hadn't found His way–just many dead ends. I had been running in many different directions, continually coming up empty. I was like the nowhere man in the Beatles' song.

Conversion at Last
Chapter Twenty-Five

It was early January 1974; I sensed I was coming to the end of where I had been for the last couple of years. I no longer wanted to hang out with my pot-smoking buddies or hit the bars. I was still smoking pot on occasion and even dropping acid occasionally, but it just wasn't creating the excitement in my spirit that it once did. I was becoming bored with the drug thing but still stubbornly clinging to it as I had nothing better to do. I felt like the fish that bit at something that looked tasty, only to find it had a hook in its mouth and doing everything it could to try and spit it out. The hook for me was the night of my Vietnam episode when I cried out to God. God had gotten His hook into me that night. I had spent the last three years trying to spit it out without success. I was worn out and exhausted from the struggle. As a fisherman jerks back on the line to set the hook after the fish bites, then lets it play a bit before reeling it in, so had I been in the hands of God. He had set the hook with the vision of my life flashing before me, only to let me go with the hook still in my mouth. Periodically, He would jerk the line and reel me in, only to let me go again. Over and over, this would happen until the struggle finally wore me down.

The drug-induced life from the past few years, which seemed so promising and adventurous initially, was now becoming a noose around my neck. I wanted out but wasn't quite sure how to go about it. The acceptance factor that had initially enticed me into the drug culture had run its course. What I needed now was true acceptance from God. Unfortunately, I had too many mixed-up ideas about God because of all I had encountered over the last couple of years. I didn't realize God was setting me up for the final catch. Just because a fisherman hooks a fish, he doesn't catch it until it is in the boat or on the shore in his net. I sensed God was determined to get me into the boat. He had been long-suffering and patient with me and wasn't about to give up.

During the previous year, my brother, Bob, and his wife had given birth to a daughter named Amie, of whom I was very fond. They had both been saved and were attending the church where we had all grown up. On a particular Sunday in March of 1974, they were going to have Amie dedicated to the Lord and wanted the whole family—including me—to witness the event. Up until this time, I had been resisting going to church. Even though I was interested in Christ and His message, I wasn't interested in organized religion. As a hippie, I had become very anti-establishment. In the back of my mind, I secretly wanted to see if it had anything to offer me. Sadly, my pride kept me from going. But the more I thought about it, the more I realized this would be the perfect opportunity without compromising my pride. So, I went. Although it was good to see many of the family friends I hadn't seen in years at our family's church, I didn't seem to be getting touched in any way during the service. However, at the end of the service, they had an altar call, one like what you hear at a Billy Graham Crusade. They began to sing one of those altar call songs like "Almost Persuaded." Before I knew it, I was putting the hymnal back in its slot and walking forward in response to the conviction I was sensing from the Holy Spirit.

Under the Power and Influence of the Holy Spirit

The conviction of the Holy Spirit mysteriously came over me. I had never encountered anything like it. I honestly felt like I was totally under the power and persuasion of the Holy Spirit and had little resistance to what was happening in my life. I am not a proponent of irresistible grace, but this was close to it. I confessed my sins and fully surrendered to Jesus Christ as my Lord and Savior, believing Him to be the Son of God, the manifestation of God in the flesh, the One who had died on the cross for my sins and then rose again from the dead.[17]

Over the previous few years, my resistance was slowly wearing down. I had many close encounters with God's grace but continually resisted. Then, like a fish, hooked that constantly fights the tug of the line until it wears out from the battle and then is caught, so was I in the hands of the Lord. The battle for my soul was over. I was too tired and worn out to resist any longer. I surrendered to what God wanted to do at that moment.

---

[17] 1 John 1:7-10 (NKJV) But if we walk in the light as He is in the light, we have fellowship with one another, and the blood of Jesus Christ His Son cleanses us from all sin. If we say that we have no sin, we deceive ourselves, and the truth isn't in us. If we confess our sins, He is faithful and just to forgive us our sins and to cleanse us from all unrighteousness. If we say that we have not sinned, we make Him a liar, and His word is not in us.

Romans 10:9-10 (NKJV) ... that if you confess with your mouth the Lord Jesus and believe in your heart that God has raised Him from the dead, you will be saved. For with the heart one believes unto righteousness, and with the mouth confession is made unto salvation.

The Bible says it is the goodness of God that leads us to repentance.[18] In my case, this was astonishingly true. Without God's goodness leading me to that moment, I'm not sure where I would be today. I will be forever grateful for His mercy, goodness, and forbearance over my lost soul. As a result, I repented immediately and entirely from all my drug use and cut myself off from all my friends who were still using.

The love and fulfillment I have experienced due to surrendering my life to Jesus Christ has by far exceeded any drug-induced experience I've ever had. The sense of purpose I have discovered, along with love, peace, joy, and contentment, outweighs anything I ever thought was possible.

Before this experience, I had become relatively isolated, which made it somewhat difficult for me to attend church for the first few weeks. I didn't like being around many people and talking with them or having them come up to me and talk. As a result, I developed a habit of coming in a few minutes late and leaving a few minutes early to avoid any conversations. Eventually, I began to get used to it and looked forward to each week's experience. I even started attending Sunday school an hour before the worship service.

As a purpose-driven person, I wasn't content with sitting and learning. I wanted to be doing something. I eventually got involved in the Bus Ministry—picking kids up on Sunday mornings for Sunday school. I would go out every Saturday and visit with the kids and their parents on my route. I was learning to face my fears and insecurities by coming out of myself.

During this season, I began to devour the Bible. I couldn't get enough of it. I would spend hours on end just reading through the gospels and the writings of Paul. I was thoroughly mesmerized by what I was reading. I began to develop a profound love for God's Word while encountering the Holy Spirit when reading. I was growing daily in this new experience and enjoying it immensely.

Shelving the Old Philosophical Ideas

One of the things that helped me during this phase was that I shelved the philosophical ideas I had picked up over the last couple of years. I knew much of what I had encountered didn't fit into the Bible and

---

[18] Romans 2:4 (NKJV) Or do you despise the riches of His goodness, forbearance, and longsuffering, not knowing that the goodness of God leads you to repentance?

Christian theology, so I decided to put them on a shelf. I didn't want what I was now experiencing through God's Word to be filtered by my previous ideologies. Therefore, I didn't discard them; I just put them away, not touching them. Eventually, I tossed them thoroughly after receiving further revelation from God's Word on what was right and wrong.

Separation from Old Friends

If I was to grow in Christ and become who God had ordained me to be, I knew I had to separate myself from all my friends. I knew that if I continued to hang around with them, I would be back to my old habits, which I was now putting behind me. So, I stayed away and didn't go around them at all. The Scripture says we are to separate ourselves from all that is ungodly and not to be unequally yoked together with unbelievers. [19] Disconnecting from our friends doesn't mean we no longer love our non-Christian friends; it simply means we no longer want to participate in whatever they do that's not right. On one occasion, a few of my friends came to see me. I told them that I had turned my life over to Christ and was no longer interested in hanging out and smoking pot with them. After that, they no longer came around. There was another occasion when I was driving to college one day. I had picked up one of my former pot-smoking buddies. He was hitchhiking, so I felt compelled to pick him up. He was smoking a joint when he got into the truck, and I started toking along with him.

No More Drugs - Ever

By the time I had arrived at the college campus and settled into my first class, high in the weed, the conviction of the Holy Spirit was upon me. It was so strong that I determined never to allow myself to get high again. As of the writing of this book, it has been about 40 years since that day. Since then, I have never smoked another joint nor taken any other drugs.

Over the years, I realized the harmful effects of drugs on me. I am thankful I got away from them before they destroyed my life. I had Hepatitis C from using needles carelessly and have significant short-term memory loss from smoking so much pot. However, a few years ago, I went through a program with the VA and was completely healed of Hepatitis C in eight weeks.

---

[19] 2 Corinthians 6:14-18

Even though the phase of my life following Vietnam was an exciting time of adventure and discovery, it was nothing compared to what I have discovered by being a committed Christian who has consecrated and dedicated my life to the purposes of God. The Holy Spirit-led life is a life of continual joy and discovery of God's purposes, which bring delight and peace to the soul.

Going to College

During this new season in my life, I began attending Wenatchee Valley Junior College. I qualified for the G.I. Bill, so I figured I might as well use it. I enrolled in the spring semester of 1974 and began attending classes.

After three and a half years of heavy drug use, I was curious whether my mind could learn and comprehend anything. However, I was surprised at how easily it all came to me. I graduated from high school with just a 2.0 grade point average, which helped me by taking woodshop and typing classes. They were easy for me. In high school, I didn't try. I just did enough to graduate. I was now getting all A's and B's in my college classes with a 3.5 grade point average. I realized that with a desire to learn, the learning process came relatively easily. I was thoroughly enjoying the learning process.

A Surprise Visit by Hobo

Shortly after my conversion, during this season, Hobo appeared at my doorstep unannounced. He had continued to live in Saskatoon all this time and was now with his girlfriend on his way back to Austin, Texas. I let them spend the night in the camper I had built. It was finally serving a purpose. We had a good talk about our times on the road together, and then they were on their way again. After that, he planned to settle in Austin, one of our favorite places we visited during our adventures together.

New Job as Orchard Foreman

During this same season, the orchardist who owned an orchard down the street from our family home contacted me and asked if I wanted to come to work for him, running his orchard. He had acquired a rare disease that was causing his bones to deteriorate, and he couldn't do much. It was a fifteen-acre orchard, and I would be doing all the work, which entailed changing the sprinklers twice a day, mowing the grass, applying spray dope to all the trees, and thinning the whole orchard with one other person whom I hired. During harvest season, I would be the person driving the tractor. My job would be to move the bins from tree to tree for the pickers and then stack them on the skid for the truck to pick them up, where they would then be taken to the packing shed.

I was in a genuine learning mode during this season of my life. I knew from my vision in Vietnam that God called me to ministry, but I had no idea how it would work out. For the time being, I was content to learn everything I could about Jesus and His ways. When autumn rolled around, I enrolled in junior college with the idea of taking general education classes I would need regardless of what direction I took. I got a schedule that consisted of just morning classes so that I would have the afternoon to work in the apple orchard during the harvest. My boss could do a little work, so he handled the crew in the morning, and I would take over in the afternoon after my classes.

During the coming winter months, I wouldn't need to work since I was receiving income from the G.I. Bill for going to school. However, once spring rolled around again, I resumed my job at the orchard. During this time, I was living in the basement of my parent's home while paying them rent.

Teaching a Bible Class and Early Influences

During this season of spiritual growth, I began teaching a Sunday school class for young adults at the church. I also started a home Bible Study on Friday evenings with another person. When I first began attending the church after that momentous day in March 1974, there wasn't a young adult group. They were in with all the other older adults. So, even though I was somewhat content with all that was going on in me, I knew God had called me to minister His Word in some capacity. I just wasn't sure how to go about it, so I took advantage of the opportunities that came my way.

During that spring, our church had a day in which high school seniors visited the district church college in Nampa, Idaho, where my sister graduated from college. I wasn't sure if it would be something I would be interested in, so I went along. Even though I was much older than everyone else, I wanted to see what the college might offer someone like me. I came away very disillusioned with the whole thing. For one thing, I couldn't understand why someone would have to go into debt and pay thousands of dollars to become a minister. I still had enough anti-establishment in me to reject such a system. I thought, "God, you must have a better system somewhere."

During this period, I had an insatiable desire for the Word of God. Unfortunately, my hunger for God's word wasn't satisfied at the church I was attending. They were good sermons, but I didn't feel like I was being fed and nurtured by God's Word as much as I needed. As a result, I began to look elsewhere. Our local Bible bookstore had a tape library where you could borrow tapes from anointed teachers and preachers of God's word and then return them.

I had gotten ahold of several cassette tapes by Bob Mumford, an excellent Christian teacher and minister, who seemed to fill the need in my life to learn God's word. So, I began to read his books as well. Among them were *"Take Another Look at Guidance," "The Problem of Doing Your Own Thing," "Christ in Session,"* and *"The Purpose of Temptation."* These books all profoundly influenced what was happening to me, especially *"Take Another Look at Guidance."*

Bob Mumford's ministry, "Life Changers," significantly influenced my life for many years. I eventually became a member of his tape club and received his teaching each month. I even had the opportunity to meet him at a church conference where he was the featured speaker.

During this season, during which I was growing by leaps and bounds, one of my mother's friends gave me a couple of books that were instrumental in shaping my early years as a committed Christian. She had given me Dietrich Bonhoeffer's book, *"The Cost of Discipleship,"* and a couple of books by Watchman Nee. All these books were instrumental in my early growth and foundation in the Lord.

As I was reading the *"Cost of Discipleship,"* I came across the chapter where he was teaching from the Book of Isaiah, the part about, *"Whom shall I send, and who will go for Us?"*[20] As I read that portion of Scripture in the book, the Lord's presence profoundly overcame me. It was so intense I knelt and prayed, *"I will go! Send me."* It was a compelling and defining Kairos moment in which I consecrated my life to the Lord.

Charismatic Christianity

Another thing that began to happen to our family during this season was our exposure to the *"Charismatic Movement."* My brother and his wife had left the church we all grew up in—The Church of the Nazarene. They were now attending a major charismatic church on the outskirts of

---

[20] Isaiah 6:8 (NKJV) Also I heard the voice of the Lord, saying: "Whom shall I send, and who will go for Us?" Then I said, "Here am I! Send me."

town called Bethesda Christian Center. They had been baptized in the Holy Spirit and were now speaking in tongues. My sister and her husband, who lived in Anchorage, Alaska, left the Nazarene church and were now speaking in tongues, too. They started attending a major charismatic church in Anchorage. Their experiences caused me to give serious thought as to whether the experience was a genuine Biblical experience.

The church I was attending was very much opposed to this type of experience. I remember going to a camp meeting during that summer where many holiness-type churches came together for a yearly camp meeting. It was in Entiat, Washington, just a few miles north of Wenatchee. During one of the meetings, the speaker powerfully preached against Charismatic Renewal. He would say, "You say it must be of God because it's growing. Well, communism is growing as well, and we know it isn't of God." Then, he had everyone in the camp meeting stand up and make a denouncement concerning speaking in tongues. I stood up and went along with it but became convicted for doing so and immediately repented for not being true to myself.

I hadn't made up my mind about the issue one way or the other but was incredibly open to it if it was the truth of God's Word. My mission for the next few months was to study the subject thoroughly. I would read books for and against speaking in tongues. I read Francis and Charles Hunter's books, *"Two Sides of a Coin"* and *"Since Jesus Passed By,"* plus other books on the subject by different authors. These books were beneficial, but I was still not sure. I also decided to start going to my brother's church on Wednesday evenings and continue with the Nazarene church on Sundays.

Around this time, my sister began sending me teaching tapes and materials from her new church in Anchorage. These teaching tapes fed my spirit, which helped convince me somewhat that there was something to the charismatic experience. She also sent me the Bible School catalog from the church she was attending. As it turned out, the church had a two-year Bible School, something in which I was deeply interested. I began to sense maybe this was where God might be leading me.

As the summer wore on, I began to think maybe I should move to Anchorage to pursue the two-year Bible College. It was called the Charismatic Bible College of Anchorage. I still was unsure about speaking in tongues, so I wanted to make sure I settled the issue in my heart and mind before making such a move. I was also very committed to my job and seeing it through the apple harvest season. So, in all probability, even if I decided to go, it wouldn't be until late that fall.

The apple harvest came and went with the Thanksgiving holiday fast approaching. I had elected not to enroll in the fall semester at the junior college as I was still unsure of my plans and immediate future. My sister sent me some more materials and teaching tapes from her new church during this time. One of the tapes she sent me was titled *"Charismatic–What Does It Mean?"* by her new pastor, Dick Benjamin. As I listened to the message, all the lights went on. I received the revelation and understanding about the baptism of the Holy Spirit and speaking in tongues. It was the deal clincher for me. Now, all I had to do was to take a giant step of faith in relationship to the revelation I had just received. I immediately drove to a travel agency and bought a one-way airfare ticket to Anchorage, Alaska. On December 2nd, 1975, I was to leave for Anchorage to enroll in Bible College. Moving to Anchorage would become a significant defining moment that would set me on course for God's destiny in my life.

God answered my simple prayer, "God, you must have another system somewhere."

I was soon to discover that He did have another plan for training young ministers rather than going thousands of dollars into debt. I was now well along the path God was charting for me. It led me to discover His plans and purposes for my life. Making this move was the adventure I had been looking for all along. I was too deceived, stubborn, and self-centered to find it earlier. I had finally found the right puzzle into which the pieces God had initially given me in the vision while in Vietnam were supposed to fit. I can't begin to express the inner peace and contentment I felt. It was by far beyond anything I had ever experienced during my drug-crazed years. The peace and happiness I have experienced are real and not temporal like I had been experiencing in the world and through drugs. The words of Jesus rang true when He said, *"Peace I leave with you, My Peace I give to you; not as the world gives do I give to you. Let not your heart be troubled, neither let it be afraid"* – John 14:27.

It has been 40 years since I walked down the aisle and gave my heart to Jesus Christ. Yet, I still have the same peace and contentment after all this time. I am so thankful for the mercy and grace of our long-suffering Father God, who doesn't give up on us even in our most rebellious states of mind.

Alaska — Becoming Established
Chapter Twenty-Six

On Tuesday, December 2nd, 1975, I arrived in Anchorage, Alaska. My sister and her husband picked me up at the airport. They had a room prepared for me to live in at their apartment until I eventually got settled enough to find my place. Flying into Anchorage was a beautiful experience as I got to see the glacier fields from the air and the beauty of the mountains. I was looking forward to exploring as much of Alaska as possible, even though my primary purpose in going there was to attend the two-year Bible College. As I stepped off the airplane, I had a real sense of anticipation and hope.

I felt like I was entering the destiny and purpose God had charted out for my life. In my heart, I knew this was the season God was going to establish me in the calling He had for me. I had taken the necessary steps of faith, and now I would watch and see what God would do. It was an inspiring time for me as I approached it with much anticipation and confidence in the faith walk I had discovered.

My sister, Bonnie, and her husband, John, had a three-bedroom apartment in the Jewel Lake area of Anchorage, located just a few miles from the church and Bible College I would attend. They also had two adorable toddlers, Jennifer and Christina. I was looking forward to spending time with them. They lived in Alaska because John worked full-time for the National Guard in Anchorage.

I hadn't seen much of my sister since my high school days. She's about 15 months older than me, and with her going to college right out of high school and me being in the army, we hadn't seen each other much in the seven years before I arrived in Anchorage. I had missed her wedding day by a couple of weeks as she got married just before I came home from Vietnam and moved to Alaska immediately.

I was looking forward to going to my new church, Abbott Loop Christian Center, for the first time, but I would have to wait until Thursday evening—two days away. I had listened to various messages from the church and its pastors for the last several months and even took a course on Evangelism from cassette-taped lessons. So, I was filled with anticipation as I waited to see what it had to offer.

Thursday evening finally rolled around, and I had a lot of anticipation and excitement in my spirit. The service was everything I had anticipated. The worship service, with the band singing contemporary praise songs rather than songs out of a hymnal, was inspiring. My spirit soared as I entered the worship experience. The preaching and teaching were exceptional as well. I liked how they incorporated God's word into the message with many Scriptures. The other big plus was that it was a church of about 1,500 people, many of whom were young adults like me. This experience was wonderfully different from what I experienced earlier in my Christian Walk. I went home elated. I thanked God for allowing me to be a part of such a wonderful place to worship and discover what He had in store for me. I felt like I had died and gone to heaven. Every service had an altar call for salvation, then for water baptism, and then another call for Spirit baptism. There would be multitudes of people who responded to each service. It was a very revival-like atmosphere.

The Baptism of the Holy Spirit

I hadn't thought too much about when I would receive the baptism of the Holy Spirit because I was so enthralled with everything I was experiencing. I knew the time to receive it was coming, though. Thursday had rolled around again, and it was December 11th. Earlier in the day, I had started to say something to one of my nieces, and I just started speaking in tongues without realizing what I was doing.

I thought, "I better go forward tonight when they have the call for the baptism of the Holy Spirit."

At the service that night, I was excited because I knew I would be going forward to receive the baptism of the Holy Spirit. I was as ready as I would ever be to receive it. So, when the pastor gave the altar call for the baptism of the Holy Spirit at the end of the service, I went forward. They took me and others who had responded to a room in another part of the building. An elder from the church spent about 15-20 minutes teaching on the subject and explaining to us how to receive. There was a team of people to help minister with the man who was doing the teaching. Once he finished, they laid hands on each of us as they began to pray for us to receive the Holy Spirit's baptism. As soon as they laid hands on me, I burst into singing in tongues, which was very unusual for me because I could never sing and carry a tune. Everyone was surprised that I received it so quickly. It was one of the most amazing experiences I have ever had. I immediately went home to my room and began to pray in tongues to ensure I had it and wouldn't lose it. The following week, I continuously locked myself in my bedroom and prayed in tongues. I wanted to ensure I was becoming fluent with the gift and not just repeating a couple of syllables.

I have always found intimacy with the Lord and the Holy Spirit by praying in this manner. I have found that praying in the Holy Spirit is a powerful weapon God has given us. It brings us into intimacy with Him and allows us to pray in agreement with His purposes and the situations for which we are praying. Frequently, when praying in this manner, my heart is fully engaged rather than just repeating meaningless syllables over and over as I sense what the Holy Spirit is praying through me. I then begin to pray in English what He is praying. Again, this is a powerful agreement in the Spirit, which He honors.

Unfortunately, many Christians who receive the Baptism of the Holy Spirit with the evidence of speaking in tongues never experience the fullness of what God intended for them because they never get past the few syllables in their initial baptism. It is a gift that must be exercised and developed to become the weapon God ordained it to be. Initially, I treated it as a toy to have fun with until it evolved into a spiritual weapon.

Other Influences

During my first few months in Alaska, I listened to many messages on cassette tapes from various speakers from the church and other guest speakers who had been to the church at one time or another. For example, I was introduced to the teachings of Kevin Conner from Australia on *"Present Truth"* and Rob Wheeler from New Zealand on the *"Parables of Jesus and the Feasts of Israel."* These powerful teachings opened my spirit to what God was saying and doing in the Church today. I honestly felt like the windows of heaven were being opened with revelation and understanding pouring into my spirit.

As I discovered later, Kevin Conner and Rob Wheeler were related spiritually to our pastor, Dick Benjamin. They had all been under the influence of W.H. Offiler, who pastored a great church in the Seattle area during the 1940s and 1950s called Bethel Temple. Rev. William Henry Offiler (1875-1957) also authored *"God and His Bible: The Divine Harmonies of Revelation."*

I was excited about beginning Bible College. I had sat in on a few classes to see what it was like but wouldn't be able to start officially until after the first of the year when the new semester started. In the meantime,

I made appointments with the church's pastors to introduce myself. I wanted to tell them I was serious about growing in the Lord and that I would start Bible College when the new semester started.

Beginning Bible College

This church operated from the gifts found in Ephesians 4:11 of apostles, prophets, pastors, teachers, and evangelists. The leading pastor was considered an apostle as they had established several satellite churches in and around Alaska and the lower 48 States. Dick Benjamin, the apostle and prominent leader, was gone much of the time, ministering apostolically to the many churches founded under his ministry. There was a prophet, evangelist, teachers, and other pastors on staff. The prophet had on his office door a plaque that said, "This isn't a non-prophet ministry." I thought that was cool.

Reading Bob Mumford's "Christ in Session" book prepared me for this type of structure. From reading his book, I already had a reasonably good idea of how these different ministries functioned. I would learn much more about this New Testament structure in the days ahead, especially after officially enrolling in Bible College.

Christmas and the New Year came and went, and I was primed and ready to start Bible College. One of the benefits I discovered was that the government approved them to allow veterans to use the G.I. Bill, which meant I wouldn't have to work. I could concentrate entirely on learning and getting involved in the church's various ministries. God answered my simple prayer when I said, "You must have something different that doesn't cost much money." The GI Bill paid for the small cost of going to Bible College, which taught the Bible.

My first day as an official Bible School student finally came. Fortunately, another Bible School student lived in my apartment complex. He was able to give me a ride to school each day. Walking would have been difficult as the weather was often below 0 degrees Fahrenheit and sometimes even as cold as 20 below. The classes were all very Bible-oriented—some covering books of the Bible while others were more topically oriented. There were also classes on Minister's Workshop and learning how to preach and teach. In the Minister's Workshop, we would learn how to conduct funerals, weddings, counseling, and things of that nature. Our teachers gave us 15 minutes to present a sermon or teach in the Preaching class. Each day, we started with Scripture memorization. We would learn one Scripture verse a day. There was a class called Praise and Worship, which taught us to worship the Lord, minister in healing with the laying on of hands, and operate in the gifts of the Spirit. Those who sang well learned how to lead us into praise and worship, and those who played instruments were part of the worship band. Essentially, the students led the worship service, and the teachers oversaw it.

As the weeks progressed, I found myself in a place of absolute contentment and happiness. I was learning so much so fast. The Lord had primed me for this season, and now I was taking full advantage of it. I was in a season where the revelation of God's Word delighted my soul and spirit. In addition, it was an excellent time to get to know the Lord in a way I had never known Him before.

During one of our praise and worship classes in my first semester, the prophetic Spirit broke out, and some of our instructors began to prophesy over many students. It was the first time I had ever received a prophetic word from the Lord. I still remember it to this day, some 40 years later. The prophecy said, "My love for God's Word would bring me into intimacy with Him." It is still true today. I have an overwhelming sense of love and respect for God's Word. I never get tired of it. I am continually amazed at the revelation of understanding He constantly pours into my spirit through His Word.

Prompted by the Holy Spirit to Get a Job

As stated earlier, I was on the G.I. Bill and received enough monthly to pay for all my expenses. Living with my sister and her husband was a big help as well. One day, a couple of weeks into the second quarter, I was in the Prayer and Praise class when I sensed the Lord prompting me to stand up and ask for a job. At the end of this class, each day, we would have a time in which we prayed for one another's needs, whatever they were. As the Lord began to prompt me to ask for a job, I began to carry on an argument with Him and let Him know that I didn't need a job. I was perfectly content to go to school every day and get involved in outreach events and other activities without worrying about working. However, I learned arguing with God doesn't do much good.

Nevertheless, He kept prompting me to stand up. Eventually, I stood up for prayer and expressed the need for a job. As I was standing there, one of the gals from the class came over to pray for me and told me they were hiring at the Sears Warehouse. She prayed, and we agreed together that I would get the job. Our Bible College schedule was from 8:00 am to 1:30 pm Monday-Thursday with Fridays off. This schedule allowed students to carry a workload while going to school.

That afternoon, following my classes, I immediately went to Sears' Warehouse to claim the job before walking in. I was hired immediately and told to start work the next day. When the Lord prompted me to ask for a job, I didn't realize that He knew exactly what I needed for the next three years while in Alaska. He knows our needs even before we ask. In this case, I was obedient to what God revealed. He saw everything from His eternal perspective and was preparing me for what I needed to do to walk in His provision for the next three years. As it turned out, it was the most perfect job I could have had during that phase of my life. I would work 20 hours a week, three hours daily, Monday-Thursday, following my classes, and eight hours on Friday with the weekends off. When summer rolled around, I would switch to a 40-hour-a-week schedule. Then, when classes would start again in the fall, I would go back to the 20-hour-a-week schedule.

During the spring and summer months, my job was to assemble bicycles and repair them. During the fall and winter months, I would oversee the toy inventory in the warehouse and send them to the main store as needed. It was a great job. Several months later, I was at work and walking down the hallway toward the bicycle repair area when I received an epiphany. I was overcome with an overwhelming sense that I was walking down that particular hallway because of the steps of faith I had taken. I realized that I was walking in a kingdom realm that had transcended the earthly realm where my feet were walking. I felt like I was walking on water. This experience was another defining moment in my life as I realized God was confirming that I was on the right path that would lead to a complete discovery of who He is and what He had in store for me. The Bible says we are in the world, but not of it, and that He translated us from the kingdom of darkness into the kingdom realm of His Son.[21][22] I knew then I was firmly established in the destiny and purpose God had charted out for my life. It was another decisive Kairos

---

[21] John 17:14-16 (NKJV) I have given them Your word; and the world has hated them because they are not of the world, just as I am not of the world. I do not pray that You should take them out of the world, but that You should keep them from the evil one. They are not of the world, just as I am not of the world.

Colossians 1:13-15 (NKJV) He has delivered us from the power of darkness and conveyed us into the kingdom of the Son of His love, in whom we have redemption through His blood, the forgiveness of sins. He is the image of the invisible God, the firstborn over all creation.

moment filled with revelation and understanding. It helped me early on in my Christian experience to sense how God worked to impart the kingdom realm into my very being. The Bible says, "The kingdom doesn't come with observation, but rather the kingdom of God is within you."[23]

Getting Involved in Outreaches

During the two years in Bible College, I took advantage of all kinds of outreaches and opportunities to prepare myself for the day when I would eventually be sent out on one of the outreach teams to start a new church somewhere. The church I had become a part of was responsible for planting well over one hundred churches between 1973 and 1990. It was referred to as a church planting factory. The church sent over a thousand people to participate in these church planting teams. They were constantly sending these teams during my three years there, which was highly motivating.

When I was in basic training at Ft. Lewis, our Drill Sergeant constantly told us we would go to Vietnam. Later, when I was at Ft. Lewis, once again, waiting to go to Vietnam, a rumor surfaced that our orders were changed to Korea. I felt disappointed because it had been drilled into me that I would go to Vietnam, and I fully accepted it. As it turned out, it was nothing more than a rumor. However, as I watched church planting team after the church planting team sent out, I was inspired to be a part of one eventually. It caused me to focus highly on what God was doing in my life.

I was genuinely involved in evangelism, which consisted of street ministry and jail ministry. Because I was free from work on the weekends, I became committed to ministering at the city jail in downtown Anchorage every week. We had two hours each week to share with the prisoners who wanted to come and listen to us. It consisted of teaching, counseling, and sharing the gospel each week. It was a great learning and growing experience.

One of the most common questions I would get asked as I ministered in jails and on the street was, "Why Jesus? What is so special about Him that sets Him apart from other great religious leaders such as Buddha, Mohammed, or Krishna? Why do you say Jesus is the only way?" My answer was quite simple. "It was Jesus who came to give Himself as a sacrifice for our sins by pouring out His blood as the atonement for our

---

[23] Luke 17:20-21

sins, not any other spiritual leaders. He was the Lamb of God who came to take away the world's sins."[24]

The Bible says in *1 Timothy 2:5-6, "For there is one God and one Mediator between God and men, the Man Christ Jesus, who gave Himself a ransom for all, to be testified in due time."*[25]

Because Jesus was and is both God and man, He is the only one who can mediate on our behalf. The reason Jesus had to pour His blood out for our sins was that the life of the flesh is in the blood; therefore, God has made it the atoning factor. It is the blood that makes atonement for the soul of humanity.[26] Jesus is the only way because He is the One Who poured His blood out on the cross to make atonement for my sins and then rose from the dead. Sometimes, someone would be sick or not show up when it was their turn.

During the Bible College season, I would be ready for any preaching and teaching experiences. In our preaching and teaching class, three people each week would have the opportunity to preach. I took full advantage of this class. Another friend and I would always have something ready when others either didn't show up on their turn to preach or weren't prepared. We would step in and take their place. Filling in for others happened quite a bit. I also began to teach a weekly Bible study at the local mission in downtown Anchorage.

True Acceptance

About halfway through the spring quarter of my first semester—after getting the job at Sears—I moved out from my sister's home. I found an apartment in the Spenard area of Anchorage with another Bible student with whom I had become good friends. His name was Keith, and he eventually became a part of the church I pastored in Roseville, California, from 1984-1997. We hit it off very well with our landlords, who were also Christians and were able to fill up two or three other

---

[24] John 1:29 (NKJV) The next day John saw Jesus coming toward him, and said, "Behold! The Lamb of God who takes away the sin of the world!

[25] 1 Timothy 2:5-6 (NKJV) For there is one God and one Mediator between God and men, the Man Christ Jesus, who gave Himself a ransom for all, to be testified in due time,

[26] Leviticus 17:11 (NKJV) For the life of the flesh is in the blood, and I have given it to you upon the altar to make atonement for your souls; for it is the blood that makes atonement for the soul.

apartments with students from our Bible College. We would load up in the car I had purchased shortly after arriving in Anchorage and head off to school each day. The acceptance I craved during my drug-crazed years was happening without even thinking about it. Not only that, but the One who mattered the most accepted me—the Lord Jesus Christ.

The Love Bug Bites

During my second year as a Bible College student, I began dating a young woman named Lydia. We had been hanging out with the same group of friends for the past year and were already good friends. Until then, I had tried not to focus on girls as I was more interested in what God was doing in my life. I wanted to stay focused, but the love bug finally bit me. We were constant companions until I left Alaska to join a newly formed church planting team in Chico, California.

Bible College Over — What's Next

By December 1977, I had finished my two years at the Bible College but would have to wait until the end of the school year in May 1978 to graduate with the class. Because I started mid-year, I was finishing up mid-year as well.

Now that Bible College had ended, I had to start thinking about what I would do next. Would I stay in Alaska in a big church where there were lots of ministries to be involved in but not many opportunities to pursue preaching and teaching? Or should I seek God to go out on a small church planting team where I would probably have many opportunities? Again, I trusted the Lord to bring it to light in His good timing. He had been very faithful in leading and guiding me on the right paths. The scripture that has been a constant source of encouragement and direction to me is Philippians 3:16.

It says, *"Nevertheless, to the degree that we have already attained, let us walk by the same rule; let us be of the same mind."*

I then elected to take a month off, go home for Christmas, and then travel to Chico, California, to visit with my sister and her family. They had moved from Alaska to Chico to be part of the church planting team.

It would be an exploratory trip for me to see if there would be much of a possibility of joining the team myself.

How God led me up so far was working well, so I determined to wait on Him for the right timing for this next phase in my life.

While home in Wenatchee for the holidays, the new pastor of the team in Chico found out I would be coming for a visit and asked me to put together a few messages on evangelism to share with the new congregation. The opportunity to teach was stimulating for me. So, I went to work during the holidays, putting all my thoughts together and preparing the messages.

During this time, Lydia and I were still seeing each other. She had gone to her parent's home in New Mexico for Christmas. On her way back, Lydia stopped in Wenatchee to see me and meet my family before returning to Anchorage. After she left, I began preparing for my trip to California, which I would travel to by bus.

Chico was an excellent experience. I was able to get a glimpse into what life would be like there. The church was small, with only about 25 people or so. It was still in the beginning stages, and we were meeting in a big room in the pastor's home. I shared the evangelism messages on three different occasions. They seemed to go over well with people being encouraged and challenged. The warm weather in the middle of winter was a real treat compared to Anchorage and even my home in Wenatchee. I could see myself there. I was content to leave it in the hands of God to make that determination.

Once back in Anchorage, I settled into my job and continued with the various outreach ministries. The church was launching a small group program, and the church leaders invited me to be one of the leaders. I was already co-leading a strong home group on Friday evenings, which had begun spontaneously. They were now asking me to join the new program the church was launching.

Over the next few months, I continued to work and lead the small group and a few other things while waiting to see the direction the Lord would lead me for the next phase of my life. I wasn't sensing that my future would be in Anchorage. But, at the same time, I didn't want to be hasty without some clear direction from the Lord.

Time to Leave Alaska

One night, something happened! I had a dream that made it clear to me that it was time to leave. In my dream, I was at work on a forklift, lifting a pallet of toys to the mezzanine, where they were stored until the main store needed them. As I was lifting the pallet, the whole pallet came loose from the forklift and came crashing down below with a load of toys, injuring two people working close to the forklift. The Lord immediately gave me the interpretation of the dream. He impressed in my spirit that it was time to leave Alaska and pursue His calling for my life. If I were to stay in Alaska, I would be out from under His covering and protection. The dream was another defining moment that moved me toward God's calling.

During the next few weeks, I made appointments with my pastors and other five-fold ministers and shared what I thought the Lord was calling me to do. Finally, it became clear that the Lord had been preparing me to join the newly founded church plant in Chico. They all heartily agreed and arranged it so I could share my testimony with the church in the near future when they would lay hands on me and send me forth. Joining the church in Chico, California, would be one more step into being firmly established in the direction God had for my life.

Lydia and I were still seeing each other and had even discussed the possibility of marriage. Unfortunately, she was neither ready for marriage nor to leave Alaska. Even though we had grown remarkably close to one another, it seemed like we would be going our separate ways for a period. For me, doing what God had called me to do was the preeminent factor in the direction of my life. At this point in my life, the most important thing for me was getting established in ministry. As stated earlier, during my hitchhiking days, there seemed to be a force within me that was constantly moving me forward into my destiny—a passion that I had now learned to identify as the Holy Spirit.

The previous three were the best years of my life. Even today, as I look back over my life, I realize that my time at Bible College in Alaska was one of the best seasons of my life. It was a time when all the confusion of entering adulthood ended. God established the direction He had charted out for my life. I was no longer a lost wandering soul but had found my way during all that I experienced following my tour in Vietnam. I was totally at peace with the direction I was going. It was exciting as I looked forward with anticipation of what God was going to do next.

Sent Out and Launched into Ministry
Chapter Twenty-Seven

It was August 1978. I had been in Alaska for almost three years. The day had finally arrived when I was to share what God was leading me to do before the congregation. I had now been home from Vietnam for a little over seven years. Seven is the number of completion and perfection. It had been quite a journey, but this phase of my journey was coming to an end. I had found my way and would be starting a new phase of life and ministry.

During the Sunday evening service, I was allowed to share. I shared how I had felt compelled by the Lord to come to this wonderful church and how God had done mighty works in my life. It was time to be sent into the harvest field He had for me. I thanked many of the people who had mentored me along the way. The elders were all called forward to pray and prophesy over me with an official send-out. One of the prophecies was interesting in that it alluded to the fact that my time in Chico would be a season of preparation, intimating I wouldn't be there that long. Tom Edmondson, the Prophet on staff, gave it. I filed it away in my mind, not giving it much attention. As far as I was concerned, I was going to Chico, California, to help establish a New Testament church that would be a thriving church in the community I would be a part of for a long time.

Lydia and I had a long conversation about our relationship and its direction. She wasn't ready to get married or leave Alaska, so we agreed to break up but remain friends and stay in touch with each other often.

Chico, California

I arrived in Chico in early September after spending a week in Wenatchee with my parents and other family members. I would still be on the G.I. Bill for six months in an internship program from the church in Anchorage. Once again, I didn't have to worry about finding a job immediately, and I would be living with my sister, Bonnie, and her family again. The church had grown to over 40 members and was still meeting in a large room in the pastor's home. The pastor was working a full-time job and trying to start a church. Overwhelmed at having to preach two services a week, He asked me to begin preaching the Wednesday evening services within a month after arriving. Preaching every week would be quite a stretch for me. I knew how to put a message together but never had to do it week in and week out with no end in sight. This kind of commitment would be a great learning experience and preparation for whatever God was preparing me for in the days ahead.

Over the next six months, I would spend my time praying, preparing messages, preaching, and witnessing at Chico State University. Because I was in the intern program with the G.I. Bill, I had to keep track of my hours for everything and file a monthly report to the church in Anchorage.

One day, while listening to a local Christian program on the radio, the Disc Jockey talked about a local concert ministry called Discovery Productions. They brought contemporary Christian music artists like the 2nd Chapter of Acts, Keith Green, Barry McGuire, Terry Talbot, Phil Keaggy, and many others to Chico. He asked if anybody in his listening audience wanted to join the ministry. Being a big fan of Christian music, I immediately called and said I would like to check it out. The next meeting was the following week, about which I was excited. The ministry became an excellent outlet for me. Our church was still small, with no other singles my age, which meant I lacked fellowship. The concert ministry consisted of single people my age except for the D.J. and two others. It was a great bunch of people. Through this ministry, we met many contemporary Christian artists of the 1970s.

Once the six-month internship ended, I had to find a full-time job. I found one relatively quickly at the Montgomery Ward store in Chico. They gave me a job as a delivery truck driver. I would deliver furniture and appliances to all the small cities around Chico within a hundred miles. I got to know the area well.

In June, Lydia came to Chico for a visit on the way to visit her parents in New Mexico. We attended "Jesus West Coast," a Christian festival on the outskirts of Chico. It occurred in a large field with many of that era's current Christian recording artists and Bible teachers. We had a great time together. During this time, we talked about marriage even though we had separated for almost a year. She had dated others during that time, just as I had. Even though I hadn't gotten serious with anyone, it was enough to prompt her to come and see me when she found out I had dated someone else. I wanted to get married when we were still back in Anchorage, but she just wasn't ready. So, after spending a few days together and experiencing what life was like in Chico, she left to visit her parents in New Mexico, where her family was living because of an Air Force transfer.

Married, October 13, 1979

We continued our courtship over the telephone, and when I again asked her to marry me, she finally said yes! We had a lovely wedding in a small Baptist church near downtown Chico, with many from our families attending. For our honeymoon, we went to Disneyland and Knott's Berry Farm. After our honeymoon, we both settled into our church. She hit it off well with all the pastor's family and their children. Other than that, it was a big shock for her. She had just come from a big church of over 1,500 people with many programs, activities, and friends her age. She was transitioning to a church of about 40, mostly older people, which made for a difficult adjustment. We both were now part of the concert ministry. Like me, we both found our fellowship with people our age there.

During our first year of marriage, we continued to be involved in the church and the concert ministry. I was still preaching every week and working full-time at Ward's. Within a few months, Lydia also got a job, and we moved into a two-bedroom apartment in the same apartment complex where we lived.

Back to College

By the time September of 1980 had rolled around, I had been thinking about going back to Jr. College to finish up my A.A. Degree. However, I only needed two semesters to complete it, and I still had a little over a year left on my G.I. Bill, so I decided to work part-time and return to college while collecting the G.I. money. I would still be preaching the weekly mid-week services as well.

I decided to get my A.A. Degree in business, thinking that it wouldn't hurt to have some business knowledge when I fully launched into the ministry. I learned accounting and bookkeeping, which has been particularly helpful over the years in ministry. The Bible college I had attended in Anchorage was non-accredited, which meant that none of the credits counted for anything as far as a regular college was concerned. However, in my book, they were far more important than anything I was getting from a secular college.

Moving On

At first, it seemed like our little church would take off. We had an addition of new families, but the families who came down from Anchorage, including my sister and her family, had elected to leave. Even though we recognized problems, we decided to stay and try to help work things out. We were committed to the church and our stream of churches that originated from Anchorage, Alaska. I was being groomed in this fellowship and felt this was the stream God had set me in. I wasn't about to give up on it at this point.

The church in Anchorage sent leaders on two occasions to find out why things weren't going well. But by the early spring of 1981, it was becoming more and more apparent to all of us that the church wasn't going to make it. During this time, Lydia and I made a trip to Citrus Heights, California (a suburb of Sacramento), to visit one of our sister churches. We wanted to see if we could move there and become a part of it. We set up an appointment with the pastor and met with him. He was reasonably excited to have us considering the move. We concluded that once I was through with school at the end of May, we would move to Citrus Heights and become a part of the sister church. This church started in 1975 as an outreach from the church in Anchorage. By this time, our little church in Chico had already closed, and we were fellowshipping at a Foursquare Church. We were still involved in the concert ministry and had the Resurrection Band from Chicago come through. Lydia and I had been reading a lot about Christian Communities like Last Days and Jesus People USA (JPUSA) in Chicago and were interested in living communally. The REZ Band was from the JPUSA community, so we were hoping to have an opportunity to sit down with Glenn Kaiser, the lead singer and one of the community's pastors, and talk to him about community life.

It was an outdoor concert with several bands, including the Sweet Comfort Band and even pro-football player Terry Bradshaw, as a speaker. He shared his testimony. It was called *"A Day in the Son."* About halfway through the afternoon, Lydia and I got to sit down with Glenn Kaiser and talk with him about community. The upshot was that he eventually invited us to come to Chicago and spend a couple of months at JPUSA and see for ourselves if it was for us.

Jesus People U.S.A.

By June, we had already closed the church. The pastor and his family would be moving back to Alaska. Lydia and I opted to take a Greyhound bus to Chicago for the summer and visit the JPUSA community. We thought that once we moved to Citrus Heights to get involved with the church there, we would be fully committed and couldn't explore other avenues of Christianity. So, we decided to take the summer away from commitments and enjoy ourselves. Upon arriving in Chicago at the JPUSA community after a horrendous ride on the Greyhound bus, we settled into a room where the occupants were on vacation. Their community was a huge old brick hotel; they had converted it into their living space in a dangerous part of town.

For protection, you were only allowed to leave the building if you were with someone. The JPUSA community had several businesses that helped support the ministry. They had carpenter crews, painter crews, moving crews, and other types of businesses. We were both assigned jobs within the community. I worked on a moving team and sometimes was designated as a floater—to do whatever around the community needed doing. They also had several ministries, such as visiting local hospitals, street witnessing, jail ministries, and much more. I went out on the street, witnessing teams on several occasions. We also worked together on their JPUSA newspaper, "Cornerstone," which they sent to thousands of homes across America. We had received it for several years and always looked forward to it. Meals were eaten together as a community in a giant cafeteria on the bottom floor of the building. Both Lydia and I took turns working in the kitchen as well. There were plenty of small group sessions during the week and a sizeable congregational service on Sundays when Glenn would usually preach.

Our original plan was to stay for two months, but after one month, we knew community life wasn't for us. So, we left for Washington to visit my family before returning to California. Unfortunately, Lydia had also gotten sick with strep throat while there, which meant a trip to Cook Memorial Hospital. We ended up spending ten hours in the waiting room of the hospital before getting to see a doctor. It was grueling. There were things we liked about community life, but there were also several things we didn't like. They were wonderful, godly people who loved Jesus with all their hearts. It was a great adventure we had the privilege of engaging in, but it wasn't for us!

We had an excellent time in Washington, visiting with my family. We had family outings at Lake Chelan with all the nieces, nephews, and other family members, but we were anxious to get home and move to Citrus Heights.

Once back in Chico, we stayed with my sister and her family, who were so good to us. When we left for Chicago, we had given up our apartment and put all our belongings in storage. We would need money to make our move, and I had quit my job with Wards before our trip to Chicago. So, we thought it would be best for Lydia to get a temporary job through her Temp agency, and I would go to Sacramento and try to get a job. I would first need a place to stay, though.

Moving to the Sacramento Area

After contacting the pastor in Citrus Heights and letting him know our circumstances and how we wanted to move there as soon as possible, he was able to find me a place to stay with a family in the church. Lydia remained in Chico until her temporary job ended a few weeks later. We discovered immediately that the church had moved to the Loomis area, another 10 miles east on Interstate 80. They had just purchased 15 acres of land and met in the old Congregational church building. The family I stayed with lived in Loomis as well. Once Lydia finished the temporary job, she joined me and the family until we found our place.

Within a couple of weeks, I landed a job with American Poly-Therm. They manufactured composite parts for defense, aerospace, sporting goods, medical, electronic, light, and heavy rail and safety industries. Several guys from the church worked there at one time or another, which helped me get the job. The one thing I didn't like about the job was that it was a graveyard shift. However, once I landed the job, we eventually found a small, two-bedroom apartment in Citrus Heights.

Over the next few years, Lydia and I got incredibly involved with our new church. It was a great church with about 125 people and was growing. There were many young people and a great worship team composed of guitars, keyboards, drums, saxophone, trombone, and trumpet players. Lydia and I eventually became the leaders of the singles group, where I would have the opportunity to teach occasionally. The church also started a Bible School to train people for ministry during this time, which allowed me to teach regularly.

There were several other churches in the California region from our fellowship of churches that had originated from Anchorage, Alaska. Our pastor oversaw these churches and would occasionally visit with them and help them along. In his absence, he would have me preach to the congregation.

Ordained as an Associate Pastor

My pastor was grooming me to become the church's associate pastor and elder. However, it wasn't long before someone else, who had been a pastor in one of our churches in Alaska, moved to our area with his family. He was a very charismatic person, becoming very influential in our church family. My pastor pulled me aside one day and informed me that he was looking to the other person, the associate pastor, rather than me. I shared this with Lydia and was somewhat upset for a short while about the whole thing, but we decided to trust the situation to the Lord and flow with it.

Over the next few months, Lydia and I continued to serve God and the church with the same enthusiasm. We continued to give of ourselves as leaders to the singles group, believing God was ultimately in charge of our destiny. My confidence was in God's calling on my life, not in how man perceived me. The other person eventually fell out of favor for one reason or another, and they ordained me as an associate pastor/elder in the church.

The following September, when I was working at McClellan Air Force Base as a civilian employee, I received a phone call from one of the church's elders to meet with him and our pastor as soon as I got off work. They informed me that our pastor was resigning and moving with his family to the Northwest while taking a lengthy sabbatical from ministry.

Becoming a Sr. Pastor

They asked if I would lead the church and serve as the senior pastor. I, of course, responded by saying, "Yes." So, the next day at work, I gave my two-week notice and began to prepare to lead as the Senior Pastor.

Over the next couple of weeks, I began to reflect upon all that had happened to me in the last few years since leaving Alaska. The prophetic word over me at my send-out service was fulfilled. The prophet had prophesied over me and said that my time in Chico would be short. Without the experience of preaching every week at our small church in Chico, I wouldn't have been prepared or ready to step into this role. I thought about what had transpired a few months earlier when my pastor told me that he was now looking at another person as his associate pastor rather than me. If I had gotten offended and left the church, I wouldn't have been perfectly positioned to lead as the Senior Pastor. Instead, I was in full-time ministry.

The church elders and our apostle from Anchorage put together a plan and time to set me in as the Senior Pastor officially. In addition, a pastor from our Seattle outreach church was assigned as a mentor to me and would be available to our church any time needed.

One of the most significant breakthroughs our church received was a few months later when a prophet from New Zealand came through. I didn't know anything about him, nor did he know our church or me. Another church recommended him to us for our fellowship. They had just experienced his remarkable ministry in the prophetic and thought we would also benefit from it. When he arrived, he requested that we not speak to each other until he delivered whatever the Lord had for our church. On the first night of his ministry, he powerfully prophesied over my wife and me. He read our mail. He began by saying that he sensed that I wasn't the church's original pastor but had taken over during turbulent times. I was already set into ministry by our apostle. Now, I was prophetically set in by a proven prophet in the body of Christ. As a result, the church fully received me as their new pastor, which made things much easier in the days ahead.

Looking back over my life since that momentous day in March of 1974, I recognize how the Lord faithfully moved me along in the destiny He had charted out for my life. The vision I received while in Vietnam continually unfolded before my eyes. Romans 1:17 says, *"For in it the righteousness of God is revealed from faith to faith; as it is written, 'The just shall live by faith.'"*

My decision to follow Christ has been nothing but a rewarding and fulfilling experience. I will be forever grateful for the prayers of my mother and father and their influence, along with others who prayed for me into the Kingdom. I also appreciate the many mentors I have had in my life. They have helped me along the way to experience the fullness of what God intended for my life—the most incredible adventure in faith anyone could have had.

Epilogue

As of the writing of this book, it has been over 40 years since I returned home from Vietnam. I am incredibly grateful for what has transpired in those years. I am married to the love of my life, my wonderful wife, Lydia. We were blessed to be moms and dads to over 20 children and teenagers who have graced our home either as foster children or simply taking kids in for a short period for one reason or another.

From this uniquely crafted family, the Lord has blessed us with "our own" sons, and we now have wonderful daughters-in-law and precious grandchildren who bring us much joy and are a part of our everyday lives, even though some live out of state. In addition, we have had two young women, Audrey (21) and Vashti (23), and Vashti's five-year-old son, living with us for the past five years, so our house is always full. They were our foster children when they were six and nine years old.

We were senior pastors of our wonderful church in Roseville, California, for 12 years. In 1997, we sensed the clear leading of the Lord to resign but continue to serve in other capacities in the church that bought our building. I'm a Bible teacher on staff teaching theology to the students in our intern program and one of the elders and staff pastors. Lydia is now the outreach benevolence pastor and pastoral assistant to our Senior Pastor, Francis Anfuso, at the church we have attended since 1997, The Rock of Roseville. My website, kenbirks.com, reaches over 7,500 people a month with the message of Jesus Christ and is a source of encouragement and help to many pastors and lay people who are also serving Jesus Christ.

In early 1985, I received a surprise phone call from Hobo, who was living in Austin, Texas. He had tracked me down to let me know he had gotten saved and was now serving the Lord Jesus Christ. God is good! He told me it was all because of my example to him. Even in my backslidden state of mind, God used me to influence his life for Christ.

I will always be grateful for the partner that Hobo was to me and for inviting me to travel with him to New Orleans from Tempe, Arizona. It was the beginning of a great friendship and a time of discovery for me. I wish I could remember more, but too many years have passed. Nevertheless, I am fortunate to have retained the stories I have written. I recently got in touch with Hobo's daughter and son on Facebook and learned that Hobo had died in 1997 in Austin, Texas. We had many great adventures, and I will always remember him fondly.

I still see Jack periodically and talk with him on the phone occasionally. He lives in Berkeley, CA, and has been battling lung cancer, which is now in remission. He is also a born-again Christian.

In retrospect, I know that God had his hand in my life. I continually stand in awe and am so appreciative of all that He has done for me. His compassion and loving-kindness towards me when I was a lost and wandering soul have caused me to love Him and His Kingdom, which keeps me continually looking forward to what He will do next in my life.

Since authoring this book, I have entered into semi-retirement and have written four other books featured in the following pages. In retirement, I have developed a wedding and funeral officiating business that keeps me busy and fulfilled, ministering to others in this unique way.

Reviews for Space and Hobo

What a fascinating read! Ken writes in such a way that you are with him at every turn of this incredible journey. Like many who have come to know Ken in the last 20 years, I read this with great anticipation and eagerness. I wondered what manner of journey could yield a man of such depth and conviction. As I began the book, my first response was: How different is the Ken I know from the young man in the pages of this book? But the more I read, the more I realized how the man Ken is today grew out of the seed of the young man in this book. Had Ken never met the One who redeemed our past, his journey would have ended in tragedy and nothingness and would hold no interest for the reader. But because Ken writes from the perspective of the redeemed, this journey is rich with God's fingerprints at every step of the way. And at a deeper level, while the particulars are Ken's unique story, the journey he describes is one that we either have or must travel.

—*Bob Guild, Associate Pastor, and Former Navy Pilot*

Have you ever thought all preachers are "goody two shoes" or can't relate to real-world problems? Have you ever thought, "Oh, it's easy for him; he's a preacher." Read this book, and you will discover the grace and patience of God for a sinner just like you. Everyone has a journey toward God, and we do not always take the straight path or do the right thing along the way. This book will encourage you to recognize God's work in you WHILE you are still a sinner and his Grace and kindness that lead you to repentance. You do not have to be a certain kind of person. God often chooses people that "religious folks" might not desire. After reading this book, you may discover you are one of those people. It is "Amazing Grace."

—*David Canipe, Friend and Musician*

I just finished *The Adventures of SPACE & HOBO,* and "Yes!" I prayed for you all those years you wandered the U.S. after Vietnam. Your mother used to call me and ask me to pray as she had no idea where you were and if you were still alive, and she was frantic with worry. But I knew the Lord would keep reminding you of how much

Reviews for Space and Hobo

He loves you, and the Holy Spirit wouldn't let you stray away without His protection and reminders.

I remember the day you talked about on page 194 of your book and how you and your mother were sitting on the right side of the church quite close to the front and in the aisle seat. I felt impressed all through the service to pray that the Lord would reach you and was so happy to see you go to the altar and finally surrender to find His peace in your heart.

Indeed, the Lord has done tremendous work in your heart and life, delivered you from hopelessness to freedom and joy in Him, and given you a ministry to help others who are hopeless and without God's peace.

—*Betty Jane Schmidt, a long-time family friend*

About The Author

Ken Birks is now a semi-retired ordained Pastor/Teacher in the Body of Christ. He is one of the pastors and an elder at The Rock of Roseville in California, where he also functioned as a Bible teacher. Ken has been a part of The Rock of Roseville since its inception in 1997. Before this, Ken was the Senior Pastor of Golden Valley Christian Center, a non-denominational, Spirit-filled church in Roseville, for twelve years.

Ken attended and graduated from the Charismatic Bible College of Anchorage, where he entered a relationship with Apostle Dick Benjamin, then the Sr. Pastor of Abbott Loop Christian Center (ALCC) in Anchorage, Alaska. Dick Benjamin has been one of the strongest spiritual influences in his life.

Ken has been married to his wife, Lydia, for 43 years. They have two adult children, Ben and Keith, and consider them their highest calling, along with the many teens and children they have been foster or surrogate parents to over the past 30 years.

Ken now does wedding and funeral officiating in the Sacramento Metropolitan area. However, he is still very much involved in various ministry activities. He has more recently begun a writing ministry.

Ken also has an internet ministry, "Sowing Seeds of Faith," located at kenbirks.com, a part of his umbrella ministry, Straight Arrow Ministries. Sowing Seeds of Faith reaches over 7,500 unique visitors a month with free Bible studies, sermon outlines, audio and video messages, and other Bible study materials to help equip saints for the work of the ministry.

Other Books by Kenneth L. Birks

Rise of the Anointed Ones
A 40-Day Devotional

Ken Birks has written a masterpiece of superb continuity. The majestic flow from theme to theme contains powerful prophetic revelation as God calls His end-time warriors to arise. I was also amazed by the poems that followed each devotional – the words were Davidic and musical – they flowed like a delightful stream with heavenly impartations. Each of these devotionals stands on its own, but together, they will propel you into a rewarding journey of experiencing God's presence in tumultuous times. Rise of the Anointed Ones is like a voice in the wilderness calling God's beloved away from all that distracts to Him who is jealous for His bride. — *Becker, Fredrickson, Guild.*

Treasurers From Above
A 40-Day Devotional

The devotionals in this book are designed to enhance your relationship with the Lord Jesus Christ in all aspects of your walk. They are meant to draw you into a deeper **understanding** of how the Holy Spirit and the Word of God work together to conform you to the image of Christ. The book encompasses many aspects of our walk with the Lord. We are encouraged in God's Word to embrace God's divine nature. The devotionals will inspire you to be all you can be in Christ. They were also crafted to embrace the beautiful promises of God so that you may receive all that pertains to the life God has given you. The aspect that separates this book from other devotionals is that each devotional ends with a biblically inspired poem encapsulating the essence of the devotional.

Other Books by Kenneth L Birks

Treasures of the Heart
Prose and Poetry Refreshing the Soul

As you read through the devotional prose and poetry found in this book, you will find a beautiful blend of timeless truths fitly applied to today's culture and challenges that fill your heart with treasures from above. The Heavenly insights will challenge you to grow in the knowledge of the Son of God.

The majestic flow from one poem to the next contains powerful prophetic wisdom and revelation that will fill your hearts and minds with the wonderful treasures God intends you to enjoy.

Prophetic Purposes
and the Zeal of the Lord

Do you believe worldwide revival is possible? Imagine what it will be like when the Church rises in the glory spoken of by Isaiah, the prophet. Just as God, in His sovereignty, brought forth the Messiah according to the timing of Daniel's prophecy, He will bring forth the prophetic purpose of a worldwide revival according to His timing. God's people, whom He planted in every city, village, town, and countryside throughout the world, will stand up as the vast army, just as Ezekiel prophesied. His prophetic purpose will be fulfilled.

With major upheaval happening all around us at an alarming rate, it's vital for followers of Jesus to know how we should respond to our present season. The values of the world are being turned upside down. If we fail to hear and respond to His trumpeting voice as it sounds the alarm, we will find ourselves falling into the traps and snares our enemy, Satan, is skillfully laying. This book gives you the keys to being ready for all that God is about to do before the second coming of Christ.

Other Books by Kenneth L Birks

**The Journey
Discovering the Invisible Path**

The Journey gives you a glimpse into God's path for your life. Whether you're just starting on your journey, in the middle, or detoured and have lost your way, this practical guidebook will shine the light on the invisible path. It leads to God's goodness, His kingdom within, and the most incredible adventure of your life.

Francis Anfuso says, "Ken makes complex concepts simple and masterfully unpacks the Bible's greatest mysteries and provides a sure foundation to build a lifetime of insight."

Richard C. Benjamin, Apostle/Pastor/Deceased

I have just read a book entitled "The Journey" written by Kenneth L. Birks. I have known my friend, Ken Birks, for 38 years. He is a man of absolute integrity. He is a diligent student of the Bible. He is a Holy Spirit-filled teacher. This book contains many scriptures referred to and identified at the bottom of the pages. In short, this book is based on the Bible. I believe Ken is also an example of his writing in this book. I recommend this book to individuals, small group leaders, pastors, churches, Bible schools, and seminaries. "The Journey" will help make disciples out of believers.

Steve Gerard, Friend

The Journey by author and Pastor Ken Birks is undoubtedly an inspired guide to "discovering the invisible path." This book is a practical writing that sheds light on the Christian path from the experience of someone (Ken) walking The Journey he has written about. It is a constructive scriptural explanation for everyday Christian guidance in an easily understandable format. It could also serve as a source for Bible study groups in that it already includes the bible study questions. Easy to read, well organized, and filled with the timeless truth of scripture to keep climbing the heavenly path!

Reviews and References

**Dr. Jay Zinn,
Founder of The Discipleship Group**

Few authors can take theology and turn it into a devotional series of divine, inspiring nuggets and poetry. Ken Birks is an author who penetrates your heart and soul to know God better.

**David Fredrickson, Sr. Pastor (Retired),
Evangel Christian Fellowship, Sacramento, CA**

Most true followers of Christ would agree that we are witnessing a time when self-serving Christianity is reaping the whirlwind of disunity, confusion, and fruitlessness. It is past time to listen to the voice of reason merely. Instead, we must respond with renewed minds, hearts, and actions. Ken's devotionals and poetry are like a voice in the wilderness calling God's beloved away from all that distracts to Him who is jealous for His bride. The reader who hears and responds will bring joy to the heart of God and encouragement to others who have put their hand to the plow.

Edward Becker, Senior Pastor, Naches Valley Community Church, Yakima, WA; Vice President, Antioch World Missions

The work in Ken's devotional books is filled with Biblical truths and spiritual revelation that flow from a heart passionate for the Savior and His precious Bride, the Church. The majestic flow from theme to theme contains powerful prophetic revelations as God calls us to arise. The words to each poem were Davidic and musical, flowing like delightful streams with heavenly impartations.

**Dr. Jim Feeney, Former Sr. Pastor
Webmaster at Pentecostal Bible Studies and Free Pentecostal Sermons Central**

I've known Pastor Ken Birks for several decades. He and I have worked in various ministerial capacities in the same family of churches. Ken is held in extremely high esteem

Reviews and References

among our many pastoral colleagues. He is a minister with a firm grasp of the Word of God, a wide variety of administrative skills, a heart for souls, a proven experiential familiarity with the gifts of the Holy Spirit, and an unwavering commitment to the work of the Lord.

John Dubler, Senior Pastor of Good Shepherd Bible Chapel, Fort Collins, CO

Ken Birks is an extremely effective teacher of Scriptures. He combines a healthy respect for the Word with enthusiasm and personal experiences that match his teaching. Ken is a man of unimpeachable integrity, and his longevity in the Body of Christ as a pastor gives credence to the hope and encouragement he brings.

Doug Hartline, Information/Technology Director, University of California

When thinking about reading a devotional, one must ask oneself two questions – is it relevant, and what makes it stand apart from the myriads of devotionals one can choose from? From my perspective, devotionals can be vital tools in improving upon our quiet time experience with God. They should be able to bring scriptural insight to us. Scripture is far more important than the words of even the most famous of authors, for it is Scripture that penetrates our souls with God's wisdom and daily guidance. Ken's work herein ensures that God's Word takes center stage and holds the most essential place so that it remains timeless and relevant.

It is the incredible prose and poetry, however, that separates his devotional books and makes them stand apart from the others. Poetry can shine a light on God's Word from a different angle in a way that helps us to look at it in a much deeper and often more profound way. It provides us with a unique ability to understand and appreciate God's Word in ways we may never have thought of before. We are suddenly confronted with beauty and clarity in our perceptions of our world and God's Kingdom.

Connect with Ken Birks Online

Social Media:
X Formally Twitter: @klbirks
Facebook: facebook.com/seedsfaith—A devotional site.
Linkedin: Linkedin.com/in/kenbirks
Instagram: @KenLBirks

Websites:
booksbyken.com
kenbirks.com
straitarrow.net

Email:
klbirks@gmail.com

Leaving Comments:
I welcome your comments. You may email me your comments at klbirks@gmail.com or leave them on the Facebook page for this book at facebook.com/klbirksbook

If you purchased this book from Amazon.com, please leave a review there.

Check out all of Ken's books and other materials at booksbyken.com.

More Pictures

My Fuel Truck

John

Me in Front of Chinook

Me Next to a Bunker

Me in Boneyard

Me on Bunker Guard Duty

More Pictures

Messing with our Monkey

Mark, Other Guy & John

Chuck & Willy Messing Around

Playing with Grenades

Kevin, Willy, and Chuck

John and Ed

www.ingramcontent.com/pod-product-compliance
Lightning Source LLC
Chambersburg PA
CBHW071156070526
44584CB00019B/2818